ONE FAMILY UNDER GOD

ONE FAMILY UNDER GOD

Immigration Politics and Progressive Religion in America

Grace Yukich

OXFORD
UNIVERSITY PRESS

OXFORD
UNIVERSITY PRESS

Oxford University Press is a department of the University of Oxford.
It furthers the University's objective of excellence in research, scholarship,
and education by publishing worldwide.

Oxford   New York
Auckland   Cape Town   Dar es Salaam   Hong Kong   Karachi
Kuala Lumpur   Madrid   Melbourne   Mexico City   Nairobi
New Delhi   Shanghai   Taipei   Toronto

With offices in
Argentina   Austria   Brazil   Chile   Czech Republic   France   Greece
Guatemala   Hungary   Italy   Japan   Poland   Portugal   Singapore
South Korea   Switzerland   Thailand   Turkey   Ukraine   Vietnam

Oxford is a registered trademark of Oxford University Press
in the UK and certain other countries.

Published in the United States of America by
Oxford University Press
198 Madison Avenue, New York, NY 10016

Library of Congress Cataloging-in-Publication Data
Yukich, Grace, 1980–
One family under God : immigration politics and progressive religion in America / Grace Yukich.
pages cm
Includes bibliographical references and index.
ISBN 978–0–19–998867–9 (pbk. : alk. paper)—ISBN 978–0–19–998866–2 (alk. paper)—
ISBN 978–0–19–998868–6 (ebook)   1. United States—Emigration and immigration—
Religious aspects—Christianity.   2. Illegal aliens—United States.   I. Title.
BR517.Y85 2013
261.7—dc23
2013004449

ISBN 978–0–19–998867–9
ISBN 978–0–19–998866–2

9 8 7 6 5 4 3 2 1
Printed in the United States of America
on acid-free paper

CONTENTS

ACKNOWLEDGMENTS

Few things in life are accomplished alone, and this book is no exception. Without the help of my friend Rachel Soltis, a volunteer and coordinator with the New Sanctuary Coalition of New York City, this study would not have been possible. Several other New Sanctuary Movement organizers also put me in touch with people, supported my work, and offered comments on this manuscript. Especially to Juan Carlos Ruiz and Amy Dalton—thank you for your ongoing support and feedback on this project, which strengthened it beyond measure. I am grateful to all of the New Sanctuary Movement families and activists for their cooperation, help, and enthusiasm about this project. While you may not agree with all I have to say, I hope much of this book rings true to your experiences, struggles, and triumphs. Many thanks also to Mizue Aizeki, Josue Bustos, Felton Davis, June Goudey, and Tom Martinez, who contributed the photographs of the New Sanctuary Movement that grace the pages of this book.

Many kind and generous colleagues offered help and guidance as I researched and wrote this book. This project started as a dissertation at New York University. Thank you to my committee members Jeff Goodwin, Craig Calhoun, and Melissa Wilde for comments, encouragement, letters, phone calls, and other forms of support. During the dissertation process, my office mates Jane Jones and Mark Treskon were the best working partners I could have asked for. Members of my dissertation writing group—Hannah Jones, Jane Jones, Sarah Kaufman, Amy LeClair, Tey Meadow, Ashley Mears, Harel Shapira, and Owen Whooley—read and reread early chapters, as did participants in the NYLON culture workshop in New York and London. I am grateful to all of them for their insights and feedback. Dom Bagnato, Candyce Golis, and Jamie Lloyd made the process easier and more fun through their skilled assistance and friendship. Sarah Damaske, Kathleen Gerson, Abby Larson, Jeff Manza, and Kim O'Neill offered helpful advice and feedback at various stages of the project. Finally, the National Science

Foundation provided funding for the research phase, making much of the travel and other aspects of the project possible.

A postdoctoral fellowship at Princeton University's Center for the Study of Religion gave me the scholar's dream: a year to focus on writing and workshopping chapters alongside some of the most knowledgeable and generous religion scholars in the world. Thank you to Bob Wuthnow, Jenny Legath, and Anita Kline at the center for their mentorship, encouragement, and support during that year. Thanks to Carol Ann MacGregor for introducing me to the Ivy's free popcorn and to Phil Haberkern for advice on balancing writing with a job search. Thank you to participants in the Religion & Public Life and American Religious History workshops at Princeton, who offered feedback on chapters. Thanks also to my informal writing group at Princeton—Annie Blazer, Jessica Delgado, Michaela DeSoucey, Kathryn Gin, Nicole Kirk, John Millhauser, Manu Radhakrishnan, Janet Vertesi, and Judith Weisenfeld. During the final writing and editing phase, Theo Calderara and Charlotte Steinhardt at Oxford University Press and several anonymous reviewers helped strengthen the final versions of the manuscript.

The contributions of colleagues were matched by the support of other friends and loved ones. During the research phase, several friends fed me and gave me couches and beds to sleep on during my months of research in Los Angeles. Thank you especially to Karolyn Mayo, Stacy Dacheux, Allan McLeod, and the Los Angeles Catholic Worker. During the writing stage, Phil Trzynka and Brett Henry offered their home in Michigan as a writing retreat, giving me thinking time that enabled me to develop and refine the arguments in this book. I am so grateful for their friendship and generosity. Thank you also to Tim and Jan Bell for unexpected companionship and laughter during those weeks, a wonderful respite from the often solitary act of writing.

Closer to home, the love and support of my spouse, my parents, my siblings, my two cats, and other family members have sustained me throughout this process. This book is about religion, immigration, and social movements, but it is also about family, the joy and pain of intimate relationships, and the transformational power of unconditional love. Thanks in large part to my parents David and Joy Bazemore, my family has always been a place of this kind of joy, support, and love. I am more grateful to them for this than words can say. Finally, throughout this project, my husband Jonathan has been both my most devoted advocate and my most insightful critic. His support helped me keep the faith during tough periods, and his close reading of this book has made it into something much better than I could have produced on my own. His quiet indignation at injustice, ability to get to the heart of a matter, and commitment to quality, meaningful work continually inspire me. Like most people, I cannot imagine life without my family. For this reason, I dedicate this book to all immigrant families struggling to stay together as they seek better lives for themselves and their children.

ONE FAMILY UNDER GOD

INTRODUCTION

On a sunny Sunday afternoon in 2007, activists on both sides of the illegal immigration debate clashed around a church in the hills of Southern California. An undocumented Mexican woman named Liliana and her U.S.-born infant son Pablito were "taking sanctuary" on the church's property as part of an activist network calling itself the New Sanctuary Movement. Legally, immigration officers could have entered the church at any time, detaining and deporting Liliana while leaving her U.S. citizen son Pablito behind. But in past sanctuary movements, officers had avoided entering churches designated as "sanctuaries," afraid of the public outcry that might result if they violated the religious spaces many Americans consider sacred. Trusting in this legacy, Liliana and her New Sanctuary partners hoped the church walls would protect her, while their detractors called for her removal from both the church and the country. Streets by nearby churches, synagogues, and mosques were quiet, but the usual calm outside of this local church was broken by shouts from anti-immigration activists for Liliana to give herself up. Minutemen and other anti-immigration activists hoisted signs reading, "Deport Liliana," "Don't Attend This Lawbreaker Church," and "Even Heaven Has a Gate," the noise of their bullhorns and their shouts of "Go back to Mexico!" disrupting the church's gathering.

Inside, church members held their weekly worship service, struggling to get past what was happening outside. A gathering of around 50 people, mostly white and middle-class, was made more ethnically diverse by the presence of Liliana and Pablito seated in their midst. Refusing to be derailed by the commotion, the congregants sang hymns and listened to the sermon. Instead of going outside and yelling back at the other group, they stayed inside and prayed for them, that they would become more compassionate toward immigrants like Liliana.

For the members of the United Church of Christ (UCC) Simi Valley, this was what it meant to be religious—to partner with the oppressed, to treat strangers as sisters, and to convince others of the rightness of their actions by behaving in what they deemed to be a loving, compassionate manner even toward those with whom they disagreed. By that point, ignoring the protest outside and praying for the protestors from inside the church walls had become routine, since the anti-immigration activists had been coming and protesting virtually every Sunday since Liliana's arrival. As long as Liliana and Pablito were with them, this was the new normal. Before its partnership with Liliana began, UCC Simi Valley was primarily a spiritual community of like-minded worshippers and a center for activism on local and national issues central to the identities and concerns of the mostly white, native-born congregants.[1] But partnering with Liliana's "mixed-status" family—a family including both undocumented immigrants and U.S. citizens or legal residents whose members are therefore in danger of being split up through deportation—transformed religion for them. Sanctuary expanded their religion into an active, costly relationship with national and ethnic outsiders who, by becoming part of their church family, changed their religious and political lives.

Following the reelection of President Barack Obama in 2012, Americans heard a lot about how the changing demographics of the United States were transforming the political landscape.[2] As both Republican and Democratic strategists scrambled to better appeal to ethnic minorities and immigrants, it became clear that immigrant communities were creating new political realities in the United States. At the same time that immigrants have been claiming their place in American politics, similar trends have been occurring in the American religious landscape. Muslims, Hindus, Buddhists, and Sikhs have been migrating to the United States in increasing numbers over the last few decades, calling for recognition in ways that require members of dominant religious traditions—Protestants, Catholics, Jews—to shift their assumptions and practices.[3] Likewise, diversity has increased within these dominant traditions: for instance, estimates suggest that Hispanic newcomers now make up approximately 35 to 40% of America's Catholics.[4] Religious newcomers are requiring religious institutions to respond somehow if they want to continue to be vibrant and relevant in "the new America" and in a world in which most religious people live outside of the U.S. and Europe.[5]

As recent studies of religious immigrant rights activism have shown, some native-born religious Americans have responded by partnering with immigrant communities to engage in immigrant rights work.[6] Despite this, the number of Americans who see immigration through a religious lens remains very small: only 7% of Americans cite religion as the most important influence on their views on immigration.[7] For most religious Americans, whether native-born or immigrant, immigration is—quite simply—not a religious issue. And though immigrant religious communities have long been engaged in immigrant rights advocacy,[8] we still know very little about how native-born religious communities are engaging with the new immigration.

During the past two decades, social scientists, the media, and the wider public have paid greater attention to religion's role in shaping politics, including movement activism, though most have emphasized the role of conservative religion and neglected progressive religion.[9] However, this research assumes that the government is the primary target of collective action among religious people—that they use "religious resources" like church buildings and membership networks to change the thing that *really* matters to them: politics. What if religious actors have a more complex set of targets than scholars have assumed? How might that change interpretations of their dilemmas, their choices, and their impact? In this book, I argue that the New Sanctuary Movement is what I call a *multi-target social movement*: a movement or movement organization that simultaneously seeks to change multiple institutions—in this case, both religious and governmental institutions. By drawing scholarly, media, and public attention to New Sanctuary's religious goals as well as its political ones, this book shows that some native-born religious people are responding to "the new America" not only by engaging in immigration politics but also by seeking to change American religion by transforming immigration into a religious issue that demands a progressive religious response.

Liliana's Family: The Path to Sanctuary

In 2007, Liliana was walking around her home, helping her husband get ready for work, when she heard a knock at the front door. When she looked through the window, she saw officers, and she wondered what could be wrong. When her husband opened the door, the officers asked for Liliana. Panicked, she realized who they were: not police officers but immigration officers. At that point, Liliana had been living in the United States without papers for nine years.

Almost a decade earlier, Liliana's family left their native Mexico, migrating to the United States legally to become farmworkers in Southern California. Still in high school, Liliana decided to stay behind temporarily, wanting to finish her degree. But once she graduated, she realized that joining her family would be harder than she anticipated. Because of a backlog in an underfunded immigration system, it would be years before Liliana would be able to reunite with her family. A desperate teenager, Liliana made a fateful choice. She decided to join her family in the United States. At the U.S.–Mexico border, she presented a falsified document she had received from a coyote—someone specializing in helping immigrants without papers cross the border. Then Liliana made a second fateful decision. She immediately told authorities that the document was not hers, never actually claiming citizenship. Without any papers, Liliana was turned back by border officials.[10] Later, determined to rejoin her family, she found a different way to migrate to the United States.

Once she reached her family in California, Liliana started a new life. She spent time with her family, all of whom were by then either legal permanent residents or U.S. citizens. Like many people her age, she got a job, and soon she fell in love and married Gerardo, a U.S. citizen. Over the next few years, they had three children: two sons and a daughter. But darkness loomed over their family as long as Liliana lacked legal status. After their marriage, Gerardo decided to petition for Liliana's lawful residency, the first step toward becoming a U.S. citizen.

Instead of receiving the good news of her approval, he heard devastating information. Immigration officials alleged that Liliana's possession of the falsified document on the border years before amounted to her claiming U.S. citizenship. Laws passed in 1996 mandated that such a misstep be punished with a lifetime ban on obtaining legal status in the United States, regardless of her marriage to Gerardo. While her lawyers contended that her on-the-spot admission that the document was not hers should have prevented the ban from being imposed, Immigration and Customs Enforcement (ICE) maintained that her possession of the document had been a claim of citizenship and targeted her for deportation.[11] Apparently there was no way for Liliana to make up for her desperate teenage mistake, no matter how long she had been in the United States, contributing to her family and her community. Gerardo's petition for her legal residency had clued immigration officials in to her case and her presence—now they knew exactly where she was.

When they came for her in 2007, Liliana and her husband begged the ICE agents to wait a few days so they could make arrangements for the children's care, especially since Liliana was still nursing their infant son. Finally, they agreed, warning Liliana not to go into hiding, a common strategy for undocumented immigrants seeking to evade capture by ICE. They warned her that if she went into hiding she would always be afraid. Liliana and Gerardo debated what to do next. She could break her promise to ICE and go into hiding, but with her children in school it would mean separation from them and from her husband—a fate not much better than returning to Mexico.

Then, Liliana remembered something she had seen on television a few days before, a story about an undocumented immigrant living in a church in Los Angeles as part of an emerging religious movement organization working for immigrant rights. While it was not the ideal solution, it would allow her to stay near her family and might give her a chance to obtain help fighting her immigration case. Liliana and Gerardo started calling every pastor and priest they knew, asking about this new group. Eventually, Liliana was on the phone with an Episcopal priest in Long Beach. She could come take sanctuary in their church. A light glimmered in her darkness.[12]

The New Sanctuary Movement

During the two years leading up to the New Sanctuary Movement's launch in 2007, U.S. immigration policy grew increasingly contentious. The difficulties facing Liliana were the new rule rather than the exception for many undocumented immigrants. Attempts to pass the Sensenbrenner Bill in 2005, strict federal legislation that would have made helping an undocumented immigrant a felony, filled newspaper headlines. In response, immigrant-led mega-marches drew hundreds of thousands of people marching for immigrant rights, from Los Angeles to Denver to Detroit. Around the same time, ICE stepped up its efforts to detain and deport undocumented immigrants, increasingly raiding homes and workplaces to round up people without papers.[13] In summer 2006, Elvira Arellano, an undocumented Mexican immigrant and president of the immigrant rights campaign La Familia Latina Unida in Chicago, took sanctuary in her church to avoid deportation and separation from her U.S. citizen son, reviving a long tradition of sanctuary stretching back to ancient times.[14] Around the country, immigrants and their supporters formed groups—both secular and religious—to mobilize in support of more immigrant-friendly reforms.

In response to the upheaval, on May 9, 2007, religious activists in Chicago, Los Angeles, New York, San Diego, and Seattle held joint press conferences in local churches to announce the launch of a national interfaith network of local activist coalitions working for immigrant rights. Calling themselves the New Sanctuary Movement, they framed their efforts as a rebirth of the 1980s Sanctuary Movement in the United States and of other acts of sanctuary throughout history. The 1980s Sanctuary Movement was a national network of churches, synagogues, and other groups providing humanitarian aid to undocumented immigrants fleeing U.S.-sponsored civil wars in Central America, especially in El Salvador and Nicaragua.[15] Participating religious communities temporarily housed immigrants in their buildings—gave them "sanctuary"—to protect them from immigration authorities until they moved on to safer, more permanent locations. The movement gained national attention and built on this publicity by challenging then president Ronald Reagan's Central American foreign policy in addition to providing concrete aid to immigrants. While its success in achieving its stated goals was limited, the 1980s Sanctuary Movement had other important consequences, such as creating an outlet for the moral outrage of progressive religious people, training a generation of activists, and building social networks that might prove useful for future causes.[16]

Because many activists during the 1980s were focused on providing aid to as many Central Americans as possible, they had few restrictions on who was eligible to receive sanctuary.[17] In contrast, following Elvira Arellano and her church Adalberto United Methodist Church's (UMC's) lead, the New Sanctuary Movement decided to give sanctuary specifically to mixed-status families like Liliana's,[18] even though they argued that all immigrants deserve compassion and rights. Early New Sanctuary families included immigrants from Latin America, Asia, and Africa, but most were young heterosexual married couples with U.S. citizen children rather than single immigrants or nontraditional families.

Another distinction between the 1980s movement and New Sanctuary was the shape of sanctuary itself. During the 1980s, sanctuary typically involved immigrants taking temporary shelter on the property of religious institutions until they could safely settle elsewhere. It was a *tactic*—a concrete practice used by movement activists to accomplish a set of goals.[19] When people referred to *sanctuary*, they usually meant this particular practice. Instead, during the first two years of the New Sanctuary Movement—the focus of this book—the term sanctuary operated as moniker, identity, and strategy for the New Sanctuary Movement, with activists only occasionally using sanctuary as a tactic. In other words, the term sanctuary encompassed a much more diverse set of practices compared to the 1980s, including Liliana's more traditional version of sanctuary as living in a church as well as loose partnerships between congregations and immigrant families still living in their own homes.[20] So while the New Sanctuary Movement built on the legacy of the 1980s Sanctuary Movement, its conception and practice of sanctuary were distinct. New Sanctuary aimed to be a religiously and ethnically diverse group of faith communities standing up for the rights of immigrants in a post-9/11

United States, a more dangerous, hostile national context for immigrants and their would-be supporters than the one that existed during the 1980s.

Religion, Immigration, and Social Movements

At face value, the story of the New Sanctuary Movement is about how religious beliefs about brother and sisterhood, compassion, justice, and the sanctity of the family can inspire movements for political change. In the New Sanctuary Movement, political goals mattered, especially the goals of creating immigration reform and ending the raids and deportations that were splitting up families like Liliana's. Shaped by leading theoretical approaches, which long emphasized the state (i.e., government) as the target of change for legitimate social movements, most studies of religion and activism have focused on how religious beliefs and other "religious resources" help people work for political change.[21] When I started the research for this book, my framework and questions were shaped by the dominance of this perspective in the study of religion and activism.[22]

But state-centered perspectives are increasingly being challenged, with researchers highlighting collective actors seeking to change targets ranging from financial corporations to culinary tastemakers.[23] People interested in religion and activism need to shift their frameworks as well, not just because of these theoretical developments but, more importantly, because of changes occurring in the religious landscape that challenge the idea that religious activists are primarily interested in political change.

For instance, though stereotypes abound of Latino and Asian immigrant religious traditions emphasizing private piety and eschewing politics, research on immigrant religious communities in the United States reveals they are engaging in community and political action, though not always using the contentious tactics typically associated with social movements and not always with a focus on the state.[24] While some immigrant religious communities draw distinct boundaries between religion and the state, others—having migrated from nations where the relationship is more fluid—are challenging the strict separation of church and state in the United States.[25] This intertwining of religious and political interests and investments muddies the waters of causal stories that depict religious resources being used to influence politics.

Though recent research has revealed a good deal about how immigrant religious communities are changing the political and religious landscapes in ways that challenge dominant approaches to the study of religion and activism, we still know relatively little about how native-born religious Americans are responding to the increasing presence and power of immigrants. Studies of progressive religious activism have grown in recent years, but most assume or explicitly contend that progressive religious activists in the United States are hesitant to contest issues of religious identity and authority and are instead focused exclusively on political change.[26] This has also been the assumption in most studies of religious immigrant rights activism.[27]

My research on the New Sanctuary Movement offers a different picture of the relationship between religion and activism today, one intimately related to the ways immigration is diversifying American religion and politics. In August 2007, a few months after its launch, I began conducting ethnographic research on the New Sanctuary Coalition of New York City. For a year and a half, I attended coalition meetings, press conferences, movie nights, public vigils, immigration check-ins, and fundraisers. For two months in 2008, I also conducted field research and interviews with the New Sanctuary Coalition of Los Angeles,[28] which provided a more complete picture of New Sanctuary's national diversity.[29] In November 2007 and September 2009, I attended two three-day national New Sanctuary Movement conferences. I also interviewed 70 people in New York and Los Angeles, both people regularly involved in New Sanctuary and people who activists tried to recruit but who never got involved, which allowed me to talk to people about what kept them from participating.[30] Because this book focuses on the New York and Los Angeles coalitions and on the first two years of New Sanctuary (2007–2009), the story it tells is limited. Every story must have a focus, and my focus on two of New Sanctuary's most central coalitions trades breadth for depth. I leave it to other researchers to document other coalitions and New Sanctuary's practices in later years.

Several "awkward" details kept emerging as I studied New Sanctuary,[31] puzzles that the assumptions of dominant, state-centered approaches to the study of social movements could not explain.[32] I began to realize that the simplest explanation was that the New Sanctuary Movement was not solely focused on changing the state. Once I embraced this idea, New Sanctuary's attempts to change both concrete religious communities and the wider public image of religion became difficult to ignore. Since the political aims of religious immigrant rights activists have already received some attention,[33] I spend less time in this book describing and analyzing New Sanctuary's political goals—which are similar to those of other immigrant rights groups— than its religious ones, since nonstate movement targets often go ignored by social movement scholars, including scholarly work on the immigrant rights movement. Still, this book's focus on New Sanctuary's religious targets should not lead to the conclusion that New Sanctuary activists did not care about political change. They certainly did, and for many this was the primary reason for their engagement.

Still, my research revealed that the New Sanctuary Movement sought not only to challenge U.S. immigration policy but also to change dominant representations of what it means to be religious today.[34] They fought to create "one family under God": to keep immigrant families united and to change the hearts and minds of religious people, turning them toward a religious worldview that embraces all people as members of one divine and human family.[35] The New Sanctuary Movement was not only a network of immigrant rights activists. It was also a group of mostly progressive religious leaders and laypeople working for religious conversion and transformation, struggling for greater authority to define religion in a public sphere often dominated by conservative religious voices.

Recognition that the New Sanctuary Movement targeted multiple institutions parallels a theoretical approach developing in the study of social movements called the multi-institutional politics approach.[36] This perspective builds on growing scholarly attention to movements and movement organizations with nonstate targets,[37] inspired in part by New Social Movement theories emphasizing the cultural, identity-based politics of many U.S. movements in the 1960s and 1970s.[38] Building on studies that explore movements with a nonstate target, the multi-institutional politics approach acknowledges that many movements not only target nonstate actors but also *simultaneously* target *multiple* institutions for change.[39] But, among social movement scholars, no one has taken up the task of expanding the multi-institutional politics approach by developing a theoretical account of movements that target multiple institutional arenas, highlighting the characteristics that distinguish them and the special dilemmas they face.

Sociologists, activists, and religious leaders need social movement theories that better account for the diverse relationships between religion and social movement activism in today's globalizing context. Recent research on the ways religion inspires and enables activism has provided an important corrective to earlier theoretical traditions, going back to Émile Durkheim and Karl Marx, that assumed religion was either a force for maintaining the status quo or was disappearing in the modern world.[40] But the shifting empirical context demands new ways of interrogating the relationship between religion and activism. For instance, few social movement scholars have explored how contemporary social movements shape religion rather than focusing on how religion influences social movements, instead creating an unnecessary and counterproductive division between "religious movements" and "social movements."[41] While a few scholars have examined religion as a target of social movements,[42] these movements have all been examples of what sociologist Tricia Bruce calls intrainstitutional social movements—movements or movement organizations whose sole target is a particular religious institution and whose participants are largely committed members of that institution.[43]

Focusing attention on the *multiple* targets of many movements and movement organizations better accounts for non-Western, non-Christian ways of thinking about and doing politics, which some scholars of religion, immigration, and globalization have been calling for in recent years.[44] For instance, some Islamic studies scholars have argued that many Islamic movements in locales like Egypt, India, and Indonesia seek not only political change but also—even primarily—the spiritual transformation of society.[45] Nancy Davis and Rob Robinson's book *Claiming Society for God* demonstrates the ways activists from a variety of religious backgrounds, both in the United States and other parts of the world, are circumventing the state in their efforts to create long-term religious and political change.[46]

Like these movements, the New Sanctuary Movement represents an example of what I call a multi-target social movement: a movement or movement organization that simultaneously seeks change in more than one arena. New Sanctuary sought to transform both the state and religion. In mobilizing religious communities, their aims went beyond the common movement strategy of organizing congregations to create a broader activist base for social and political change. This was part of New Sanctuary's endgame, but it was not the sole part. Instead, they also sought to mobilize religious congregations in order to challenge dominant, largely conservative, religious authority in the United States and to transform the religious and spiritual lives of those involved, moving them toward a more progressive, global, inclusive religious vision. In the framework of multi-target social movements, the supposed dichotomy of religious movements versus social movements becomes muddied. In the remainder of this book, I will show how analyzing the New Sanctuary Movement as a multi-target movement, with the simultaneous goals of changing multiple arenas, helps make sense of decisions and struggles that otherwise seem puzzling, demonstrating the potential of this perspective to provide a fresh lens for interpreting a variety of movements, both past and present.

Making Immigration a Religious Issue

In Los Angeles, Pastor Michaels's [47] church was one of many that, for both political and religious reasons, decided to take a public stand in support of undocumented immigrants by joining the New Sanctuary Movement and offering to house an immigrant family in their church building. While Liliana and Pablito lived in Pastor Michaels's church for a while, after several months they moved into UCC Simi Valley, a church an hour north of Los Angeles that had recently joined New Sanctuary. Also a mainline Protestant church with some activist experience but little prior experience with immigrants, the advantage of this church over Pastor Michaels's was mostly location— it was much closer to Liliana's former home and therefore to her husband and her other children. But it also became a target for the anti-immigration activists in the hilly suburbs north of LA. So while it was closer to family, it also presented new frustrations, both for Liliana and for her religious partners, in a setting less equipped than urban areas to deal with disruptive activism. During the weekly protests by anti-immigration activists outside of the church, local police came to "protect" the church from damage by the protesters. In 2008, they unexpectedly sent a bill for police protection of $40,000 on to the shocked leadership of the church.

Liliana and Pablito did not live in the church building. Instead, they lived in a house on church property, up a hill just behind the church (Figure I.1). Each week after the service ended, UCC Simi Valley members and other New Sanctuary activists from area faith communities and partner organizations

FIGURE I.1. Liliana and Pablito in sanctuary in 2007. (Photo by June C. Goudey.)

escorted them back to the house, protecting them in case one of the anti-immigration activists tried to come onto the property and make a "citizen's arrest"—a tactic they had attempted before. On this ritual walk, they often talked or joked with each other, but sometimes there was silent recognition of the dangers involved. The intimacy created through the church's relationship with Liliana and Pablito was both motivated by their religious commitments and changed the shape of those commitments.

Once inside the parish house, they could usually relax a bit, shutting the door behind Liliana as she entered her sanctuary. Thanks to her religious partners, she was safe on church property, protected from ICE, from anti-immigration activists, and from others who sought to deport her—assuming ICE chose to continue respecting the historic practice of church sanctuary despite the lack of laws prohibiting their entry. But she was also trapped in separation from her husband and other children, unable to visit family, work, or even go to the store without risking detention by officials. Because of her public involvement in the New Sanctuary Movement, ICE knew exactly where she was, and they might pick her up if she left her "sanctuary," as they did with Elvira Arellano after she left sanctuary in 2007. If Liliana had gone into hiding rather than joining New Sanctuary, she may have evaded ICE's detection and attention, reuniting with her family after a short time. Instead, when my research ended in 2009, Liliana had been living in sanctuary for over two years, effectively stuck on church property with no end in sight.

How did a group of well-meaning activists create a situation in which, rather than experiencing a concrete change in her status, Liliana had been trapped in a church for two years? Since immigrant rights organizations existed before New Sanctuary's launch, why did activists create their own distinctly religious activist network rather than joining existing organizations? Why did the growing group of activists choose a controversial, questionably legal strategy like sanctuary in the midst of an increasingly hostile political climate? Why did they focus only on giving sanctuary to mixed-status families like Liliana's when they claimed to represent all undocumented immigrants equally? Why, despite their initial emergence as an interfaith coalition of native-born people and immigrants, did they end up a largely white, middle-class, native-born, Christian network? And what, if anything, does New Sanctuary's religiosity have to do with all of this? The remaining chapters of this book depict the courageous ways that religious activists are responding to the new political and religious realities associated with immigration to the United States today while also portraying the conflicts and complications accompanying attempts to change both political and religious realities at the same time.

1 THE NEW SANCTUARY MOVEMENT

A thin man with graying hair stands behind a church podium, wearing a collared shirt, blue jeans, and his signature cowboy boots. It is difficult to say which is more famous and admired in the world of progressive religious activism—the place or the man. Riverside Church, a member of the New Sanctuary Movement, has long been a center for religious activism. Martin Luther King, Jr., railed against the Vietnam War from its pulpit, and Nelson Mandela spoke there after his release from prison in South Africa. The man in boots is Rev. John Fife, a Presbyterian pastor from Tucson and one of the founders of the 1980s Sanctuary Movement. Today, he is well-known for his work with No More Deaths, an organization working along the U.S.–Mexico border to provide humanitarian aid to migrants crossing the Sonoran desert into the United States.[1]

Rev. Fife has come from Arizona to New York to give the key-note address at the 2009 national gathering of the New Sanctuary Movement. He opens with a joke: "At first I resented the term 'New' Sanctuary Movement. It implies that the rest of us are old."[2] People laugh as he continues, "Then I realized it's appropriate. Sanctuary is always new. But it has an ancient history." New Sanctuary activists around the room listen intently as Fife gives a short rundown of this history, from the use of temples in Ancient Israel to protect people from blood feuds to the comparatively modern abolitionist movement and the Underground Railroad.[3]

Like many preachers and longtime activists, his voice has a musical quality, strong and impassioned at one moment and quiet and reflective in the next. He talks about the effects of today's immigration policies, comparing the growing number of immigrant deaths in the desert due to increased border enforcement to lynchings during the Civil Rights Movement, labeling the deaths "lynchings in the desert." He says, "For those of us who would be faithful, collaboration [with the government] is a betrayal of our faith...God still rules. God will have the last word." The speech ends on a playful but rousing note: "And so we gather as the 'new' movement in the centuries-long sanctuary movement. And this is the word of God: the bastards will not win in the end!" Laughter fills the room, and as Rev. Fife steps back from the podium loud applause erupts. Activists around the room rise from their metal folding chairs, smiling and clapping as Rev. Fife makes his way down the stage steps and toward the door, shaking hands and hugging people along the way.

As Rev. Fife's speech implies, the New Sanctuary Movement was a religious response to the growing crisis around undocumented immigration in the United States, building on the legacy of a religious movement of the past. Many of its members reported being motivated by their religious beliefs to work for justice for immigrants. They could have done this by joining existing immigrant rights organizations. Instead, the early group of activists that formed the New Sanctuary Movement chose to form a separate, distinctly religious movement organization focused on immigrant rights.

Social movement scholars have tried to uncover the reasons behind the emergence of social movement organizations. Dominant approaches focus on the ways that political opportunities, organizational resources, and the development of a revolutionary consciousness enable movement emergence, most assuming (or occasionally explicitly asserting) that the state is the target of legitimate social movements.[4] While these three factors explain some aspects of the New Sanctuary Movement's emergence, as I will show in this chapter, they do not adequately explain why activists created a new, distinct religious network rather than joining more established immigrant rights organizations.

The Birth of the New Sanctuary Movement

During the decades leading up to 2007, increasing numbers of immigrants came to the United States and stayed without proper authorization. At the same time, public hostility toward immigrants increased, laws became stricter, and enforcement grew harsher. In response to these crises, the New Sanctuary Movement officially started on May 9, 2007, with joint press conferences in Los Angeles, New York, Chicago, San Diego, and Seattle. Launched the same day that the Comprehensive Reform Act of 2007 (S.1348) was introduced in the U.S. Senate, it had obvious political aims. New Sanctuary hoped to draw attention to the struggles of mixed-status immigrant families in the lead up to the Senate vote.

At the launch, clergy in their collars, skullcaps, and yarmulkes stood alongside mixed-status immigrant families, preaching that God calls people to "welcome the stranger" and that God's care for families requires religious people to work to keep immigrant families intact. They stressed the Golden Rule teaching that many religions share—the Christian version is "do to others as you would have them do to you"—arguing for more love and compassion in the immigration debate.[5] They explained that their new network was being organized through faith communities, with people of faith advocating with and for immigrants. In other words, in their appearance, organization, and arguments for political change, they were explicitly religious.

The 2006 decision of undocumented Mexican activist Elvira Arellano to move into her Chicago church inspired the revival of the legacy of "sanctuary": the practice of temporarily providing refuge for fugitives in houses of worship, whose long history had its most recent and well-known incarnation in the United States during the 1980s Sanctuary Movement. Following her example, local coalitions began forming around the country, most framing themselves as a religious response to the immigration crisis and made up primarily of faith communities and clergy. Many coalitions had or were seeking at least one *sanctuary family*—a mixed-status immigrant family who agreed to make their immigration case public by joining New Sanctuary and partnering with one of the member congregations. Sanctuary families typically included an undocumented parent undergoing deportation proceedings and a U.S. citizen spouse or child—in other words, they were families who would be split up if U.S. immigration and deportation policies did not change. The New Sanctuary Movement lifted up sanctuary families' cases as examples of the familial separations happening every day due to immigration policy, arguing for the necessity of a more just system.[6]

For much of its use throughout history, sanctuary typically involved providing refuge in houses of worship to people fleeing government authorities.[7] During the 1980s Sanctuary Movement, which Rev. Fife helped lead, most people taking sanctuary were recent arrivals from Central America who needed transportation, housing, resettlement assistance, food, and clothing—fleeing violent civil wars, they entered the United States seeking humanitarian aid as much as residency or citizenship.[8] Churches and synagogues housed immigrants on their properties, protecting them against capture and deportation until they could be moved to a safer place. At various points in history, this form of sanctuary has been either a legally protected practice or one that was widely allowed despite the absence of legal protections for houses of worship engaged in sanctuary.[9]

But the New Sanctuary Movement parted ways, in many respects, from past practices of sanctuary. In contrast to the 1980s, when the Sanctuary Movement worked with recent arrivals, the New Sanctuary Movement highlighted the struggles of long-term U.S. residents with local family and community ties, careers, and homes. These immigrants did not need humanitarian aid or a place to hide as they looked for a safer long-term location. Instead, they sought legalization and naturalization that would allow them to continue living and working in the U.S. locales they already called home. As a result, New Sanctuary activists struggled to reimagine sanctuary to meet the demands of a new political environment.[10] A few local coalitions had people living in houses of worship, but most New Sanctuary families resided in their own homes with their own families and worked in their usual jobs. Instead of taking temporary shelter in a religious building, they went about their daily lives, partnering with local congregations called *sanctuary faith communities* that provided legal, financial, and spiritual support, through practices like accompanying immigrants to their check-ins with Immigration and Customs Enforcement (ICE).

Much New Sanctuary organizing happened (and continues to occur) at the local level. However, the bulk of this book is based on the first two years of the New Sanctuary Movement, a time when a good deal of organizing was occurring nationally as well, both before and after the failure of the comprehensive immigration reform legislation that was one of the group's initial emphases. The New Sanctuary Movement never had many paid staff members, with volunteers from local religious groups comprising the steering committees and doing the majority of the everyday work. In addition to coming together during several national gatherings, local coalitions worked together nationally through conference calls, a national newsletter, and occasional emails. Until 2009, there was always at least one paid national staff member, though the specific people filling staff positions—and their duties—changed over time. During its first two years, the New Sanctuary Movement held three national gatherings, one each in Chicago, Los Angeles, and New York. These three cities were the main hubs of the national New Sanctuary Movement during that time, which grew to include between 25 and 30 local coalitions in 2008. This book focuses on two of them—Los Angeles and New York—not to systematically compare them but to offer a fuller picture of the national network's diversity.

The Los Angeles New Sanctuary Coalition

From 2007 to 2009, the Los Angeles New Sanctuary coalition was primarily made up of members of another organization, what social movement scholars would call a "movement midwife" because of its provision of resources that helped give birth to the coalition.[11] Clergy and Laity United for Economic Justice (CLUE) and its executive director, Rev. Alexia Salvatierra, played a central role in mobilizing people in the Los Angeles area, a process I will discuss in greater detail later. There were four families in public sanctuary in the LA area (i.e., unlike in cases of private sanctuary, their presence and status had been made known to the media and government authorities),[12] all of them living in churches, something that was typical of the Sanctuary Movement in the 1980s but less common in the New Sanctuary Movement.

The Los Angeles coalition was organized according to what its members called a cluster model. Each faith community with a family living on its property was known as a host congregation, and multiple nearby faith communities took on a supporting role, as in the case of Liliana. Since there were four families in sanctuary, there were four clusters in the LA coalition. In 2008, between 15 and 20 religious communities were regularly involved in the Los Angeles coalition, and many more had signed a pledge of support for the group. Most of these groups were mainline Protestant congregations, though a few were Catholic, evangelical Protestant, or Jewish.[13] Many were affiliated with CLUE, were immigrant congregations, or had a history of religious activism.

All four of the sanctuary families in LA originally migrated from Latin America. As mentioned before, Liliana was originally from Mexico. While she and her young son Pablito were living at a church in Simi Valley outside of Los Angeles, her husband and her two other young children were still living in their home. Everyone in the immediate family had legal status except Liliana. Another Mexican immigrant in sanctuary, José, had two sons and lived in several different churches in the LA area during the coalition's first two years. A third immigrant, Juan, lived in one church for the majority of the time he was in sanctuary. Originally from Guatemala, he migrated to the United States during the 1980s when his country was in upheaval. While he applied for political asylum at the time, a letter that came to his home about his court case was in English, and he could read only Spanish at the time. After some bad advice from a lawyer, his case was dropped and he was not able to obtain asylum. Juan's mother had legal status in the United States and was an ongoing advocate for him and for the other immigrants in the LA coalition. Juan was married and had several children who were U.S. citizens, and his landscaping business provided their livelihood.

The fourth immigrant in sanctuary in LA was a Guatemalan immigrant named Yolanda. She had lived in Los Angeles for years and had a daughter in her late teens who was an American citizen. Yolanda was a longtime member of an area church, and her own church decided to give her sanctuary. Church members worked for months to turn an upstairs educational space into a small apartment for Yolanda and her daughter, even installing a shower. If deported, Yolanda would have been separated from her daughter, sent to a country where she no longer knew anyone and had not lived in years.[14]

The four immigrants in sanctuary in LA lived in churches in part because they felt they had no further legal avenues through which to fight their deportation orders. If they had stayed at home in their houses with their families, they could have been detained and deported at any time. It was only under this urgent situation that they decided to take what came to be called physical sanctuary in the New Sanctuary Movement, especially since once they did so there was no certainty about when they would be able to leave the church buildings again.

The New Sanctuary Coalition of New York City

During the first two years of the New Sanctuary Coalition of NYC, families did not take physical sanctuary like Liliana. Since the immigration cases of most of the six NYC families still had some hope of being addressed through legal appeals, they were able to stay in their homes and continue working at their jobs. As a result, sanctuary in the New York City coalition took a different form. Faith communities partnered with mixed-status families and offered them support, accompanying them to immigration check-ins, providing legal or financial assistance when necessary, or sharing spiritual and moral support and friendship. Between one and three congregations typically partnered with each family, and the coalition as a whole offered additional support where needed rather than using a cluster model of support.

Like the LA coalition, preexisting organizations helped the New Sanctuary Coalition of NYC get started. In particular, a secular immigrant rights organization called Families for Freedom (FFF)—an NYC organization founded and led by members of mixed-status immigrant families—supported the coalition's initial mobilization efforts, especially through providing some of its own member families as sanctuary families for the coalition. However, FFF's role was more limited than CLUE's because, as a secular organization, it did not have the religious activist membership or networks needed to mobilize people around sanctuary.

As of 2009, between 10 and 15 faith communities were regularly involved in the New York City coalition, and many more had signed a pledge of support. As in LA, most of these congregations and clergy representatives were mainline Protestant, though a few were Catholic, evangelical Protestant, Jewish, or Muslim. Most either had a long history of religious activism or were majority-immigrant congregations who felt compelled to do something about the immigration crisis.

In NYC, the six families in sanctuary were more diverse in their national origins than those in LA. At the time of the coalition's launch in May 2007, there were two sanctuary families in the coalition: a Haitian immigrant named Jean and his wife and children (Figure 1.1); and a Chinese immigrant named Joe and his wife and children. Years ago, Jean migrated to the United States legally, green card in hand. But an old criminal conviction coupled with changes to immigration law stripped him of his former legal status, making him deportable. Joe and his family were seeking asylum, but it had not yet been granted. A second Chinese family in the coalition, an undocumented couple named Sam and Sandra[15] who had a U.S. citizen child, also sought asylum. Another family, a Jamaican immigrant named Roxroy and his common-law wife and citizen children, was also part of the early New Sanctuary Movement. Amina,[16] an undocumented woman from Senegal, also joined the coalition after her undocumented husband was deported, leaving her alone to provide for their six U.S. citizen children, her own deportation potentially imminent. Lastly, an undocumented Guatemalan woman named Patty, married to a U.S. citizen named Jarrett, also joined New Sanctuary.

FIGURE 1.1 New York City sanctuary immigrant Jean at an immigrant rights march in 2008. (Photo by Mizue Aizeki.)

Several months after joining, Patty became pregnant and later gave birth to a U.S. citizen child.

As these details on the New York and Los Angeles coalitions demonstrate, the national New Sanctuary Movement was a diverse network in its early years. Its membership included immigrants from many national backgrounds and religious activists from a variety of traditions. Likewise, its sanctuary practices varied widely, from occasional legal aid to daily interaction and physical protection from ICE. Though its shape varied around the country, New Sanctuary activists shared a commitment to bringing faith communities and immigrants together to improve the lives of undocumented immigrants in the United States, an uphill battle in the hostile political climate of the mid-2000s.

U.S. Immigration Politics in the 21st Century

The history of the United States is a history of immigrants. From the European settlers who took the land of Native Americans to the largely Italian and Irish immigrants of the 19th century to the mostly Latin American, African, and Asian immigrants of today, people have migrated to this land seeking new beginnings. Still, immigrants to the United States have almost always been met with a combination of fear and prejudice.[17] In 2006, just before the New Sanctuary Movement's emergence, Americans were evenly split as to whether immigration has a positive or a negative impact on American society. Nearly half of Americans agreed that the growing number of immigrant newcomers threatens traditional American customs and values, while 45% said that newcomers strengthen America.[18]

The simplest explanation for the controversy over immigration, both in 2007 and today, is that immigration has been on the rise in recent decades, creating concern among those that favor limiting the number of immigrants to the United States. As of 2007, about 38 million immigrants were living in the United States, or around 12.5% of the total population.[19] As recently as 1970, these numbers were much smaller: 9.6 million immigrants and 4.7% of the total population. As Figure 1.2 demonstrates, there has been a steady, steep increase in immigration over the past few decades.[20] Despite this recent trend, as a percentage of the population, immigration was still *lower* in the mid-2000s than at several other points in the nation's past. Immigrants in the early years of the 21st century made up a lower percentage of the total U.S. population than they did at the turn of the 20th century, for instance. But the relatively low numbers of migrants during much of the 20th century,

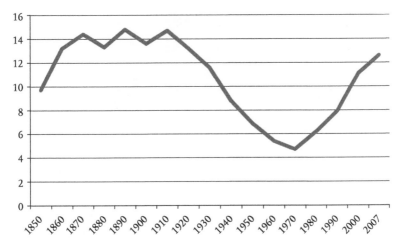

FIGURE 1.2 Foreign-born as a percentage of total U.S. population, 1850–2007. (*Source:* United States Census.)

followed by an abrupt rise in recent years, is one of the reasons that immigration policy has become so controversial. Because the percentage of immigrants dropped to a very low level in recent decades (within most American adults' lifetimes), in the mid-2000s people raised in an environment relatively absent of immigrants were being confronted with something unexpected and unfamiliar.

But there are additional reasons behind the tension around immigration over the last decade. Immigrants started settling in more midsize cities and suburbs, venturing outside of traditional gateways like New York City and Los Angeles. States, cities, and towns that had little prior contact with immigrants were suddenly forced to share their communities with newcomers, in some cases for the first time. Many of these localities did not have the resettlement resources that traditional gateways did, a situation spurring conflict and tension between citizens and immigrants in these communities.[21]

As they relocated to these areas, recent immigrants brought cultural diversity to previously homogenous communities, but they brought higher levels of racial and ethnic diversity as well. After the passage of the Hart-Cellar Act eliminated national quotas in 1965, a much larger proportion of immigrants to the United States began migrating from Latin America, Asia, and Africa compared with the past, when most immigrants had European ancestry.[22] As Figure 1.3 demonstrates, the decline in the percent of immigrants hailing from Europe between 1960 and 2007 was drastic, as was the increase in the percent of immigrants originating in Latin America and Asia.[23]

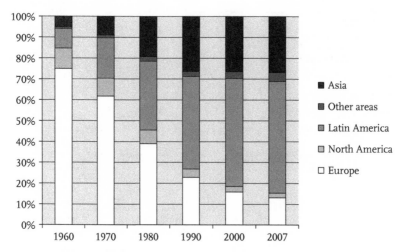

FIGURE 1.3 Region of birth of the foreign-born, 1960–2007. (*Source:* United States Census.)

Thus, between 1960 and 2007, immigration patterns shifted from a primarily white immigrant population to an immigrant population made up primarily of people of color. Some scholars argue that these trends were and continue to be so dramatic that they are contributing to a major reconstruction of racial categories in the United States, a process that parallels the changing racialization of Jewish and Italian immigrants during the 20th century.[24] These patterns diversified communities with little experience with racial and ethnic diversity, resulting in new tensions and conflict in the mid-2000s, embodied in practices like media constructions of Latino immigrants as threats to the health of local American communities.[25]

Finally, both in 2007 and today, much of the anti-immigrant sentiment is directed at a particular group of immigrants—those variously referred to as illegal, undocumented, or unauthorized immigrants.[26] The number of immigrants living in the United States without permission from the government—whether they crossed the border illegally, overstayed visas, had Legal Permanent Resident (LPR) status revoked due to a criminal conviction, or failed to be granted asylum, among other reasons—grew by approximately 40% between 2000 and 2007, from an estimated 8.5 million to 11.8 million.[27] However, most of this growth occurred during the first half of the decade, with the population of undocumented immigrants stabilizing between 2005 and 2007 at between 10.5 and 12 million, or approximately 30% of immigrants in the United States.[28] In 2008, three out of four undocumented immigrants were born in Latin America (59% in Mexico, 11% in Central America,

7% in South America, and 4% in the Caribbean), while 11% were from Asia and less than 2% were from the Middle East.[29]

Like immigrants more generally, undocumented immigrants became more geographically dispersed over the last decade. While longtime destination states like New York, Texas, and California still claimed the largest number of undocumented immigrants, an unprecedented number began residing in states like Georgia, North Carolina, and Virginia, increasing tensions in these places. Undocumented immigrants also made up around 5.5% of the total U.S. labor force in 2007, a rapid increase from 4.3% in 2003.[30] Though some pundits and comedians have argued that these jobs are ones that do not interest American workers, some anti-immigrant forces have contended that the largest problem with undocumented immigration is its effects on the American labor force.[31]

While all of these trends were important aspects of the context that gave birth to the New Sanctuary Movement in 2007, one of the most significant was the growth in the number of U.S. citizen children with an undocumented parent, which grew from 2.7 million in 2000 to 4 million in 2008, an increase of 48%.[32] These children have often been disparagingly referred to as "anchor babies" by anti-immigration activists, a term implying that undocumented immigrants intentionally give birth to children in the United States, hoping that their children's citizenship will help them obtain legal status—a contention vigorously challenged by immigrants' supporters.

In the mid-2000s, these well-publicized trends drew attention from both sides of the political aisle, with practically everyone agreeing that so-called illegal immigration was a problem that must be addressed even while they disagreed about how best to deal with it.[33] While in 2006 immigration as a whole was somewhat undesirable among many Americans (only 17% supported an increase in legal immigration),[34] the rise in undocumented immigration was even more contentious. In the mid to late 2000s, significant percentages of Americans perceived undocumented immigrants as job stealers, threats to American culture, dangerous criminals, or potential terrorists.[35] These negative stereotypes about undocumented immigrants became increasingly reflected in strict legislation and enforcement practices that were reminiscent of xenophobic reactions to increased migration in America's past.[36]

Legislative Change and Increasing Enforcement

As immigration levels rose dramatically during the 1990s, the U.S. government began seeking new ways to regulate the increasing flow of migrants, resulting in the passage of the Illegal Immigration Reform and Immigrant Responsibility Act (IIRAIRA) in 1996. The IIRAIRA represented a major shift in immigration policy, replacing a largely discretionary system with mandatory detention and deportation, not only for people without papers but also for legal permanent residents—green card holders—convicted of a newly broad range of minor offenses.[37] Prior to 1996, the legal status of LPRs was revoked only in cases of aggravated felony.

The law was applied retroactively, making immigrants with LPR status and criminal convictions eligible for deportation (like NYC sanctuary immigrant Jean), regardless of the understandings in place when they migrated, when they were tried, and when they served their sentences. Immigration and civil rights lawyer Ira Kurzban argues, "Within a period of approximately thirty years, we went from the 1960s civil rights act for the foreign born... to the Illegal Immigration Reform and Immigrant Responsibility Act of 1996, which literally rewrote the immigration laws to severely restrict due process and most forms of immigration relief."[38] This legislative change contributed to what some have conceptualized as a pre-9/11 expansion of immigration enforcement.[39]

After the September 11 attacks in New York, Washington, D.C., and Pennsylvania in 2001, things became even worse for undocumented immigrants. Though the 1996 law was significantly stricter than other laws of recent past, its implementation had not been a national priority before 9/11. Rising levels of fear and racism following the attacks made the United States less welcoming to outsiders, and the immigration system began changing again in major ways. The Federal Bureau of Investigation (FBI) and the Immigration and Naturalization Service (INS) started conducting raids soon after 9/11, detaining South Asians, Arabs, and North Africans and deporting many of those they detained.[40] In 2003, the INS and other immigration agencies became housed under the newly formed U.S. Department of Homeland Security (DHS). This was a watershed moment—all immigrants became defined, in legal and unequivocal terms, as threats to the security of the United States. The former responsibilities of the INS were divided among three new government agencies: U.S. Citizenship and Immigration Services (USCIS); U.S. Customs and Border Protection (CBP); and Immigration and Customs Enforcement (ICE).

By 2004, the newly formed ICE had laid out a 10-year goal referred to as Operation Endgame to remove all undocumented immigrants from the United States. To carry out this new mandate, the budgets for immigration enforcement ballooned. Between 1985 and 2002, spending on immigration enforcement had already more than quadrupled, growing from $1 billion to $4.9 billion. The largest increases came during the year following the passage of the IIRIRA and following the September 11 attacks.[41] By 2007, the budget for CBP (the agency within DHS tasked with the border-related enforcement functions of the former INS) had grown to almost $8 billion, with ICE's budget at $4.5 billion, for a total of $12.5 billion on immigration enforcement and border protection budgeted for the year—an increase of almost $8 billion in 5 years.[42]

These changes in funding, policy, and policy implementation strategies led to huge increases in immigrant detentions and deportations. In the mid-2000s, ICE stepped up its strategy of raiding the workplaces, homes, and shopping centers of immigrants. In 2006 alone, raids and other enforcement operations led to the deportation of approximately 280,000 people: a 32% increase from 2003.[43] After 2006, intensive raids, detentions, and deportations only increased, with even more undocumented immigrants detained or deported without warning, leaving families and homes behind.

In 2007, ICE detained one and a half times as many immigrants as in 2001, with the number growing from 209,000 to 311,169 people.[44] This rise in detentions paralleled increases in deportations. From 1988 to 1997, approximately 490,000 people were forcibly sent back to their country of origin from the United States. In the following decade, 1998 to 2007, that number multiplied more than four times to over 2.2 million deportees, with 320,00 deportees in 2007 alone (see Figure 1.4).[45] Over the period stretching from 1997 to 2007, more than 100,000 of the millions deported were the parents of U.S. citizen

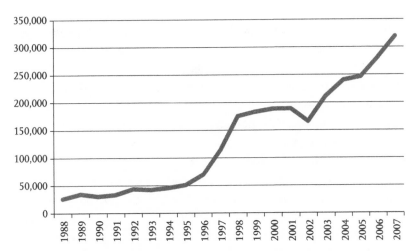

FIGURE 1.4 Number of people deported from the United States, 1988–2007.
(*Source*: U.S. Department of Homeland Security.)

children.[46] A 2009 Human Rights Watch report estimated that over one million family members were separated by deportation from the United States between 1997 and 2007.[47]

In sum, the late 1990s and early 2000s brought about punitive changes in immigration policy and enforcement, spurred on by legislative actions designed to curb undocumented immigration and perhaps legal immigration as well. By the middle of the first decade of the 21st century, more immigrants than ever were coming to the United States. However, more than ever were also being detained and deported. Together, this created an increasingly volatile political context surrounding immigration in the United States, one embodied by the storm surrounding the 2005 passage of H.R. 4437, popularly known as the Sensenbrenner Bill.

The Sensenbrenner Bill, Political Threats, and Immigrant Rights Mobilization

As undocumented immigrants faced ever more difficult realities in the United States, with raids, detentions, and deportations increasing around the country, legislators were debating how best to continue reforming immigration law at the federal level. On December 16, 2005, the U.S. House of Representatives passed H.R. 4437, the Border Protection, Anti-terrorism, and Illegal Immigration Control Act of 2005, also known as the Sensenbrenner Bill because of its sponsor, Rep. Jim Sensenbrenner (R-WI). The Sensenbrenner Bill toughened sentencing for those convicted of document fraud (e.g., false social security cards used to obtain work and pay taxes), increased penalties for employing undocumented workers, and made it a crime for anyone to knowingly assist an undocumented person living in the United States.[48] An outcry erupted from immigrant rights groups across the country after the bill's passage. Even in light of what they saw as increasingly harsh enforcement of current immigration laws, this new legislation came across as particularly ruthless. It not only punished undocumented immigrants for seeking what supporters called honest work but also penalized anyone providing them any form of aid, including humanitarian groups.

Following the bill's passage, immigrant rights groups began organizing in opposition to the legislation, particularly since it was expected to reach the Senate for debate in February or March 2006. On February 14, 2006, activists in Philadelphia organized a walkout known as A Day Without Immigrants, a protest designed to show how the local economy would suffer if immigrants left their jobs, homes, and schools.[49] In early March, mass protests around the country began in earnest, with approximately 30,000 people marching in Washington, D.C., and close to 100,000 marching in Chicago.[50]

On March 16, 2006, Tennessee Republican Bill Frist introduced an immigration reform bill in the Senate that shared some stipulations of the Sensenbrenner legislation (S.2454), calling it the Securing America's Borders Act. Fears that the debate would produce a bill that would incorporate some of the harsher aspects of the Sensenbrenner Bill continued to rise, so immigrant rights groups escalated their efforts, fighting to keep the Senate's version of the bill more moderate. On March 25, 2006, many observers were stunned when 500,000 people took to the streets of Los Angeles (along with tens of thousands more in other cities) demanding fair and humane immigration reform.[51]

The Senate debate lasted for several weeks before stalling in mid-April. In the meantime, the power of showing the value of immigrants to American society through organized protest, demonstrated by the marches in Philadelphia, Chicago, Los Angeles, and other cities, was catching fire in national immigrant rights circles. On May 1, 2006, in conjunction with international May Day celebrations of workers' rights, cities around the country organized demonstrations, asking immigrants to leave work, boycott stores, and take other actions that would highlight the ways the American economy depended on them.[52] Modeled on some of the earlier protests and similarly called A Day Without Immigrants, more than a million people participated in marches around the United States, with around half a million protestors each in both Los Angeles and Chicago. By some estimates, it was the largest day of protest in U.S. history.[53] Preexisting immigrant community groups, like Spanish language media organizations and Latino Catholic parishes, helped mobilize individual protestors, but new immigrant rights organizations were also formed and strengthened as part of the planning for the marches.

On May 25, 2006, the Senate approved a bill (S.2611)—the Comprehensive Immigration Reform Act—that included a possibility for a path to citizenship for some undocumented immigrants, excluding many of the harsher provisions of the Sensenbrenner Bill.[54] Immigrant rights groups saw the Senate's refusal to affirm the House's legislation as a victory and dedicated themselves to building up their ranks and mobilizing more widely. However, the bill ultimately died without passing, spelling an end to any comprehensive reform that might have provided relief to immigrants and their families and reminding activists of how much work still needed to be done.

Over the following year, immigrant rights groups worked with supportive legislators, such as Senator Harry Reid (D-UT) and Rep. Luis Gutiérrez

(D-IL), to introduce comprehensive immigration reform legislation in the Senate and the House in 2007. New immigrant rights groups emerged as part of these efforts—including the New Sanctuary Movement. When immigrant rights activists learned that the Comprehensive Immigration Reform Act of 2007 (S.1348) would be introduced in the Senate in May, they began tailoring parts of their campaigns and organizations toward influencing the legislation's content and passage while recognizing that its passage was not guaranteed and therefore that their strategic visions must be long-term. After CIR failed for the second time in two years during summer 2007, immigrant rights groups—including the recently formed New Sanctuary Movement— had to reassess their strategies and goals in light of the closing of a window of political opportunity and the continually increasing threats to immigrant well-being in the form of raids and deportations.

The Importance of Political Context

In the decades leading up to the New Sanctuary Movement's emergence in 2007, significant changes occurred that deeply affected the U.S. political landscape. There was an immense rise in immigration in general, in the number of nonwhite immigrants, and in the number of undocumented immigrants. For reasons related to xenophobia, racism, nationalism, and cultural and economic concerns, these increases created a tense political environment around the issue of immigration. Americans were split on the issue of whether continued immigration was good for the country or not. At the same time, trends of increased immigration created a need for new types of policy to regulate these increases. In the mid-2000s, this took the shape of increased enforcement of existing laws in the form of rising raids, detentions, and deportations of undocumented immigrants, a situation resulting in the separation of a million family members from each other. Fear became rampant in many immigrant communities, who often felt targeted by authorities and distrusted by their neighbors even if they personally had legal status.[55]

The passage of the Sensenbrenner Bill in 2005 was the proverbial straw that broke the camel's back. Political threats to immigrant communities had become so great that immigrants and their allies felt it necessary to respond in new and more powerful ways. These rising threats created a political context encouraging the emergence of a national movement for immigrant rights. Indeed, a national immigrant rights movement began to gain prominence in 2006, and in 2007 the New Sanctuary Movement also emerged as a national network of movement organizations responding to the threatening political context. Thus, as dominant social movement approaches would predict, political context helps explain why the New Sanctuary Movement emerged when it did.

However, this cannot fully explain why the New Sanctuary Movement emerged as a new, distinct religious network given the existence of many other groups already working for immigrant rights. The tightening authority of the state over the lives of immigrants required a response from immigrants and their supporters, but not necessarily a separate religious one. The next question, then, focuses on the extent to which religion provided motivation for mobilization around immigrant rights.

Religious Commitments as Call to Mobilization

After the national May Day marches of 2006, immigrant advocates around the country spent the next couple of months talking about how to build on the momentum created by the marches, seeking a next step, a theme to organize around, a leader. In December 2005, just after the passage of the Sensenbrenner Bill, Cardinal Roger Mahony, the archbishop of Los Angeles (the largest Catholic diocese in the United States), had written a letter to then president George W. Bush. The letter expressed his deep concern about the bill's passage, particularly its insistence that aid workers refuse charity to undocumented immigrants. This portion of the bill outraged many religious people, who saw it as a limit to their religious freedom. An excerpt of the letter reads:

> One could interpret this Bill to suggest that any spiritual and pastoral service given to any person requires proof of legal residence. Are we to stop every person coming to Holy Communion and first ask them to produce proof of legal residence before we can offer them the Body and Blood of Christ? Speaking for the Catholic Archdiocese of Los Angeles, such restrictions are impossible to comply with. The underlying basis for our service to others, especially to the poor, is the example, words, and actions of Jesus Christ in the Gospels. The 25th chapter of St. Matthew's Gospel does not simply invite us to serve others in the name of Jesus, but offers such service as a requisite to the Kingdom of God.[56]

After quoting several verses from the 25th chapter of the Gospel of Matthew, he implored President Bush to seek other, more compassionate means of immigration reform rather than throwing his support behind the House legislation.

Cardinal Mahony had a long history of working with immigrants in the context of religious ministry.[57] During the years following his ordination in 1962, he ministered to largely Hispanic farm workers in California. After he was made bishop, he was appointed in 1975 by the California governor as chair of the first California Agricultural Labor Relations Board, which involved mediating between Cesar Chavez's United Farm Workers and state growers. Thus, when he wrote to President Bush about the needs and the rights of immigrants, he was speaking from a plethora of experiences regarding immigration as a pastoral issue, not merely a political one.

Cardinal Mahony's objection to the Sensenbrenner Bill was not merely an objection to the state of political affairs in the United States. It was also a rejection of the dominant view of religion in the early 21st century. He argued that the Sensenbrenner Bill was mistaken not only because it was unfair to immigrants but also because it restricted his ability to practice what he saw as true religiosity, which had been neglected due to the dominance of other, more nationalistic and legalistic forms of religion popularized by the religious right. Cardinal Mahony's sermon served as a rallying call for religious activists around the country, a challenge not only to defend immigrants but also to defend a more compassionate and global vision of religion. Similarly, the first Latina bishop in the United Methodist Church (UMC), Bishop Minerva Carcaño, voiced strong and public support for Elvira Arellano when she took sanctuary in a UMC church in Chicago in 2006, further arousing the consciousness of religious people around issues of immigration.[58]

Social movement scholars argue that developing a revolutionary consciousness involves discovering the need to work for change and the conviction that change is indeed possible.[59] If either of these two elements is missing, it is less likely that people will spend the time and effort required for involvement in social movement activism. In the case of the New Sanctuary Movement, while many New Sanctuary activists reported having long been motivated by their religious beliefs to get involved in social justice activism more generally, Cardinal Mahony's sermon and Bishop Carcaño's actions served as "aha moments" for many people regarding immigration by asserting the relevance of religion for immigrant rights issues and of immigrant rights for religion.

Still, being motivated by one's faith to work for immigrant rights does not necessitate starting a distinct religious movement organization. Religiously motivated activists can be found in many movement organizations, whether religious or secular. Before (and after) the birth of New Sanctuary, many religious activists chose to participate in established immigrant rights organizations that were not organized around religious identity. Similarly, some activists already participated in forms of religious immigrant rights activism that were regional or denominational. However, these parts of the immigrant rights movement did not necessarily meet the need for a national, religiously inclusive network of immigrant rights activists.

The Immigrant Rights Movement

Encouraged in part by Mahony's willingness to challenge government policing not only of immigration but also of religion, in 2006, many native-born and immigrant religious people were cultivating the required revolutionary consciousness to advocate for immigrant rights. Fortunately, the growing number of immigrant rights organizations provided ample opportunities for religious activists to get involved in the push for more immigrant-friendly policies. Struggles for the rights of immigrants to live and work in the United States without fear and prejudice have a long history, often tied to issues of labor.[60] The best-known modern example of U.S. immigrant organizing is the United Farm Workers of America movement (UFW), founded and led by Cesar Chavez and Dolores Huerta during its heyday in the 1960s and 1970s. At the time, the UFW's "resourcefulness" trumped its lack of resources,[61] enabling it to grow into a sizeable, powerful challenge to California growers that culminated in the 1975 passage of the pro-immigrant Agricultural Labor Relations Act.[62] The movement's strategy of focusing on labor laws as a way to improve immigrants' lives was so successful that it came to dominate the culture of immigrant rights activism even after the UFW's influence declined.[63]

During the 1990s and early 2000s, a great deal of immigrant rights advocacy took place via organizations and coalitions formed around workers' rights issues.[64] Former UFW activists worked during this period to build alliances between labor unions, nonprofits, religious groups, and Central American solidarity organizations that formed during the 1980s.[65] The American Federation of Labor and Congress of Industrial Organizations (AFL-CIO), Service Employees International Union (SEIU), and other groups organized campaigns like the Active Citizenship Campaign in 1995 (immigrant voter registration drive) and the Immigrant Workers Freedom Ride in 2003 (a national immigrant rights event designed to resemble Civil Rights freedom rides).[66] Using strategies and tactics such as voter registration, local "know-your-rights" workshops, consumer boycotts, and occasional large-scale events like the Freedom Ride, immigrant rights activism took place mostly on a local scale, oriented toward changing community policy and employer practices.[67]

Thus, while immigrant advocacy has been an important part of the American political landscape for many years, the mobilization of what we think of today as the national immigrant rights movement is largely the product of political changes in the 1990s and 2000s. The growth in undocumented immigration, the rise in detentions and deportations since the events of 9/11, and attempts to pass legislation imposing increased regulation on immigration all served to motivate people to action in the mid-2000s.[68] Particularly following the passage of the Sensenbrenner Bill in 2005, existing and usually localized immigrant social service and advocacy groups felt an urgent need to step up and speak out on behalf of the rights of migrants, resulting in the national marches in May 2006.[69] The Senate's subsequent refusal to affirm the House's legislation was seen as a mark of success by immigrant rights groups, a sign that encouraged people to organize for further actions.[70]

These marches were not spontaneous acts by angry crowds of individuals. Rather, immigrant rights organizations from around the country, such as the Coalition for Humane Immigrant Rights of Los Angeles (CHIRLA) and the New York Immigration Coalition, helped mobilize individual activists for these events and for later fights for comprehensive immigration reform in the U.S. Congress.[71] These existing organizations provided a ready chance for religious activists inspired by Cardinal Mahony's sermon to get involved in the work for immigrant rights. However, religious identity and religious motivations are central for many religious activists, suggesting that they might prefer participating in an existing *religious* immigrant rights organization to joining a secular one.[72]

Religious organizations and identities play an especially pivotal role in the lives of many immigrants, suggesting that immigrants and their partners might prefer religious forms of protest. Participation in ethnic religious groups enables recent immigrants to assimilate into their new context, providing social and cultural capital, emotional support, and other tools essential for survival and success.[73] Within these religious communities, immigrant groups often develop religious and ethnic identities that differ somewhat from those they shared in their country of origin, since discrimination or lack of access to public goods may structure their experiences in new and distinct ways. This is why sociologist Prema Kurien talks about an American Hinduism: the experiences of Hindus in the American context are different enough from their experiences in India to create a form of Hinduism that is uniquely American.[74]

Because of their shared experiences, which often involve some type of political, social, or cultural exclusion, many immigrant religious communities engage in public issues, usually through involvement in local community groups or ethnic advocacy organizations.[75] These organizations often focus on local or state-based issues rather than national issues, and since immigrant religious groups are themselves often ethnically homogenous their activist goals frequently center on the interests of their particular ethnic group.[76]

The immigrant rights marches of 2006 were an exception to this general pattern. Organized in response to the Sensenbrenner Bill and the national political context it represented, the marches mobilized immigrants and their partners from a variety of ethnic groups, though some data suggest that Latinos were by far the largest group of participants. For instance, in the Chicago march, 82% of marchers were Latino, and 46% were Latino Catholics who reported frequently attending church.[77] While the immigrant rights marches were not "religious," a large number of religious immigrants participated in the marches. And though very few of the "frequently attending" Catholic participants in the Chicago march said they came to the march with someone from their church (3%), other data suggest that some Catholic clergy and immigrant parishes advertised the marches, encouraged churchgoers to participate, or even took a more direct role in organizing processions and other public actions.[78] So while it is unclear how many religious organizations played a direct role in the immigrant rights marches, many played an indirect role by making churchgoers aware of the marches and by connecting the marches to religious issues through advertising for them in church buildings.

In addition to indirect forms of support, many religious groups were involved more directly in faith-based immigrant rights efforts around the time of the 2006 marches. In 2005, the U.S. Conference of Catholic Bishops launched its Justice for Immigrants campaign, whose work focused on educating Catholics about the injustices facing immigrants and advocating for more just immigration policies.[79] Similarly, in early 2006, Hispanic evangelical leaders joined together to form the Hispanic Coalition for Comprehensive Immigration Reform (HCFCIR), a national coalition of Hispanic evangelicals opposed to the Sensenbrenner Bill.[80] At the same time, some mainline Protestant denominations and congregations were involved in humanitarian work along the U.S.–Mexico border, engaging in Posadas Sin Fronteras and other cross-border religious forms of protest.[81] And Muslim groups like the Council on American–Islamic Relations (CAIR) were working to support immigrant Muslims and to advocate on their behalf, though they often did this from a more secular perspective in public due to anti-Islamic sentiment in the United States.[82]

In other words, religious people were working for immigrant rights well before the launch of the New Sanctuary Movement, and at least some of those efforts were explicitly religious. Still, most of these existing efforts did not necessarily translate well to the national stage. Border activism was regionally, ethnically, and religiously restricted, with its focus primarily on Mexican and Central American, and largely Christian, immigrants and advocates.[83] Though the Justice for Immigrants campaign and HCFCIR were both focused on national organizing, their respective Catholic and evangelical identities and institutionalizations excluded immigrants and supporters from other religious backgrounds. The focus on Latinos restricted the scope of both organizations as well, a problem for religious activists who wanted to create a more inclusive and representative national religious movement for immigrant rights in a context where immigrants come from a multitude of ethnic and religious backgrounds.[84] As a result, some religious activists chose to concentrate their efforts elsewhere. They opted to build on the resources of existing interfaith and interethnic religious organizations, especially interfaith labor organizations, to form a new immigrant rights network with an explicitly religious—and explicitly interfaith—focus and framework.

The Role of Interfaith Labor Organizations

According to dominant social movement perspectives, preexisting organizations provide resources that are essential to mobilizing any serious challenge to state authority and power.[85] If political threats and revolutionary consciousness push people to act but they do not possess the resources necessary for mobilization, a movement or movement organization is much less likely to emerge.[86] In the case of New Sanctuary, several preexisting organizations provided the resources necessary for mobilizing a new, national interfaith activist network. In particular, two large interfaith and interethnic labor organizations played central roles in mobilizing the New Sanctuary Movement, along with the help of several smaller organizations and campaigns.

Interfaith Worker Justice (IWJ), an organization dedicated to increasing the religious community's involvement in workers' rights issues across the United States, started in Chicago in 1996. A similar organization, Clergy and Laity United for Economic Justice (CLUE), began in LA during the same year, focusing its efforts first on LA and later expanding to a statewide organization. Through their emphasis on workers' rights, these organizations put religious leaders, even those ministering primarily to white, middle-class communities, in direct contact with immigrants. Particularly in California, with its historically large and growing population of immigrant workers, CLUE members' engagement with issues of workplace justice inevitably led to encounters with the special difficulties experienced by immigrant workers, particularly those who were undocumented.[87]

The situation that IWJ and CLUE activists saw on the ground in 2005 and 2006 greatly troubled them. They heard stories of undocumented immigrants being exploited by employers—paid very low wages and denied legal protections in the workplace. Even immigrants with legal status were worried, stressed, and feeling unwelcome in the United States because of the vitriolic tenor of the immigration debates, particularly following the passage of the Sensenbrenner Bill.[88] Because of their dedication to workers' rights advocacy, many CLUE and IWJ staff and affiliated activists realized that they needed to respond somehow to the turmoil surrounding immigrant rights in the United States. However, their organizations were committed to workers' rights in general, not to immigrant rights specifically. If they chose to focus too much energy and resources on immigrant rights campaigns, they could threaten their organizational goals, identity, and member support as well as funding support from labor rights groups like unions. Of course, CLUE and IWJ activists could have joined existing organizations that *focused* on immigrant rights, volunteering or serving as advocates for those organizations. Instead, they joined with other similarly minded activists around the country to form a new immigrant rights network that would focus on immigration from an *interfaith religious* perspective, using their existing organizations to help get this new group up and running.

In this way, CLUE and IWJ served as movement midwives[89] by helping give birth to New Sanctuary through providing the resources necessary for mobilization. These resources included things like money, meeting space, leadership, office supplies, and legitimacy but also things like membership lists and social networks for recruiting new participants. These two organizations, along with the national progressive Christian organization Sojourners, sponsored the first national meeting of potential New Sanctuary activists in Washington, D.C., in 2006.

While CLUE and IWJ had large membership networks that helped launch the New Sanctuary Movement, a smaller organization acted as a symbolic movement midwife: La Familia Latina Unida (LFLU) in Chicago, a coalition of Latino mixed-status families in danger of being separated by deportation. Elvira Arellano, an undocumented Mexican immigrant, helped establish LFLU as an outreach of the immigrant rights organization Centro Sin Fronteras and of her Chicago church, Adalberto United Methodist Church.

When she was ordered to appear for deportation in August 2006, the church offered to give her sanctuary. She accepted, moving into the church with her young son Saul, a U.S. citizen whose health problems required that he remain in the United States for treatment. Elvira's actions, supported by LFLU and Adalberto UMC, provided an image of a possible option for responding to the immigration crisis in an explicitly religious way (Figure 1.5).

In New York City, there was no faith-based workers' rights organization that played an equivalent role to IWJ or CLUE in other parts of the country.[90] Instead, in New York, several long-term religious activists, most of whom had worked with immigrant populations or were immigrants themselves, used their personal networks to explore possible ways of organizing in response to the growing threats facing immigrant populations. In 2006, the new pastor of the historically activist Judson Memorial Church, Rev. Donna Schaper, came to New York from Florida, where debates over undocumented immigration were difficult to ignore. Her networks led her to a recently formed nonprofit organization called Families for Freedom. Founded in 2002, FFF was a "multiethnic defense network by and for immigrants facing deportation

FIGURE 1.5 Protestors at a May Day immigrant rights march in Los Angeles display a poster of sanctuary immigrant Elvira Arellano and her son Saul. (Photo by Josue Bustos.)

in New York" that sought to change laws and policy implementation to end deportation and its negative effects, such as splitting up families.[91] While Families for Freedom was a secular organization, its organizers were excited to form a coalition with religious leaders. They ended up providing a very important resource for the New Sanctuary Movement: contacts with immigrant families that could potentially become sanctuary families. At the same time, Catholic priest and Mexican immigrant Juan Carlos Ruiz was working for a New York–based organization called Asociacion Tepeyac, a largely Catholic nonprofit network founded in 1997 by Mexican community leaders. With approximately 40 organizations in its network, it advocated for the welfare and rights of Latino immigrants, especially those who were undocumented. Ruiz also worked with FFF and was in conversation with them about crafting a response to the crisis. Families for Freedom brought Rev. Schaper and Ruiz together, and the roots of a New York–area New Sanctuary coalition began.[92] Thus, instead of a single existing religious activist organization playing a central role in mobilizing activists around a coalition in New York, a few key religious leaders used their own, their partnering organizations', and their churches' resources and networks to mobilize a small group of activists around the issue.

The case of the New Sanctuary Movement confirms the widely accepted social movement perspective that the resources of preexisting organizations matter for mobilization. But the preexistence of immigrant rights organizations with a religious identity was not enough for the activists who formed New Sanctuary. They could have joined these existing religious immigrant rights groups, but they did not. Instead, they built on the resources of existing interfaith and interethnic labor organizations to create a new national activist network for immigrant rights that was explicitly interfaith. While casual observers might interpret early activists' decision to create a new interfaith immigrant rights network as an effort to mobilize the resources of faith communities to create the broadest base possible for political change, their decision was about more than creating new immigrant rights activists, as the next chapter will show.

Conclusion

At the beginning of this chapter, I described Rev. John Fife—a veteran of the 1980s Sanctuary Movement—speaking at a New Sanctuary Movement gathering, tying together the two groups with the common thread of sanctuary. But aside from giving this speech, Rev. Fife rarely participated in the New

Sanctuary Movement. Long before New Sanctuary began, Rev. Fife helped start an organization called No More Deaths, a group of mostly religious activists working to provide humanitarian assistance to migrants crossing the Sonoran desert into the United States. The activists who started the New Sanctuary Movement could have poured their energy into existing groups like No More Deaths in Arizona, CHIRLA in Los Angeles, or the New York Immigration Coalition, mobilized by their religious faith and working on behalf of immigrants. But they wanted something else.

This chapter has shown that political threats, organizational resources, and the development of a revolutionary consciousness connecting religion to immigrant rights all played a role in the New Sanctuary Movement's emergence. But while these factors help explain why and how the network emerged when it did, they do not fully explain why it emerged as a new religious activist network. These same factors also explain the mobilization of the broader immigrant rights movement, made up largely of existing advocacy organizations, both religious and secular, that future New Sanctuary activists could have joined. Instead, they decided to form their own explicitly interfaith group focused on immigrant rights. To understand the emergence of this distinct group, we must examine the New Sanctuary Movement's targets, which included not only government targets like policymakers and enforcement officers but also other targets for change.

2 CHANGING HEARTS AND MINDS

"To have a home, make a home. To be at home, give a home to others," Donna Schaper told her congregation during a Sunday sermon, gathered in the sanctuary of Judson Memorial Church, the headquarters of the New Sanctuary Coalition of New York City. "The spiritual argument is not about 'Us' settled giving 'Them' immigrants a home. That is paternalism and acts as though we have nothing to gain from welcoming immigrants." Quoting the writer of the Book of Ecclesiastes, a biblical text known for its representation of existential angst, she continued: "The writer says we are all going to suffer one way or another at one time or another. The human condition is the human condition, and it doesn't matter whether you are settled or immigrant. Trouble plans to knock on your door. Time and chance happen to us all. The text may sound depressing at first but in fact it is not," she concluded. "It says that we are all part of one family and may as well act like it."[1]

Well-educated, white, and middle-class, Rev. Schaper's demographics matched those of most of Judson's church members. Many of Judson's members were also progressive religious activists. Located in New York's bustling Greenwich Village, the church worked on a variety of community issues, from needle exchange programs to lesbian, gay, bisexual, and transgender (LGBT) rights. On a Friday, visitors to Judson might have witnessed the performance of a new play. On Saturday, curious students from nearby universities could attend teach-ins on the Palestinian–Israeli conflict.

But while Judson was heavily involved in the surrounding community, it was more than a community center. On Sundays, Judson's sanctuary was home to worshippers, people who embraced its message of social justice not just as political vision but also as central to their *religious* vision of salvation. This religious vision, one of inclusion and hospitality, is key to understanding the puzzle raised in the last chapter. My ethnographic research reveals New Sanctuary activists with multiple concerns and commitments, ones that were not restricted to changing immigration policy.

Beyond Political Goals

When the time came for Judson to find a new senior minister several years ago, Donna Schaper seemed like the perfect fit. Rev. Schaper was one of the first women trained by legendary community organizer Saul Alinsky, working in the Temporary Woodlawn Organization (TWO) on housing issues on Chicago's South Side. Wherever she has lived over the years—Arizona, Miami, Massachusetts, Connecticut—progressive religious activism has been central to her ministry. "I've done housing, I've done micro lending, peace, women's issues," she told me back in 2008, as we sipped cups of coffee. "Things that require political solutions or economic solutions. That draws me more than 'social issues,' although God knows I've been drawn into the social issues over the years as a religious woman, as the right has developed. You know, stand up for gay people, stand up for women when absurd things were being said about them."

Ordained in the United Church of Christ, over time Rev. Schaper has developed a vision of what religious life, and religious community, should be. Calling it "public ministry," she taught courses on this vision to seminary students at a well-known theological school in California and started a training program for public ministers at Judson after she arrived in 2005. "People don't understand this about people on the left like me. This is really religion, not politics for me," she explained to me. "Now does that mean that my religion is the equivalent of my politics? No. Not at all. I'm a great fan of Oscar Romero, who as a Roman Catholic bishop in El Salvador always said to never let your religion be as small as your politics. Always keep a transcendent place where you can judge your own politics, those of the state, and especially those if you have a victory. That God is larger than any one point of view." So while she is drawn to issues with political ramifications, for her, these issues are ultimately about more than politics.

At Judson, Rev. Schaper has trained young people, especially seminarians, in this vision of public ministry, one that seeks to change the way *religion itself* is envisioned and practiced, not just politics. For many at Judson, this was a natural continuation of the church's long legacy of activism. But Rev. Schaper's most recent foray into religious change—the New Sanctuary Movement—moved beyond the church's traditional commitments to what scholar Jeff Stout calls "lifestyle liberal" issues like the arts, LGBT rights, and the environment.[2]

Before coming to Judson, Rev. Schaper pastored a church in Miami. "Immigration is everything there. The whole economy is under the radar.

People make jokes about the Miami airport, like, 'Boy, you get off the plane here, it feels a lot like the United States.'" In Miami, her congregation was full of immigrants, something she could relate to as an immigrant from Germany, though her experiences as a European immigrant differed in important ways from those of her Hispanic congregants. When she got to Judson, she felt compelled to share their experiences with her white, middle-class, mostly native-born church members, many of whom had limited ongoing interaction with immigrant communities. "I read scripture as totally saying that God is found in the stranger and the outsider. You know, Jesus in Matthew says, 'When I was outside, you let me in.' It's very clear. It could say, 'When I was an immigrant, you let me in.'"

Along with preaching sermons on the theme of immigration, Rev. Schaper set about trying to change her congregants' religious visions through writing on the topic.[3] Around the time of New Sanctuary's emergence, she wrote a particularly provocative piece called, "Who's the Illegal, Pilgrim?: Based in the Story of the Good Samaritan and Moses Being Picked Up in the Reeds." An excerpt reads:

> Behaving ourselves, working hard and respecting culture and history are not what makes us "American." Or Good. Being a person who can fish a baby in a basket out of a stream, especially if that baby is not yours or even yours ethnically, makes a person good. Stopping by to assist a fallen Samaritan, especially if you are not a Samaritan, is what makes a person good. The scripture is pretty clear about these crossovers. Nationalism doesn't seem to impress God the way it impresses people.
>
> If you want to be an American, after being good, that is fine. But Nationalism is not what makes people good. Nationalism often does just the opposite. Scripture loves to tell stories about people behaving in transnational ways, like the Good Samaritan or Pharaoh's daughter.
>
> Immigration is not a political or social matter at its core. It is spiritual and personal at its core. If you believe the lies of nationalism and self-righteousness, if you believe that you deserve good children or good papers, then you have another thing coming. It is just a question of time when you will stand in the need of grace yourself.[4]

As this excerpt shows, for Rev. Schaper, immigration was ultimately a spiritual problem, one in which people perceived themselves and their fellow citizens as more deserving of grace, mercy, compassion, and love than people of other nationalities and ethnicities, especially ones who have been labeled "illegal" by the government, media, and pundits. This American religious culture, which she saw as ethnically segregated and overly tied to nationalism, was so ingrained in local religious communities that at times it even emerged in a progressive bulwark like Judson.

Rev. Schaper was frustrated by the type of civil religion that sacralizes the nation, with chosenness, blessedness, and brother and sisterly love ending or diminishing at America's national borders.[5] Instead, her vision of public ministry involved a move from religious nationalism to religious globalism:[6] to emulating the biblical figure Miriam by caring about others' children as though they are one's own, even if they are the children of undocumented immigrants. In a religious global culture, religious communities would embrace all people as children of God, equally worthy of care and compassion regardless of religion, nationality, legal status, race, or ethnicity.

But when she came to Judson, she was not satisfied with preaching sermons, training public ministers, and drafting religious essays on moving from nationalistic religion to a more transnational, global religion. She looked for ways to get involved in the immigration struggle, to partner with immigrant communities. That is how she found Families for Freedom, how she met Juan Carlos Ruiz, and how she helped found the New Sanctuary Movement. Particularly in its early days, Rev. Schaper and Judson became the central actors in the New Sanctuary Coalition of New York City, making them prominent in the national New Sanctuary Movement as well. In Los Angeles, one of the other centers of New Sanctuary, local leaders shared some of the characteristics of Rev. Schaper and Judson, but they differed in important ways as well.

Thousands of miles away, members of San Juan Church[7] stand outside in the bright Los Angeles sun, forming a long, two-by-two line. A hundred yards in front of them, on the sidewalk at the edge of church property, stands a journalist and a handful of anti-sanctuary protesters, waving American flags and holding signs reading "Deport Illegal Aliens." Slowly, the church members amble forward, circling around the church as they sing quietly in Spanish, as though they are working a spell of protection over Juan, the Guatemalan immigrant taking sanctuary inside. While the anti-sanctuary sidewalk protesters are all white, the church members are all Latinos, many first-generation immigrants. Several clergy march with the church members: the Anglo Lutheran bishop, the Anglo priest from a neighboring church, the church's Latino immigrant pastor, and Rev. Alexia Salvatierra, a fellow pastor and fellow Latina. Tall and thin, with long, flowing hair, she stands out in the crowd, her appearance as striking as her energy is palpable. The church group walks slowly and sings peacefully, stopping to pray for the anti-sanctuary protesters, that God would "change their hearts and minds" to make them more welcoming and loving. One of the anti-sanctuary protesters comments, with considerable chagrin: "Whoever organized this really knew what they were doing."[8] As the procession winds its way into the church, the church's pastor turns toward the protestors and says, "God bless America." Surprised, the protestors respond, "God bless America," as the pastor closes the church's door so the worship service can begin. According to Los Angeles New Sanctuary leaders, the protestors never showed up at the church again.[9]

Rev. Salvatierra is the founder of Clergy and Laity United for Economic Justice (CLUE), one of the organizations that helped start the New Sanctuary Movement. "We had been involved in workers' rights, but because 70% of the low wage workers in Los Angeles County are immigrants, we had bumped up against different kinds of immigration issues. So, primarily Social Security and unmatched letters, immigrant workers' freedom rights, those kinds of issues," she recalled over coffee in 2008. "But when the Sensenbrenner Bill passed, it sent waves of shock and trauma and horror throughout the immigrant community because even workers that are not undocumented know people that are. And it was such—even for people that are documented—it was such a manifestation of rejection for them, and of hatred. And that's how they experienced it."

While CLUE's name suggests that both clergy and laity are equally involved, in practice most of its regular participants were ordained religious leaders. They joined the picket lines at strikes, donning their clergy collars and stoles and decrying the immoral practices of union-busting employers. But they also organized their own events, and these had a different flavor. Instead of yelling, they prayed; instead of arguing or reasoning with opponents, they mentioned God's care for "the least of these." In other words, they used religious language and actions in public. The anti-sanctuary activist was right. These were smart tactics given religion's public legitimacy in America. But for Rev. Salvatierra, praying for opponents in public was more than a smart tactic for political change. It was a step toward transformation in the American religious landscape as well (Figure 2.1).

Like Rev. Schaper, Rev. Salvatierra was trained in the Alinsky tradition, continued today by organizers of the Industrial Areas Foundation (IAF). The IAF organizes one of the largest networks of congregation-based organizing

FIGURE 2.1 Rev. Alexia Salvatierra and other New Sanctuary activists pray at a May Day immigrant rights rally in Los Angeles. (Photo by Josue Bustos.)

efforts in the United States, and it has received a good deal of attention from scholars in recent years, most recently in religion scholar Jeff Stout's book *Blessed Are the Organized*.[10] As Stout's book shows, Alinsky's model is based on identifying shared interests, with a particular focus on empowering communities to recognize their own self-interests in contrast to the interests of the individuals and groups dominating them. Ultimately, the goal is to move from a newfound awareness of the power dynamics structuring their lives into action that will reshape the distribution of power in communities, creating more equitable arrangements.

After completing her organizer training, Rev. Salvatierra traveled to the Philippines and worked alongside indigenous Catholic activists. The experience transformed her views about the nature and purpose of organizing. "They were dying for their faith," she told me of the Filipinos she knew there. "It was not simply self-interest. They would say, 'All children are my children.' That's why they died," she said. "Love can be a more powerful motivator than self-interest."[11]

Back in Los Angeles, Rev. Salvatierra looked for a way to put what she had learned in the Philippines into practice, a formula for a different kind of congregation-based organizing. She called her approach faith-rooted organizing, in explicit contrast to the term faith-based organizing commonly used by the IAF and similar groups. "Faith-*based* organizing can be just like any other type of organizing; it just happens to be in religious communities," she explained during a 2009 training session. "In faith-*rooted* organizing, we are guided by our sacred faith traditions at every step of the process, from analysis of goals to strategies to sustaining leaders."

At the 2009 national gathering of the New Sanctuary Movement, she held a workshop on the approach, leading participants through the process of identifying "the special skills that people of faith can contribute that others may not have." After instructing activists to name their own interests and hopes, she asked them to go a step further, identifying God's dreams. "The question of *God's dream* is important in faith-rooted organizing, because it might challenge your own personal dream," she told them. "And it's not that we have to get power from targets. That's Alinsky's model. That's the world's truth, not God's." She continued, "God's truth is that we need to recognize the power we already have, the power from God, and live it out."

In *God's Heart Has No Borders*, sociologist Pierrette Hondagneu-Sotelo includes a chapter on some of the immigrant rights work in which CLUE activists and Rev. Salvatierra have been involved.[12] By her account, CLUE activists might have been motivated by their faith traditions, but they were solely interested in political change, particularly in transforming immigration policy. Using this interpretation, their purpose for mobilizing religious organizations was to create a broader base in advocating for political change. But Rev. Salvatierra's commitment to faith-rooted organizing, to identifying and working toward religious and spiritual goals alongside political ones, demonstrates the multiplicity of Rev. Salvatierra's and CLUE's aims, at least in their work in the New Sanctuary Movement.

When word began to spread back in 2006 that there might be a chance for comprehensive immigration reform in the coming months, Rev. Salvatierra and other progressive religious activists, mostly clergy, began looking for a way to organize on both a local and national level. They ultimately started the New Sanctuary Movement, with CLUE serving as the group's fiscal sponsor for its initial stages and forming a national steering committee. But changing legislation was never the sole goal of many of the activists, including Rev. Salvatierra. In 2007, she wrote a short piece for *God's Politics*, a blog sponsored by Jim Wallis and *Sojourners*, the national Christian magazine. In the piece, called "Sanctuary Breaks an Unjust Law," she spoke directly to the blog's religious audience, writing:

> When I was doing missionary work in Southeast Asia, I attended a service in a language that I didn't speak. It was an amazing moment; I felt the depth of our connection as brothers and sisters in Christ, beyond all of our differences. When we got to the line, "Forgive our debts as we forgive our debtors," I was struck by the insight that one of the deepest roots of our connection is the common experience of God's mercy...Someone had compassion on us—literally "com" (with) and "passion" (feeling)—someone felt with us, felt our pain as if it was his pain, our hopes and dreams as if they were his hopes and dreams.
>
> For many of us, the decision to provide sanctuary is rooted in the impulse of the heart to love as we have been loved—to hear the cries of Liliana and Joe and Mae and Jose and Jean's children and respond with compassion.
>
> Yet, the act of sanctuary is more than simple charity...We read in Hebrews that those of us who provide hospitality have entertained angels unaware. To offer sanctuary is to recognize that the strangers in our midst are blessing us, in clear and mysterious ways.[13]

The New Sanctuary Movement was designed not only to create political change (e.g., to achieve comprehensive immigration reform or to stop raids and deportations). As Rev. Salvatierra's comments and writings suggest, the New Sanctuary Movement's goals went beyond achieving "our dreams" to achieving "God's dreams," working toward spiritual and religious transformation that enables participants and witnesses to feel "the depth of our connection as brothers and sisters in Christ, beyond all differences."

When I interviewed her in 2008, Rev. Salvatierra finished our conversation with a story. "A man came from Fox on the day of Liliana's reception [into the church]," she said. "From Fox News?" I asked, thinking I knew where the story was headed. I assumed this would be a tale about a conservative reporter bent on showing the evils of "illegal immigrants" and activists' disdain for him as a political enemy. She confirmed that yes, the reporter was from Fox News, before continuing, "They were doing a special on 'The Heroes of ICE,' and he just wanted to put a minute in about Sanctuary, just for a counterpoint. He had a crew cut, he looked like a Marine—he was obviously full of his own way of seeing the world. He was supposed to spend five minutes there, and he spent like an hour and a half listening to Liliana. And then he said to me afterward—he was very upset, and he said to me: 'Is this happening to a lot of people? Is this common?' And I said, 'Yes.' And he said, 'Well, people need to know about this.' And I said, 'Well, that's your job.' You know, I feel like that's what Sanctuary's all about. He'll never see it the same way," she said. "So, I really believe in conversion," she concluded. "I think that's at the heart of faith-rooted organizing that makes us different from secular organizing. We believe in conversion. People are not just what their class makes them."

An Inclusive Religious Vision

Like Rev. Schaper and Rev. Salvatierra, many early New Sanctuary activists were clergy with years of experience as progressive religious activists. And like them, they were motivated to start and join a religious immigrant rights organization due to both political concerns and religious ones. As a result, the New Sanctuary Movement sought not only political change; it sought to change hearts and minds as well. In particular, activists hoped to form an activist network that would change the hearts and minds of members of native-born faith communities like Judson, moving them toward awareness of and concern for undocumented immigrants as part of their religious vision. This is why even existing religious immigrant rights organizations, like the Catholic Justice for Immigrants campaign, would not do. To embody a truly inclusive global religious vision, the activists who started New Sanctuary needed an interfaith religious network, a point I explore in detail in Chapter 7.

The earliest official statement of the New Sanctuary Movement, circulated among the burgeoning group of activists gathering in early 2007 before the group's official launch, listed its goals as:

1. To take a united, public, moral stand for immigrant rights
2. To protect immigrants against hate, workplace discrimination, and unjust deportation
3. To reveal the actual suffering of immigrant workers and families under current and proposed legislation to the religious community and the general public

As this statement of goals demonstrates, from the earliest days of New Sanctuary, activist efforts focused on seeking change in immigration policy, concrete religious communities, and the larger religious community, which they often referred to using the religiously inclusive term people of faith. This statement of goals was mostly an internal statement, used to make sure leaders in the emerging network were on the same page about the importance of political and religious change. After the official launch, the statement of goals shifted somewhat as it became geared toward recruits, ordinary members of congregations who were both the medium and the target of change. The New Sanctuary Movement Pledge, a mission statement New Sanctuary activists used to draw in new participants during its early years, asked those signing the pledge to "covenant" to:

1. Take a public, moral stand for immigrants' rights
2. Reveal, through education and advocacy, the actual suffering of immigrant workers and families under current and proposed legislation
3. Protect immigrants against hate, workplace discrimination, and unjust deportation

In this version of the pledge, education and advocacy were presumably directed at everyone, including oneself, rather than at "the religious community and the general public," since most of the recruits were themselves members of religious communities and therefore one of the targets of change.

By the 2009 national New Sanctuary gathering in New York, religious goals remained important, as the following story shows: In a large room at Riverside Church, activists break into small groups divided by region to talk about the vision for their work. After everyone comes back together, a spokesperson reports on each group's discussion (Figure 2.2). The following day, Rev. Salvatierra arrives with a compilation of the previous day's reports, grouping New Sanctuary's focus into six categories: leadership and capacity building; growing the base; community organizing; building alliances; political change; and change lives. Kim,[14] a white woman in her 20s, copies the categories onto an easel of butcher paper as Rev. Salvatierra reads them aloud from a sheet of paper. Once a page is full, Kim rips it off and passes it to Carolyn,[15] a New Sanctuary activist from California who works with Rev. Salvatierra as an employee of CLUE. Carolyn holds up the most recent pages so that the crowd can read what is written as Kim continues to scribble furiously on the original easel of paper.[16]

When Rev. Salvatierra reaches the "change lives" category, she says, "CIR is not our only goal. We don't stop with the political because we're rooted in faith." She continues, listing mini goals as her scribe writes them on the easel for everyone to see. "We want families to be whole. We want to make the world better for generations to come. We want one human family. We

FIGURE 2.2 Liliana's husband watches as fellow New Sanctuary activists discuss goals at the 2009 national gathering. (Photo by Tom N. Martinez.)

want to build a radical utopia of love and justice." One of the papers slips from Carolyn's hands, and a member of the crowd calls out, "Is our human easel getting tired?" Everyone laughs, grateful for a little down-to-earth comic relief to ease the prospect of responsibility for cosmic spiritual transformation. As the group discusses moving forward with a shared statement on the vision for New Sanctuary's work, Rev. Salvatierra asks, "Can we get an amen, clap, or a straw vote to affirm the plans we have articulated together here?" One man, a white, middle-aged layperson, asks, tongue-in-cheek: "Does this include the goal of the kingdom of God?"

As this story demonstrates, two years after New Sanctuary's launch, religious goals like "building a radical utopia of love and justice" remained important. But as it also suggests, the focus on religious change was contested, particularly as the New Sanctuary Movement expanded over the first two years to include laypeople and people new to religious activism. Among some rank-and-file members, among laity (as opposed to clergy), and among immigrants, New Sanctuary's religious goals sometimes seemed like a distraction from the changes in immigration policy they hoped to make. However, the shift away from religious goals toward more political goals was not an easy one to make, not only because leaders prized these goals but also because religious goals were built into the identity and core strategies of New Sanctuary, as the next two chapters show.

In light of the religious goals of the progressive religious activists who formed and subsequently provided leadership in the New Sanctuary Movement, the puzzle that emerged in Chapter 1—the decision to create an explicitly interfaith response to the immigration crisis rather than to join existing secular immigrant rights organizations or regional or denominational faith-based organizations—makes more sense. While religious activists who cared about immigrant rights could have joined these organizations, either as individuals or as faith community allies, existing organizations typically focused solely on changing immigration policy or changing one particular type of religious community, such as Catholic parishes. Instead, many early New Sanctuary activists saw widespread religious and spiritual change as an important goal as well, not only because converting the hearts and minds of members of religious communities could eventually lead to a change in politics but also because they cared about the shape of religious institutions, identities, and cultures *in and of themselves*. To pursue goals not only of more inclusive immigration policies but also of a more inclusive American religious culture, early New Sanctuary activists needed to create their own explicitly religious network of movement organizations and, specifically, an *interfaith* network.

Belief in and commitment to a God of inclusion and hospitality is core to the moral worldview of many progressive religious Americans, particularly the group often referred to by scholars as liberal Protestants. According to religion scholar James Wellman, for many evangelical Protestants, a Christian is someone who has been "saved" by professing faith in Christ, though many emphasize that the fruits of a personal relationship with Christ are love and justice. In contrast, many liberal Protestants define Christians first and foremost as people who emphasize Jesus's welcoming, forgiving, justice-seeking behaviors and teachings in scriptures, de-emphasizing the importance of doctrinal beliefs (though many also profess faith in Christ).[17] Since inclusion is, to a large degree, definitive of the liberal Christian vision, when confronted with undocumented immigrants, leaders in progressive religious traditions more generally might be especially likely to approach the issue from this religious framework of inclusion.

The New Sanctuary Movement emphasized the presence of a religious global thread in the scriptures of many religious traditions, even if it was not commonly espoused by religious Americans. At a New Sanctuary gathering in New York, a rabbi reminded the crowd: "We are commanded to love the stranger more than 30 times in Hebrew scripture. Only once are we commanded to love our neighbor." Similarly, speaking at a mosque in San Gabriel, California, an imam involved in New Sanctuary told his fellow Muslims, "Prophet Muhammad (peace be upon him) migrated from hostile Makkah to the friendly Madina. The people of Madina not only welcomed them with open arms, but treated them like their own blood brothers and sisters. They even divided their wealth with the immigrants. This is a great example of true Akhuwah (brotherhood and sisterhood) in human history." He continued, "It is an example for us: how to treat people who are fleeing from hostile land and coming to our community. Prophet Muhammad (peace be upon him) told us: 'The strangers are guests of God. They are angels. Treat them well.'"[18]

Christians in the New Sanctuary Movement pointed to Jesus's parable in Matthew 25, where he blesses his faithful followers for a job well done, saying, "I was a stranger, and you welcomed me." But the story of the Good Samaritan, which Rev. Schaper mentioned in her essay, offers another important example of Jesus challenging national and ethnic boundaries. In this story, after Jesus instructs listeners to "Love your neighbor as yourself," a particularly wily man asks, "But who is my neighbor?"—possibly hoping to avoid putting this teaching into widespread practice. Rather than providing a direct answer, Jesus tells the story of a Samaritan, a member of a despised ethnoreligious group nearby, showing how the Samaritan cared for an injured Jewish man as though he were his own brother. One interpretation of the parable is that your neighbor is anyone who needs you, perhaps especially those you would consider strangers or even enemies.

But while the religious global is arguably a central part of all three Abrahamic religious traditions, isolationism and lingering ideas about manifest destiny have often dominated the American religious context.[19] Sociologist Robert Bellah has written at length about civil religion in America, highlighting the ways American religious symbols and institutions have been used to strengthen and sustain national identity and solidarity.[20] While the concept of civil religion has been widely debated and criticized,[21] many politicians end every speech with "God bless the United States of America," bumper stickers around the country proclaim the same message, and many Protestant churches display an American flag at the front of the sanctuary. These realities suggest that many Americans continue to see their country as special in the eyes of God. Indeed, almost half of all Americans still agree that America is the "last best hope for mankind," and 60% of white, native-born Americans agree that "America holds a special place in God's plan," sentiments reminiscent of themes of manifest destiny and Christian nationalism.[22]

In contrast, sociologist Peggy Levitt's book *God Needs No Passport* suggests that many immigrants to the United States are what she calls "religious globalists."[23] Living a largely transnational existence, these immigrants are highly religious, but in a way that is not restricted by national boundaries. Maintaining intimate relationships with people in multiple nations, it is harder for them to imagine that some of these people should count as brothers and sisters, favored by God and worthy of rights and compassion, while others should not. Instead, they point to teachings in a variety of faith traditions about all people being made in God's image. Levitt divides religious globalists into two categories: *exclusivists* see their religious community as extending beyond national boundaries but as including only members of their own faith tradition; *inclusivists* see their religious community as including all people, regardless of nationality or faith tradition—their common tie is not a shared faith but a shared status as children of God. To a large degree, the New Sanctuary Movement embraced the latter of these two definitions, even though it included people who were theological exclusivists when it came to salvation (i.e., people who view all people as children of God but only members of their own traditions as eternally saved). In many ways, this image of religious globalism mirrors the vision of the "beloved community" that has been part of progressive religious activism since the Civil Rights Movement.[24] But even more than the notion of the beloved community, which while globally inclusive in theory has in practice often been associated specifically with racial justice, the religious global vision is intentionally and self-consciously transnational, focused on breaking down even national borders between human beings. When I refer to *religious globalism* throughout this book, it is the inclusive vision of religious globalism that I am referencing.

As Rev. Schaper's essay on the Good Samaritan captured in clear language, New Sanctuary sought to convert people from a variety of faith traditions from a religious nationalism that holds up America and Americans as special in God's eyes to religious globalism, which embraces a theological idea present in many religious traditions: that *all* people are children of God and equally worthy of care and compassion. In other words, they did not create a religious movement and organize congregations solely to create a broader base of support for changing immigration policy. The state was an important target for them, but they hoped to change the character of their *religious institutions* as well. Convincing ordinary religious people and communities to "welcome the stranger" as though they were instead a brother or sister who deserved a good job, health care, and respect as much as their neighbor down the street, and indeed to begin to experience them in that way, was an important goal of New Sanctuary.

But their religious goals were not restricted to changing concrete and diverse types of religious communities. The New Sanctuary Movement also sought to transform broader religious culture. Through reaching out to media outlets like Fox News as Rev. Salvatierra did, whose viewers tend to be theological conservatives as well as political conservatives, New Sanctuary activists hoped to change the religious visions of "people of faith" writ large.[25] In this sense, New Sanctuary's target was an "imagined community"[26] made up of religious Americans from a variety of faith traditions, all of which have threads of the religious global in their teachings and histories. For this reason, more denominational efforts like the Catholic Justice for Immigrants campaign[27] or regional, mostly Christian efforts like Posadas Sin Fronteras[28] were insufficient vehicles for achieving the religious goals of many early activists. Instead, through the work of New Sanctuary, they hoped not only to transform the hearts and minds of religious individuals and their faith communities but also to change religious discourse around the United States, shifting the dominant religious voice from one emphasizing preference for Americans, laws, borders, and boundaries to one emphasizing inclusive brother and sisterhood.

Multi-target Social Movements

During its first two years, the New Sanctuary Movement was not solely focused on changing immigration policy or even on keeping immigrant families together through halting raids, detentions, and deportations. The aims of New Sanctuary also included *religious* change, in particular the transformation of individual faith communities and of American religious culture. In other words, New Sanctuary did not merely have religious goals: it *targeted* religious institutions and religious culture as sites for change (see Table 2.1). Recognition of New Sanctuary's religious targets, in addition to its political ones, helps solve several important puzzles, ones that state-centered approaches to the study of social movements have traditionally neglected.[29]

In the past, much social movement research assumed that the goal of any serious movement or movement organization is to change public policy, ignoring other possible targets.[30] But as more recent scholarship has noted,

Table 2.1 New Sanctuary Movement Targets, Goals, and Strategies

Institutional Fields	Targets, Goals & Strategies			
	Religion		The State	
Specific Targets	Local Congregations	Imagined Religious Community	ICE Agents	Policymakers
Goals	Globally Inclusive Congregations	Religious Discourses of Hospitality	Halt Deportations, Keep Families Together	More Liberal Immigration Policy
Strategies	Sanctuary	Family Values	Sanctuary	Family Values

power and authority do not reside solely in the state.[31] This book follows in the line of growing attempts to better recognize the variety of targets that social movements and movement organizations seek to change, treating them as worthy of analysis and as sources of essential knowledge about how social movements actually work in practice.[32]

While social movement scholars are increasingly challenging dominant perspectives, arguing that legitimate social movements and movement organizations might aim to change markets, culture, or other targets,[33] none has clearly distinguished between movements that primarily focus on a single target (whatever that target might be) and movements that split their focus between multiple targets. The New Sanctuary Movement suggests that theorizing this distinction is essential to understanding the different sets of challenges and opportunities facing movements and movement organizations that simultaneously seek change in multiple institutional arenas. The emerging *multi-institutional politics approach* to social movements comes closest to doing this,[34] acknowledging that movements and movement organizations might have multiple targets without further distinguishing, naming, defining, or theorizing such movements.

Because it had goals of changing several arenas simultaneously, I call the New Sanctuary Movement a *multi-target social movement* (MTSM), distinguishing it from movements and movement organizations that focus solely on changing public policy, on transforming a single institution, or on multiple goals within a single arena such as politics, religion, or economics. For the purposes of conceptual distinction, I term the latter *single-target social movements* (STSMs). Building on other widely accepted definitions of movements and movement organizations,[35] I define MTSMs in the following way:

> Multi-target social movements are organized collectivities working to simultaneously challenge or defend multiple sources of existing authority, whether institutional or cultural. These challenges need not be equally important in the collectivity's work, but they must all be considerations in its decision-making.

Thus, the term multi-target social movements can refer to either broad-based, national movements or to nascent movement organizations and activist networks like New Sanctuary that are part of larger movements: their distinctive feature is their focus on multiple targets of change.

Distinguishing between multi-target and single-target social movements is essential because institutional targets shape movement emergence, the institutional cultures of movements and movement organizations, the actors they must recruit, and the decisions they make about mobilization, collective identity, strategies, and tactics. There may be very few movements and movement organizations that target only a single institutional arena—this remains a largely unanswered empirical question since much prior scholarship assumed that legitimate social movements were focused on changing the state. MTSMs and STSMs are best conceptualized as what Max Weber called ideal types: as categories on the extreme ends of a continuum along which the vast majority of movements and movement organizations fall (see Figure 2.3).[36]

A particular movement may also move along this continuum over time as its targets and goals adapt to changing contexts or its membership base changes. Where a movement or movement organization lies along the

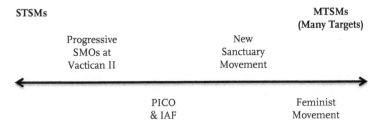

FIGURE 2.3 Continuum of single-target and multi-target social movements.

continuum at any point in time will shape its dynamics, including which institutional contexts influence its mobilization, the number of institutional cultures with which its strategies must resonate, and the numbers of different constituencies it must seek to recruit. Thus, a multi-target social movement with many targets (e.g., the Feminist Movement, which arguably targets culture, religion, corporations, the government, and other institutions in seeking greater rights for women and other historically underrepresented groups) will face greater dilemmas than a group like New Sanctuary (which targets religion and the state), which in turn faces greater dilemmas than groups further along the continuum toward single-target movements. The remainder of this book develops a theory of multi-target social movements, revealing how the recognition of New Sanctuary's multiple targets sheds additional light on decisions that otherwise seem awkward, confusing, irrational, or counterproductive.

The multiple targets of a particular MTSM need not include religion or even the state. Sociologist Elizabeth Armstrong's book *Forging Gay Identities* argues that the gay and lesbian rights movement was committed to changing targets other than the state, in particular American culture.[37] She develops a cultural-institutional approach to the study of social movements, calling for movement scholars to pay greater attention to the ways that movements and movement organizations long seen as seeking political change may have been seeking other types of change—in this case, cultural change—as well. As this example demonstrates, naming, defining, and theorizing multi-target movements has the potential to provide additional insights not only about relatively unexamined movements but about well-known social movements as well.

Relating this specifically to religious activism, in some ways it is understandable that social movement scholars, many of whom are religiously unaffiliated, would emphasize political change as the ultimate, meaningful goal of any effort to change other arenas like religion. But for many religious people, who are invested in the future of religious institutions and identities, changing religion is not just a means to a different end: it is an important end in itself. For instance, religious studies scholar and progressive religious activist Charles Marsh critiques social movement scholars and activists for ignoring the religious and spiritual aims at the root of many examples of modern religious activism.[38] And while religious institutions have less power in society than they once did, as sociologist José Casanova has shown, they are by no means irrelevant sources of power and authority in today's world, even in largely secular nations like the United States.[39] Also, it is not necessarily true that religious identity matters only for those whose religious identity is the primary organizing identity in their lives, as has been assumed at times.[40] Even religious people who organize their lives around multiple identities often still care a great deal about their religious identities.[41] Ignoring these kinds of empirical realities leads social movement scholars to the wrong conclusions about not only movement goals but also movement emergence, collective identity, strategy, tactics, and outcomes.

Recognizing this gap, several recent studies examine movements and movement organizations that target religious institutions for change.[42] Tricia Bruce's account of Voice of the Faithful, a movement organization made up of Catholics responding to the clergy sex abuse scandal, emphasizes its focus on changing a single target: the Roman Catholic Church. She calls these movements or movement organizations intrainstitutional social movements, arguing that they "target a specific, bounded institution (rather than the state or society at-large)."[43] Like intrainstitutional religious movements, multi-target movements may seek to change religious institutions of which they are a part.

Table 2.2 Ideal Types of Religious Social Movements

	Multi-target Movements	Single-Target Movements	Intrainstitutional Movements
Definition	–Challenge multiple sources of authority simultaneously	–Primarily challenge one source of authority, usually the state	–Challenge one source of authority based in an institution of which activists are committed members
Relationship between Religion and Activism	–Religious change, whether cultural or institutional, can be one of several goals –Religion is likely to simultaneously act as resource and constraint on goals	–Religious change can be sole goal, but these movements are typically known as religious movements rather than as social movements –Religion can act as resource or constraint	–In religious institutions, religious change is the sole goal –Religion provides resources but ultimately constrains, leading to replication or absorption

However, multi-target movements are not focused on a single institution as the target for change, so they may be simultaneously working to change institutions where they are insiders and ones where they are outsiders. In Table 2.2, I highlight the differences between the ideal typical categories of multi-target movements, single-target movements, and intrainstitutional movements.

The New Sanctuary Movement was not unique in its combination of both religious and political targets, a fact hinting at the potential usefulness of the concept of multi-target social movements as a tool for analyzing a variety of movements and movement organizations. For example, the Plowshares Movement, an international network of mostly Catholic antiwar activists, arguably had both political and religious targets. Though sociologist Sharon Erickson Nepstad's accounts of Plowshares do not focus on theorizing its targets, her work demonstrates that many of the activists were committed Catholics who hoped that their acts of witness would change the Catholic church's stance on war and militarization while at the same time influencing political policy through persuading policymakers and the public of the immorality of war.[44]

Not all religious social movement organizations have religious goals. In fact, this is one of the important differences between the New Sanctuary Movement and some other instances of faith-based organizing in recent years. For instance, Jeff Stout's account of the IAF focuses on congregations coming together to address shared problems in their local communities, activity he believes is central to democratic life.[45] Similarly, the work of social scientists like Paul Lichterman, Heidi Swarts, and Rich Wood highlights the efforts of faith-based community organizations, focusing on how religious groups are working toward political change that can potentially strengthen democracy.[46]

According to these analyses, many religious communities are engaging in progressive activism, but while they seek to mobilize religious participants to create social change and at times even target multiple institutions simultaneously, their targets for change are more often political institutions than religious ones.[47] This adds another layer to the central question of this chapter: why did the New Sanctuary Movement emerge as an explicitly religious movement organization? Put another way, why were religious targets important for New Sanctuary activists, even though they appear to be less central for some other progressive religious activists like participants in the IAF? As organizations focusing largely on local and regional concerns (though these local and regional groups occasionally join together to address national issues), faith-based community organizations like those in the IAF network are less influenced by both the threats and opportunities of a shifting national religious context, the impetus for the religious goals of many New Sanctuary activists.

The Religious Context

Though the importance of political context to the emergence of movements challenging the state is well-known, a few scholars have also explored how cultural context shapes movements and movement organizations, findings relevant to the study of religion, as one aspect of culture. In her analyses of Vatican II, sociologist Melissa Wilde emphasizes the importance of cultural context, arguing that the degree to which culture and organizational forms mesh with the movement environment helps determine the effectiveness of movement organizations, with culture sometimes enabling and sometimes limiting activism depending on those environments.[48] In a review of existing scholarship on movements, sociologist Rhys Williams also calls for more attention to the cultural contexts of social movements and the ways they can both constrain and provide opportunities for mobilization and social change.[49] However, fewer studies explore the ways cultural context enables or demands the very *emergence* of movements with cultural goals. As one element of culture, the same might be said of religion. Little research exists illuminating whether and how religious context enables or demands the emergence of movements and movement organizations with religious goals.[50]

If political context determines, at least to an extent, mobilization for political change, then we might expect expanding opportunities or increasing threats in other institutional arenas to shape the emergence of movements and movement organizations seeking to challenge those same institutions. In the case of the New Sanctuary Movement and its religious goals, this means examining whether shifts in the local and national religious context might help explain New Sanctuary's emergence as a new, national interfaith network seeking religious change.

At its early events and on its website, the New Sanctuary Movement distributed a pamphlet called "For You Were Once a Stranger: Immigration in the U.S. Through the Lens of Faith."[51] The pamphlet included letters from two Christian clergy, reflecting on what was theologically necessary for change in the treatment of immigrants. Archbishop Charles Chaput of Denver described an email he received following a series of immigration raids at meatpacking plants across the country. He quotes the Catholic parishioner as writing the following in his email to him:

Sorry Bishop: No sympathy (from me) for the illegal alien criminals arrested by ICE. In fact, I hope their offspring starve to death. I do not pray for illegal aliens. I pray for their victims. I have no problem with God, and He has no problem with me. I hope their families starve to death, and it's crap like this that drives Catholics away from the Church.[52]

While it is unlikely that most religious Americans would have agreed with the harshest parts of this email—surely few would hope that anyone's children would starve to death—the sentiment that there is an "us" and a "them," even in the eyes of God, a national and ethnic division that separates the deserving from the less worthy, was much more widespread in native-born religious communities, at least as New Sanctuary activists perceived it. Confronted with xenophobia and hatred of foreign-born people in some of their congregations, some religious leaders worried that a lack of meaningful interaction with undocumented immigrants in the context of religion kept congregants from seeing them as fellow children of God.

In many ways, these religious leaders were right about the lack of interaction between American religious communities and people from other nations. In his book *Boundless Faith*, sociologist Robert Wuthnow chronicles the global engagements of American Christian communities over the past couple of decades.[53] He argues that during the first decade of the 21st century the religious world was becoming more "flat," writing: "There is no longer a distinctly American Christendom from which to engage in activities aimed at spreading the gospel to those in other parts of the world who are outside the fold."[54] As the explosion of new technologies and the globalization of markets increased transnational connections in other areas of life, churches also began to seek new ways to engage with people across national borders. These trends revived certain strands of religious globalism in Christian tradition, though—importantly—only in a minority of religious communities.

Though Wuthnow believes important changes have been taking shape in American Christianity due to globalization, he also finds that in the mid-2000s most churches were still primarily focused on the local. Only 12% of church members said their congregation focused a great deal on people living outside of the United States.[55] Also, only 24% of churches had been involved with more than two "transcultural" activities in the past year, such as international mission support, antiwar activities, or a short-term mission trip.[56] This confirms other research on the localistic worldview of churches.[57] According to sociologist Nancy Ammerman, in the mid-2000s 83% of church partnerships were with local organizations, while only 17% were with national or international organizations.[58] Finally, even the minority of churches that were comparatively transnational in orientation often focused primarily on missionary work—what Peggy Levitt calls exclusivist religious globalism—rather than on more inclusivist forms of transnational religious connections.[59]

So while the visions and practices of local religious communities in the United States were becoming more global in some ways, providing increased opportunities for American congregants to have meaningful interactions with foreign-born people, in the mid-2000s the majority remained focused on their fellow Americans rather than on people born or living outside of the United States. While this was certainly less true for immigrant congregations,[60] this research nonetheless suggests that the identity of the average American congregation continued to be local or national rather than global.

In addition to seeking to transform local religious communities, making them more attuned to global concerns, on the national religious stage many early New Sanctuary activists hoped to offer a religious voice that challenged the dominance of the religious right's vision of religiosity in the U.S. public sphere. There has long been overlap between the religious right and religious nationalism.[61] Still, the hope was not only that they could convince religious people to see immigrants as their brothers and sisters but also that they could persuade religious people that social justice for all who are oppressed was central to the religious vision, thereby opposing themselves to the more rule-oriented religious vision of the religious right. These goals were often implicit and were contested even among early New Sanctuary activists, but they nevertheless played a role in shaping the New Sanctuary Movement's emergence and the shape it took in its early years.

During the 1990s and 2000s, the rising prominence and power of the religious right created increasing threats for some of the many religious Americans who did not identify with conservative religion's religious and political goals. These threats made collective religious identity more salient for some religious people, making it more likely that their mobilizations around political issues might take on aspects of a collective identity struggle as well. In the 1950s and even the early 1960s, when the Civil Rights Movement began to emerge, the American religious landscape was relatively established. Mainline Protestant groups such as Episcopalians, Presbyterians, Methodists, and Lutherans still held much of the religious power in the country, not yet having lost their hold on public institutions like universities and even some businesses.[62] But during the late 1960s and 1970s, the general upheaval in

American society accompanying the Civil Rights Movement, the feminist movement, the anti-Vietnam movement, and other significant changes also led to an era of religious change. Increasing secularization of public institutions and the beginnings of decline in denominational memberships were the partial results of these decades—a disestablishment of mainline Protestantism in America.[63]

This period led to a major restructuring of American religion, in which denominational affiliation became much less important than in the past.[64] Instead, people's primary religious identities became less associated with denomination than with groups of people that shared their general beliefs and attitudes, creating a division between religious conservatives and religious progressives. While this represented an important departure from the past, much of this new division still overlapped with denomination. For example, though more theological and political diversity exists within evangelicalism and within mainline Protestantism than is often recognized, members of historically mainline Protestant denominations are more likely to be liberal or progressive theologically and politically than members of historically fundamentalist or evangelical Protestant denominations are.[65]

So though religious liberals and progressives, largely found in mainline denominations, continued to participate in public action around political issues, after the 1960s and early 1970s they lost much of their former power and authority in public institutions, forcing them to take more private, often "quieter," approaches to social change.[66] Part of their lack of public response to disestablishment may have been due to shock and an inability to immediately respond. Their declining numbers also forced them to focus more energy on the health of their own denominations.[67] However, mainline Protestants did not immediately fight back by publicly asserting their collective religious identity in part because the threats from other religious groups over what it means to be religious were not yet sufficiently strong to merit this type of action.

By the late 1970s and 1980s, that situation changed dramatically. During this period, religious conservatives gained increasing power and prominence in American public life and politics, with the rise of the Institute for Religion and Democracy in the late 1970s and early 1980s, the election of Ronald Reagan, and the formation of the Moral Majority and the Christian Coalition as major public assertions of conservative religious identity.[68] The increasing visibility of the pro-life movement and the "family values" movement, one of whose main platforms was opposition to LGBT rights, also put forward a public image of the religious citizen as a theologically and politically conservative one emphasizing issues of personal morality, especially rules governing gender and sexuality.[69] The 2000 election of religious conservative George W. Bush as U.S. president, with broad support from religious conservatives around the country,[70] merely cemented the growing public religious norms and understandings that to be religious meant to be theologically and politically conservative, despite the actual presence of diverse religious voices within faith communities, particularly nonwhite Christian communities. Indeed, some sociologists have argued that one of the reasons for the rise in Americans claiming no religious affiliation in recent years may be the widespread cultural association of religiosity with political conservatism.[71]

While divorcing oneself from public religious affiliation was one possible response to this religious context for religious people who were not conservative, another possible response was to fight back by reasserting a different kind of public religious identity. People who were more committed to their religious identities and institutions, perhaps clergy in particular, would be more likely to take this route of further embracing their identities as religious and politically progressive than to throw out their religious identities altogether. For those who had an interest in controlling the definition of what it means to be religious—whether conservative or progressive—the recent shifts in public religious assumptions in this regard would have caused either joy or immense frustration.

Particularly in 2006, when New Sanctuary first began to mobilize, the dominance of the religious right's voice on the national stage was urgently felt by some religious people. With President George W. Bush and his motto of "compassionate conservatism," the religious right arguably had its most powerful religious-political spokesperson in U.S. history. But even after Bush left office, controversy remained high. For religious people who did not identify with the religious right, their norms, values, meanings, and definitions of what it meant to be religious were being increasingly threatened because of the shifts in the relationship between religious institutions in America over the past few decades.

For people who were committed to their religion—as many religious progressives are, despite stereotypes to the contrary[72]—these threats in the national religious discourse made one's religious identity more salient, not less so, making it more likely that collective religious identity struggles might emerge as an important aspect of any *national* mobilization of religious activists, potentially moving mainline Protestants away from the more "quiet" form of activism that had characterized them in the recent past.[73] By putting their religious identity at the forefront of such actions, they could contest the authority of the religious right's religious vision in the public sphere by arguing that living out one's religion *primarily* means working for social justice and compassion rather than adherence to a particular set of rules about personal morality.[74]

In another part of the "For You Were Once a Stranger" pamphlet, a Protestant pastor from Indiana, Rev. José F. Morales Jr., reflected on the often inward-looking state of American Christian culture, arguing that it needed to be transformed:

> What's at the core of the [immigration] debate, in my opinion, is a *cultural fear* that grows out of cultural hegemony, and cultural idolatry…Immigration is not a threat to national security; it is a threat to national identity…The cultural fear of the cultural majority is addressed by appeals to religion—in this country, by appeals to their Christianity. And I will specify—*their* Christianity. For, interestingly enough, numbers show that the majority of African, Arab, Persian, and Latin American immigrants are Christian; and yet, these forms of imported, un-Americanized Christianity are not good enough for this republic and their religion. As a Christian, I challenge their cultural-civil form of Christianity because, as I see it, it is not Christianity…People of faith should be at the forefront in naming the fear, and illegitimizing [sic] it…And it is only by knowing the "other" and by loving them that fear is replaced by compassion and solidarity, which are core values of the sanctuary movement.[75]

Rev. Morales highlights the need for and the challenge of cultivating a less *American*, more inclusive, global religious discourse at the national level. According to Rev. Morales, the dominance of a particular, nationalistic form of Christianity was threatening *true* Christianity, whose focus is compassion and solidarity without regard to national borders. These types of sentiments were not restricted to Christians in the New Sanctuary Movement. In the same pamphlet, Hussam Ayloush, Southern California executive director of the Council on American–Islamic Relations (CAIR) and member of the Interfaith Worker Justice (IWJ) board of directors, is quoted as saying, "Islam looks at all of us as immigrants on the earth. All of earth belongs to God and we are God's guests. In that sense, we are all immigrants. We are guided by our religious teachings which declare all human beings are dependents of God."[76]

In addition to these more general threats to an inclusive religious culture, two specific conditions created an ideal context for the emergence of an activist network with religious goals. First, Cardinal Mahony's sermon, discussed in detail in Chapter 1, was a response to the threat that the Sensenbrenner Bill posed to a conception of religious life that includes charity and justice as central religious practices. As such, it was a call to defend not only immigrants but also a particular view of religion. Second, at the time, the religious right was not talking about immigration—while anti-immigrant organizations included religious people in their ranks, no major anti-immigrant groups were giving religious reasons and justifications for their positions. This created an opportunity for progressive religious people to establish a pro-immigrant view as the appropriate religious position, challenging the dominant image in America of religion as conservative.

The case of the New Sanctuary Movement and the religious context in which it emerged suggest that religious context may shape the emergence of movements and movement organizations with religious goals in ways that are similar to the effects of political context. In particular, expanding opportunities to spread one's religious vision and increasing threats to one's religious authority and power create an environment in which movements with religious targets may emerge.[77] At certain times and places, religious power and authority are more contentious than others, leading to increased salience of struggles over what it means to be religious.

What I call religious context can be distinguished from political context by the institutions involved and the discourses circulated by those institutions. Whereas the political context typically involves governmental institutions,[78] the religious context refers to religious groups and the public discourses circulating among such groups.[79] The New Sanctuary Movement's emergence as a national network of interfaith movement organizations was partly an attempt to struggle over religious power and authority made more prominent and necessary because of the highly contentious national religious context in the 2000s. This focus on national religious threats differentiates the New Sanctuary Movement from progressive religious organizing that primarily happens at local and regional levels, such as the IAF. These activists may be less inclined to target religion because their work focuses less often on the national level and therefore does not have to contend to the same extent with dominant national assumptions about what it means to be religious.

These distinctions between religious and political contexts (though there is overlap between the two as well) are especially important in understanding how the emergence of multi-target social movements differs from what we know about the emergence of state-centered movements. For a multi-target social movement like the New Sanctuary Movement to emerge, there must be significant shifts in *multiple institutional contexts* in approximately the same time and place, such that actors feel it necessary or desirable to respond by seeking change in multiple arenas. This means that movements with many targets will likely be rarer than movements with fewer targets, such as single-target social movements. Additionally, activists contemplating mobilization must have accurate information about multiple contexts to be aware of and respond to these changes, making it more likely that multi-target social movements will be started by activists with deep ties to multiple institutions and identities.

The Soul of the Nation

An investment in changing religious institutions and culture for their own sake, not just for the sake of political change, distinguishes multi-target social movements like the New Sanctuary Movement from many religious activist efforts, an insight that first fully hit me during a conversation with Rev. Donna Schaper one morning at her home in Judson Church's rectory. The rectory sits on a quiet, tree-lined street in Manhattan, two floors in an old brownstone. Inside, the walls are filled with colorful art and the rooms with plants, the fruit of Rev. Schaper's avid gardening. Rev. Schaper and I are meeting to talk about New Sanctuary, and we park ourselves in the light-filled kitchen. Her golden retriever barks and wags his tail excitedly, jumping up on my knees, begging for attention. "If you keep petting him, he'll keep petting you," she warns, a smile betraying her amusement. "You'll notice that I do like this," she says, putting up her hand and laughing. "It means, 'Go away, Kofi. You bother me.'"[80]

But as we begin talking about the New Sanctuary Movement, Kofi finds his way to her side of the table, and she smiles as she scratches his ears. Scripture permeates the conversation. "'When I was a stranger, you gave me a place,'" she says, quoting a biblical passage. "Imagine tribes in ancient Israel taking care of people who weren't of their own tribe! Or a God who would mandate that kind of behavior! The Qur'an is filled with it too, and I've been studying that just so I can really make the argument that God is not the private property of any nation, race, people. There are no 'illegals' in the eyes of the universal God."

"What really concerns me at the bottom of this is the kind of people I minister to—which are white, wealthy, you know, upper class people, by and large, as am I—we will not find God if we don't welcome the stranger," she continues. "So when we say, 'Go home' or 'We don't need you here,' we're not just saying that to an immigrant. We're saying, 'God, we don't need you here. You go home now. We've had enough.' And that really bothers me. This is the idolatry of the rich that's—that really hurts them. And I'm here to minister to my kind of people. So if we're going to take that point of view, we're in trouble. Big trouble."

By now, Kofi has calmed down, plopping down by Rev. Schaper's feet and resting his head on his paws. She sips her coffee for a moment before she continues. "I think the word 'sanctuary' is a very important choice, and I think it's very effective. One of the reasons I'm doing it is it feels like a very effective religious strategy as opposed to the whole question of—the New York City Immigration Coalition does great politics. And I love working with them, but to us this is not just about politics. I mean, we won't be happy if we get a fabulous immigration reform. We want people's hearts to turn. And that is the really important piece. It's important to the soul." Leaning toward me, she insists, "And I don't say that instrumentally. This is not, 'Oh, the best way to impact this is to be religious.' I don't mean it that way. I mean: the stakes are the soul of the nation."

3 SANCTUARY AS RELIGIOUS CONVERSION

Most days, Joe chops fish and vegetables at an Asian fusion restaurant in Brooklyn. In this bright, simply decorated eatery with inexpensive fare, his wife works as a waitress while he cooks in the back. Joe migrated to New York from China in 1996. He came to the United States as an unaccompanied minor: he was 17 years old at the time and his parents stayed behind in China. Joe found work in the food service industry shortly after his arrival in the United States, and for close to a decade he labored in New York City kitchens. Seeking integration into his new country, he also enrolled in English classes. During those years he met Li,[1] a fellow Chinese native who arrived in New York in 2000. They married in 2005 and had their first child soon after, feeling free to have several now that they were not restricted by China's one-child policy.

But in late 2005, a chance incident jeopardized their life together. On a trip to Vermont with Joe's cousin, a trooper pulled them over for speeding. He asked to see everyone's IDs, and Joe's cousin—a U.S. citizen—showed his driver's license, was ticketed, and released. But Joe and Li had no IDs to display. The trooper detained them, assuming they might be in the country without authorization.[2] After being held in Vermont, they were moved to a jail in Massachusetts. Joe and Li were detained separately, restricted from talking and even writing to each other. Instead, they had to send letters to relatives, who would mail them back to them. Joe was detained for three months and Li for four and a half. All this time, Li was unable to nurse their six-month-old baby, who stayed with Joe's aunt while they were detained.

Though they were eventually released, afterward they were under the close watch of Immigration and Customs Enforcement (ICE). Their lawyer appealed their deportation orders, arguing that they both had applications for asylum and that the government had to let those applications run their course before they took any actions to deport them. If deported, Joe and Li would have been separated from their three U.S. citizen children. Another possibility was that one would be granted asylum and the other would not, potentially separating them as a couple.

As part of the New Sanctuary Movement, Joe's family went public with their case, hoping to draw attention to the millions of immigrants like themselves who contributed to the economy, followed local and state laws, loved their children, and cared for their home and neighbors. In other words, for more than a decade, they resembled exemplary U.S. citizens in practically every way, except that they did not have papers. Their situation was very different from the one faced by the Central American refugees who received sanctuary as part of the 1980s Sanctuary Movement. During that era, refugees fleeing civil wars flooded across the U.S.–Mexico border, often with nothing but the clothes on their back. They had no jobs, no money, and often no family with them. In desperation, they were searching for temporary aid—food, water, medical care, a roof over their heads, and a place of protection from Immigration and Naturalization Service (INS) until they could recover and locate a more permanent home.

In contrast, in the mid-2000s, many undocumented immigrants resembled Joe and Li. They had lived in the United States for years. They owned their own homes and had jobs and families in the United States.[3] They were contributing members of communities. They did not need temporary aid, and they would have preferred not to take shelter in religious buildings—that would mean giving up the lives they had worked so hard to build. In other words, they did not really need what sanctuary had traditionally provided. They needed only papers, a change in their status, a stay on their deportation orders. And while there might have been some strategies and tactics that could have helped them get these things—working with immigrant rights lawyers, lobbying for change in federal, state, and local laws—it is unclear how the traditional practice of housing an immigrant in a church could have helped keep families like Joe and Li's together or could have changed the policies that threatened to separate them.

New Sanctuary was formed in part to support 2007 efforts to pass comprehensive immigration reform (CIR) legislation, which might suggest that publicizing the cases of families like Joe and Li's was a good political strategy for changing legislators' minds about the necessity of reform. But it was not, in fact, a good political strategy, and many activists realized this. Some early New Sanctuary activists believed from the beginning that sanctuary was a poor strategy for their political goals, since there was no guarantee that CIR would pass. Even if it did, the bill's stipulations meant that it would not result in a change of status for many of the families taking sanctuary as part of the New Sanctuary Movement.

Given the political context, the choice of sanctuary is puzzling. Why did early activists choose sanctuary? Were they unaware of or confused about the political context and sanctuary's lack of fit for it?[4] Did they read the context accurately, deciding on sanctuary for nonrational, so-called expressive purposes that nonetheless contradicted their actual goals?[5] Or could their strategic choices be better explained in another way? In what follows, I show how the concept of the multi-target social movement helps explain what otherwise appears to be a strange decision about strategy. In doing this, I show how multi-target social movements make strategic choices, how the process differs compared with other forms of movement activity, and what this can teach us about strategic decision-making in social movement organizations.

Native-Born Congregations in America

The Lutheran Church of the Good Shepherd, one of three congregations that formed a sanctuary partnership with Joe and his family, sits at the corner of a busy intersection in the southwest end of Brooklyn. A small bell tower rises into the air next to the main entrance of the stone building. An old wooden sign out front lists the times for the main services. For much of its history, the church and its members have resembled most American churches: the primary focus has been on worship and building relationships among members and the local community.[6] The "History" section of its website reads:

> There are many stories to be told—of a missionary to India, war bond drives, help to the Red Cross, dedication to the study of the Bible, assisting a young seminarian in Bali, stocking food pantries...our choirs singing at Radio City and performing Gilbert & Sullivan operettas in our Great Hall...the ballet performances, Wild West and Gay Nineties shows. We can't forget the flea markets, boutiques, strawberry festivals, cake sales, Anniversary Day Parades. And, so much more.[7]

The bulk of the examples—from flea markets and cake sales to war bond drives and Bible studies—paint a picture of engagement with fellow church members, local neighbors, and occasionally American traditions of citizenship more broadly. At least one of the two mentions of connections in other nations is an instance of support for a fellow American traveling to another country rather than for people of different nationalities.[8]

While its location within the diverse five boroughs of New York may imply that it is a place of racial and ethnic diversity, when it joined New Sanctuary, Good Shepherd was mostly a church of white, native-born people with limited *intimate* experience with recent immigrants. In 2006, the year before the New Sanctuary Movement started, 96% of the church's baptized members were white.[9] Part of this homogeneity is a reflection of what Martin Luther King Jr. called the most segregated hour in America: 11 o'clock on Sunday mornings. Only 7.5% of U.S. churches have at least 20% participation from people of other races and ethnicities besides the dominant race in the church.[10] But while the racial and ethnic breakdown at Good Shepherd was partly a reflection of larger religious trends, it was also a reflection of the surrounding neighborhood, an area known as Bay Ridge.

Around the time of New Sanctuary's launch, the neighborhood was far whiter than New York City as a whole: 79% of Bay Ridge residents were white compared with the city's 44%. In addition, the immigrant population in Bay Ridge was smaller than average, with only 30% of Bay Ridge residents being foreign-born compared with 36% in the city more broadly. [11] As a neighborhood church, Good Shepherd largely drew its membership from the surrounding area, an area lacking much of the racial, ethnic, and global diversity characterizing New York immigration as a whole.[12] And since a subway ride into downtown Manhattan from Bay Ridge takes over an hour, Bay Ridge is more insular than many New York neighborhoods.

So while Good Shepherd is located in one of the most diverse cities in the world, before it joined New Sanctuary many of its members did not encounter that global diversity in regular, intimate ways. Despite the church's membership in a local PICO community organizing group that included immigrant congregations, many church members had not engaged directly in that work, and the PICO group was so large that even those who had been involved had not necessarily had ample opportunity to develop intimate relationships with immigrants. Like most majority-native-born congregations, Good Shepherd was relatively segregated by citizenship status, containing few new immigrants and, despite occasional ministry to the local Russian community, limited opportunities to interact with new immigrants in intimate, prolonged ways.[13] As a result, local relationships and concerns usually took precedence over others, particularly ones transcending national borders.[14] When their website stated, "We are a family and we worship together, work together, laugh together, cry together and reach out to all who would join us," that family had primarily been one of white, native-born people sharing the intimacies of their spiritual lives with each other.

At the New Sanctuary Coalition of New York City launch on May 9, 2007, Good Shepherd's pastor, Rev. David Rommereim, stood beside Joe and his family. Good Shepherd's members had just signed a sanctuary pledge partnering them with Joe's family and with two majority-immigrant congregations playing a supporting role in his case. They were not exactly sure what sanctuary would involve in the beginning, especially given most members' lack of experience with the current immigration system. As Pastor Rommereim told me later:

> We kept saying that we didn't know where it's going to go. And I tried to develop the skill of being very conscientious, that we don't know exactly. So my job is to be the host to ambiguity but to give confidence that it will be okay. And I looked at those kind of leaders that can go into the unknown with confidence—traditionally that's called faith but nowadays it's just that you don't have the exact answer. What is the answer? Well we know the values, we know what we're about, we know what we mean when we say we're a Christian community. Where the sanctuary movement will end up we don't know and neither did it or does it. We're still working on it.

For Good Shepherd and for many churches like it, joining the New Sanctuary Movement required a leap of faith. With little intimate experience with immigrants and a history of focusing on local and national concerns, partnering with undocumented immigrants was a step into the unknown for Good Shepherd. But as the last chapter showed, early New Sanctuary Movement leaders hoped participation would influence the character of religious communities themselves, expanding their notions of spiritual brother and sisterhood.

For the first few months, the congregation had to figure out what a sanctuary partnership would look like, since Joe and his family were living in their own home rather than in the church. They worked seven days a week in a restaurant in another part of Brooklyn, so it was hard for them to make it to the church on weekdays. Instead, they came to services on weekends, where they worshipped and talked with congregants. Church members got together for dinner at their restaurant, trying to support them and check in on their situation. Pastor Rommereim explained, "That's just building relationships. And it takes time."

But perhaps the most important, most intimate shared experience was the experience of the immigration check-in, when Joe or his wife had to check in regularly with immigration officials. Each time, they were in danger of being detained and deported. Attending these check-ins with Joe and Li was emotionally trying, as church members experienced the emotional roller coaster many undocumented immigrants must ride on a regular basis. Pastor Rommereim accompanied Joe on many occasions: "We go down and check in. They [Joe and his wife] may check in at different times, which turns out to be nice because at least one parent is going to be there [with the kids]. I've been down there when parents are there and they say, 'Can we check in at the same time?' And I wish they had counsel to say, 'Don't check in at the same time,' because then it's over [if they're both detained] and then your kids go directly to welfare or the foster system."

Pastor Rommereim's story unintentionally reveals the trouble with sanctuary as a movement strategy for political change. By providing connections to legal advisors and serving as advocates at immigration check-ins, Good Shepherd's members helped Joe and his family, but there were thousands of other immigrant families in New York who received little benefit from the practice of sanctuary. And even sanctuary's ability to protect Joe and his family from separation was limited. As Pastor Rommereim acknowledged, "We know that this isn't the Middle Ages [when churches had a legal right to provide sanctuary]. You can come here, and we can provide sanctuary, but anybody can come and take you. We don't have any legal status and we don't pretend to say we do."

Pastor Rommereim recognized the limits of sanctuary as a strategy for political change and for the protection of immigrant families. He was not alone. From the beginning, New Sanctuary activists were aware of the lack of fit between sanctuary as a movement strategy and the current political context around immigration. Theories of strategic choice that blame a misreading of the political context for the choice of politically inappropriate strategies are therefore insufficient for explaining the choice of sanctuary.[15] If one conceives of the New Sanctuary Movement as a network of movement organizations whose sole purpose was changing immigration policy and its enforcement, then the choice of sanctuary as the organizing identity and main strategy of the New Sanctuary Movement seems a strange one indeed. But the intimacy cultivated through the sanctuary partnership between Joe's family and Good Shepherd's members suggests that the strategy may have been a better fit for New Sanctuary's religious goals. In what follows, I will show that the New Sanctuary Movement's combination of religious and political targets is key to understanding its choice of sanctuary as moniker and core strategy.[16]

Sanctuary and Strategic Decision-Making

In late 2007, a Good Shepherd member who had been interacting with Joe and his family for several months as part of the New Sanctuary partnership began attending coalition-wide meetings. Her experience getting to know Joe and his family as part of their sanctuary partnership—worshipping together, going to check-ins together, eating together—had given her a new perspective not just on immigrant rights but also on religion itself. At the end of one of the meetings, she told the group, "This is the first time I have felt there was a purpose to being a Christian." This church member was not involved in New Sanctuary because of a prior commitment to immigrant rights and a desire to express those views. Rather, she had experienced a change in her religious identity and commitments because of her participation in New Sanctuary.[17]

When I asked her how initial activists chose to mobilize around sanctuary, Rev. Alexia Salvatierra responded, "This is a weaving with many strands, a work of the Holy Spirit. There were people in many places at the same time with a similar vision." This similar vision was not always a vision of sanctuary, though. Finding the perfect strategy for both the political goal of changing immigration policy and the religious goal of making religious communities more accepting of national outsiders was a challenge. They needed what I call a *crossover strategy*: a strategy with resonance and efficacy in multiple institutional settings. Early activists tried out several possible strategies and tactics in 2006, such as education sessions in congregations on immigration and trips to Washington, D.C., to lobby politicians for comprehensive immigration reform. But none of these alternatives provided an adequate marriage of the religious and the political to reach and transform native-born congregations.

Sanctuary's Legacy

As the name New Sanctuary Movement indicates, this was not the first activist group to engage in something known as sanctuary, a practice with a long history of joining the religious and the political. Offering refuge in places deemed sacred to people being pursued by the government or other authorities is a practice stretching back to ancient times.[18] In fact, many New Sanctuary activists referenced the traditions of ancient Israel as both a religious reason for their actions and as a moral justification for them, citing passages in the Hebrew Scriptures as instituting sanctuary, such as this passage from the Book of Numbers:

The LORD spoke to Moses, saying: Speak to the Israelites, and say to them: When you cross the Jordan into the land of Canaan, then you shall select cities to be cities of refuge for you, so that a slayer who kills a person without intent may flee there. The cities shall be for you a refuge from the avenger, so that the slayer may not die until there is a trial before the congregation.[19]

According to the Hebrew Scriptures, by the time of King Solomon, a tradition of altar sanctuary had also developed in Israel. In the book of I Kings, after Solomon's brother tried to overthrow him, the brother took refuge at the altar. Solomon pardoned his brother and let him go free, making the important shift to houses of worship and sacred spaces as places of sanctuary.

In addition to the traditions of sanctuary found in the sacred texts of ancient Israel, sanctuary is also found in ancient Roman literary accounts. Romulus, the mythical founder of Rome, is said to have built a temple to a god named Asylaeus (from which the word asylum is likely derived). In this temple, servants, debtors, and even murderers could reportedly take refuge.[20] In the Christian tradition, the first legal reference to sanctuary is found in the Theodosian code (392 AD). At that time, fugitives could find rest in churchyards and surrounding areas, but not inside churches themselves. The practice of sanctuary continued throughout the centuries with varying rules and stipulations, some allowing sanctuary within religious buildings and others that did not. During the 16th century, Henry VIII established eight towns in England as sanctuary cities. But because of conflicts between church and state, the practice of sanctuary was abolished by Parliament in 1624 and has not had legal sanction in England since.[21]

In the United States, sanctuary has no legal grounds: it never has. If fugitives take refuge in houses of worship, officers have every legal right to enter the building and arrest them. Despite this, practices of sanctuary emerged at several junctures in U.S. history. During the Civil War, churches participated in the Underground Railroad, hiding fugitive slaves from the South as they escaped to the North. A century later, churches, abbeys, and monasteries gave refuge to draft resisters and AWOL soldiers opposed to the Vietnam War.[22]

But among many progressive religious activists in the United States, sanctuary is best known for its use during the 1980s as part of the Sanctuary Movement, a religious response to U.S. financial and military support of civil wars in Central America and the aftermath of that involvement.[23] In May 1981, Jim Corbett, a Quaker in Tucson, Arizona, started having run-ins with INS officers. Corbett and his wife were farmers, their house and land not far from the Mexican border. A few months before, they had been meeting more and more Salvadorans trekking across their land after struggling across the Sonoran desert, fleeing Central America for their lives. Back home, U.S.-trained and funded death squads had targeted them for their race, status, or politics, raping, torturing, and murdering their neighbors and families.[24]

Corbett discovered that the refugees he met were being deported before their applications for asylum could even be processed. He concluded that the Ronald Reagan administration feared the wider public would learn about the violent consequences of its training and funding of right-wing dictators and death squads. These refugees were inconvenient witnesses to U.S. culpability. Corbett and a group of fellow concerned citizens initially resisted by bailing Salvadorans out of detention, often using their own money. After their release, they transported recent border-crossers from the border to Tucson, offering them safety in their own homes. But it soon became clear that this was not a long-term strategy. They had neither the room nor the funds to protect the deluge of immigrants flowing across the border.

In fall 1981, Corbett called Rev. John Fife, the pastor of Tucson's Southside Presbyterian Church, hoping the church would agree to begin housing immigrants there. Though Fife was a veteran of religious activism, he hesitated at first. However admirable, this was not simply civil disobedience—offering sanctuary in a church could be interpreted as a felony. But Corbett told stories of the Salvadorans he had encountered and of the dangers they faced. Soon, Fife became convinced that sanctuary was both moral and necessary. With his encouragement, Southside's leaders voted to shelter undocumented immigrants in their church.

When INS agents caught wind of what was going on, they were incensed. Threatened by officials, Corbett, Fife, and Southside remained resolved to act. Calling an emergency meeting, Fife pointed out an alternative to just waiting around to be arrested for their actions. If they went public about their activities, they "could claim the high moral ground," openly explaining themselves to the media, their denominations, and the public.[25] Excited by this idea, they agreed to publicly declare Southside a "sanctuary for refugees."

After building media interest and support from other churches, Southside held a press conference on March 24, 1982. They hung two signs on the front of the church, which translated from Spanish read: "This is a Sanctuary of God for the Oppressed of Central America," and to INS agents, "Immigration, Don't Profane the Sanctuary of God."[26] Close to 40 reporters and TV crews showed up to cover the growing story of an emerging Sanctuary Movement. During its first year of sanctuary, Southside gave refuge to 1,600 Salvadorans on their way to more permanent homes in other parts of the United States and Canada.

In the beginning, Southside was open about its activities and legal violations. They even sent a letter to INS, explaining what they were doing and why they felt compelled by their Christian faith to do it. By 1983, over 45 churches and synagogues around the country had proclaimed themselves to be public sanctuaries, and over 600 groups had endorsed the movement. The movement started operating much like a new underground railroad—activists transported refugees from church to church until they reached waiting family or friends. The Sanctuary Movement grew throughout the 1980s, even getting membership bounces from the eventual arrests of Fife, Corbett, and several other activists in 1984 and 1985. By 1987, the number of public sanctuaries reached 400. But after Reagan left office in 1988, George H. W. Bush changed course in Central America. As the sense of urgency decreased, the Sanctuary Movement faded, ending for the most part by the mid-1990s.

Unlike prior incarnations of sanctuary throughout history, which tended to be private acts of charitable aid, 1980s sanctuary activists realized their actions had the potential to make political waves. By *publicly* housing Central American refugees in their religious buildings and giving them a media platform for sharing their stories, activists not only saved their lives but also called public attention to the consequences of what they saw as violent and misguided U.S. foreign policy, using sanctuary as a social movement strategy for widespread social change.[27]

Despite the lack of legal grounds for sanctuary, throughout sanctuary's history in the United States, authorities have rarely intervened, even when well aware that someone was taking sanctuary in a religious building. Because of religion's long-standing authority and legitimacy in the U.S. public square, breaking down the door of a church, pushing aside a pastor, and dragging out a suffering immigrant have been seen as undesirable moves, to say the least. This concern undoubtedly weighed especially heavily on the minds of immigration officials in the early 21st century when the New Sanctuary Movement began, even compared with the 1980s. By the late 2000s, anyone with a smart phone could capture negative photos or videos and broadcast them widely on YouTube or other websites at a moment's notice. Apprehending a fugitive by breaking into a church was not only bad manners: it was bad public relations.

Still, in the first decade of the 21st century, there was little legal protection for those engaging in sanctuary in the United States. For immigrants taking sanctuary the risks were especially high. Once you had publicly taken sanctuary, immigration officials knew your status and they knew where to find you. As Pastor Rommereim explained, New Sanctuary activists did not know what to expect when they revived sanctuary. They were unsure of whether ICE would enter churches to apprehend sanctuary immigrants or whether activists themselves might also be arrested. At the very least, religious communities were risking the types of prosecutions faced by Fife, Corbett, and the other sanctuary activists in the 1980s. But in reality, by the mid-2000s the political context was significantly more treacherous for those who would engage in sanctuary, and the needs of immigrants in the 2000s differed from those in the 1980s as well.[28]

Choosing Sanctuary

Sanctuary's long history of engaging both religious and political institutions makes it a good example of a *crossover strategy*. As mostly clergy and experienced progressive religious activists, the people who formed what would become the New Sanctuary Movement had *cultural repertoires*—tool kits—that included sanctuary. In other words, they were familiar with the practice, with its legacy as a movement strategy, and with how to use it as a tool to reach their goals.[29] They knew it had a long religious history and that it had been used for immigration-related battles in the past. And they knew how direct experience with immigrants during the 1980s had transformed religious communities like Tucson's Southside Presbyterian Church, unintentionally expanding its circle of religious concern.

Several early activists who formed the New Sanctuary Movement had been involved in the 1980s Sanctuary Movement. Even those who had not been involved were at least familiar with the practice of sanctuary as a well-known contemporary example of progressive religious activism. Regarding the 2006 deliberations around sanctuary among the group of early activists who later formed New Sanctuary, one activist said:

> You know, you're talking of people who have had, in most of our cases, you know, 20 and 30, 40 years of political activity. We know what to do...[My church] made the decision not to be a sanctuary church at the time [in the 1980s]. Even though we had far more refugees than anybody else did, but we, because some of our programs were funded with public monies—We just didn't want to jeopardize anybody, you know. So we were very active in all the, you know, the protests against the wars [in Central America] and everything else. But we just never declared ourselves a sanctuary.

This person was very familiar with the practice of sanctuary and what it had historically involved, despite the fact that his church chose not to become part of the Sanctuary Movement in the 1980s. Other early activists were similarly knowledgeable about sanctuary and other religious-political strategies because of their long history as activists—their cultural repertoires helped them "know what to do."

Further, sanctuary also held a *special* place in the tool kits of several early activists. At the 2007 national New Sanctuary Movement gathering, an activist from the 1980s exhibited nostalgia for the earlier movement, saying, "The first movement was the most profoundly transformative experience of my life, personally and politically," and expressed his hope that the new movement "will create community like the first one." Similarly, a Los Angeles priest, whose church had played a central role in the 1980s Sanctuary Movement, pushed for the choice of sanctuary from the beginning, hoping to renew the transformative power of the earlier movement.

Despite sanctuary being religiously and politically *resonant*, activists were initially doubtful about using it because many people did not believe it to be an *effective* strategy for the current political and legal context. This was the case both before and after the failure of comprehensive immigration reform in 2007. While New Sanctuary was formed in part as a short-term attempt to influence this legislation, many activists saw sanctuary as a poor strategy even for the group's short-term political goals. Furthermore, they realized that CIR might not pass and that, if it did not, their campaign would need to continue. In other words, many early activists recognized that sanctuary was a less than ideal fit for both its short-term political goals and, in the event of the failure of those goals, for more long-term political strategy.

Indeed, sanctuary was an even poorer fit for its political goals after CIR's failure than it was at the time of the New Sanctuary Movement's launch, when a potential endgame for at least some of the sanctuary immigrants was in sight. Once CIR failed, sanctuary's utility for political change was even more limited, as the tactics associated with the strategy of sanctuary had few direct implications for legislative change that might provide relief for sanctuary immigrants or might end raids and deportations. As one organizer in Los Angeles related:

At that point Fr. Rosario[30] was pretty much a steady drumbeat in LA about "we have to go back to the Sanctuary Movement." But that had been the historic sanctuary congregation which had been known for having all kinds of people sleeping there, you know, thousands of undocumented members, and we think that it probably made sense for his church to do some form of sanctuary. But I think I had the image of, you know, opening the doors and thousands of people coming into each congregation and not being able to do anything for them. And people who really actually didn't want shelter or need shelter or social services or anything but papers. You know, so it was like I thought we were gonna be sitting ducks, and we're gonna have lots of people come into our congregations and then ICE is gonna come in and pick them all up. And what good will that do? So no, I really didn't see it as something that was going to work.

Early activists perceived the needs of immigrants to be different compared with the 1980s. They also recognized that immigration enforcement was more stringent under ICE than it was under the 1980s agency INS. In other words, they believed that sanctuary was not the best choice for their political goals of ending raids and deportations and changing immigration policy.

In many ways they were right to be concerned. In a political environment in which sanctuary providers and recipients might both face serious legal repercussions, sanctuary's past association with civil disobedience made it difficult for activists to attract widespread support among congregations, support that was necessary to build a large enough coalition to attract the media attention needed to influence policy. And sanctuary partnerships focused the efforts of congregations on single families, meaning that they had far less time and energy to focus on the ways that raids and deportations were affecting immigrants on a broader scale. In other words, sanctuary was indeed a poor fit for their short-term political goals, both of influencing CIR in 2007 and of shaping other policies after CIR failed. In the long run, sanctuary had political potential. It could empower members of marginalized groups by making them visible, training them as organizers, and expanding their social networks. And by asserting religion's moral authority, it could also assert the moral illegitimacy of the state. But in the short run, its utility for New Sanctuary's political goals was limited.

Having recognized sanctuary's lack of viability for reaching their political goals, early activists could have adopted more politically efficacious strategies, such as organizing churches to participate in immigrant rights marches—a strategy that some religious immigrant rights activists had already embraced and that had arguably worked in preventing the passage of the Sensenbrenner Bill.[31] The fact that they did not suggests that there were other concerns driving their decision to choose sanctuary.

In his book *Getting Your Own Way*, sociologist James Jasper identifies a variety of the strategic dilemmas collective actors face in decision-making, arguing that some of these dilemmas are rooted in tensions between goals, audiences, and the different arenas in which groups operate.[32] He writes that "few strategic conflicts unfold in only one arena" since conflicts often "spill" from one arena to the next, an argument that highlights how activists' decisions about strategy must recognize the rules that structure those different arenas if they want to operate strategically within them.[33] This need for familiarity with a particular arena or institution's rules and cultural understandings would be especially important when activists are intentionally targeting multiple arenas, seeking not only to operate successfully within them but also to change them.

The more politically efficacious strategies New Sanctuary could have adopted (e.g., organizing churches to participate in marches) might have enabled them to operate within the political arena, but they did not fit the "rules" of the religious arena as closely. In other words, these other strategies were not crossover strategies—they had far less religious resonance and less power to work toward religious change than sanctuary, despite its shortcomings as a strategy for political change. This was a problem given activists' commitment to a religious-political approach. For instance, one early activist, a mainline Protestant pastor in LA, described his commitments in this way:

When Jesus walked here on this earth and became incarnate, I mean it's really ordaining what's here and present in front of us. Not just to look to the Lord somewhere else but to say, "thy will be done here on earth as it is in heaven." And you know, in looking at his ministry, it was clearly a political ministry in that to build the kingdom of God was to reverse the religion of the day and to call into question the hypocrisy of the temple leaders and things like that.

Like many of the early activists, for him, the core of Christianity was about both religious and political change—a political *ministry* of "building the kingdom of God" and "reversing the religion of the day." So while activists recognized the potential problems with sanctuary, in that the current context made it a less-than-perfect strategy for reaching their political goals, their commitment to challenging the religious status quo made it more attractive. As a practice with a long religious-political history, sanctuary provided the greatest possibility of simultaneously seeking political and religious change, making it difficult to give up on the strategy.

Making Sanctuary New

Just as the nascent group was debating whether to choose sanctuary given its inadequacies, in late summer 2006, news broke that an undocumented Mexican immigrant named Elvira Arellano was taking sanctuary in her Chicago church. Word traveled fast among progressive religious activists about this revival of sanctuary. The attention Arellano's story received both in religious and political circles convinced many activists that sanctuary had the religious resonance they sought. But more importantly, Elvira's experiences with the local congregation where she was in sanctuary—her own, mostly Latino congregation, whose members became closer as a result of her constant presence in the church[34]—made them realize just how important sanctuary could be for changing hearts and minds, given its ability to increase intimacy between sanctuary immigrants and hosting congregation members.

Elvira's example made them think about the possibility of using the religious resonance and name of sanctuary while reimagining its meaning and shape to better fit both their political and religious goals. In her analysis of the New Sanctuary "movement midwife" organization Clergy and Laity United for Economic Justice (CLUE), sociologist Pierrette Hondagneu-Sotelo argues that *radical accompaniment* was one of the main strategies used by CLUE activists in their workers' rights campaigns.[35] Rev. Salvatierra told me that over time she was able to see a vision of sanctuary in the New Sanctuary Movement that involved the radical accompaniment of mixed-status immigrant families. For Rev. Salvatierra, stepping outside of the common understanding of sanctuary and reimagining it as radical accompaniment enabled her and other early activists to finally embrace sanctuary as the best available strategy for working toward both their political and religious goals. Describing her conversations with other activists about the possibilities of a new form of sanctuary, Rev. Salvatierra said, "And that shifted for me, a little bit, my sense around sanctuary. Because it was more of a sense that, yeah, you know, there is something about that sacrificial stance of saying I'm going to accompany you, even if it means that I break the law, that has enormous moral power."

According to this new vision, the New Sanctuary Movement would differ drastically from the 1980s Sanctuary Movement. While some immigrants would live in church buildings, practicing the traditional or physical type of sanctuary, the essence of sanctuary would be the creation of intimate relationships between congregations and mixed-status families—often, between nonimmigrants and immigrants. Ideally, this would involve religious congregations partnering with the family of an undocumented immigrant undergoing deportation proceedings. The newfound flexibility in the definition of sanctuary would allow undocumented immigrants to keep living in their own homes and communities rather than forcing them to pick up and leave everything to move into a church. But by partnering with a church, synagogue, or mosque, often one that had little experience with undocumented immigrants, they not only could receive the legal, financial, or spiritual support they needed but also could give congregations what *they* needed by providing immigrants a platform to share their stories with nonimmigrant congregants, potentially changing the religious community's sense of its own mission and vision.

CLUE activists started working alongside Fr. Rosario and other advocates for sanctuary as strategy, sharing resources and agreeing on the reframing of sanctuary as the broader and more ambiguous radical accompaniment rather than as the historic, much more specific tactic of protecting people from law enforcement by sheltering them in houses of worship. Once they agreed on sanctuary as strategy in late 2006, the developing coalition of Los Angeles activists had to decide who would be selected for sanctuary in its reimagined form of radical accompaniment. If the point of *new* sanctuary was to create relationship, then the model of one congregation giving sanctuary to hundreds of immigrants would not work. Instead, they decided to select immigrant families who, as Rev. Salvatierra put it, "incarnate in their own lives the brokenness of the system and who are willing to be prophets and to reveal that."

These families would be diverse to represent the diversity of immigrants in the United States. They would be mixed-status families in which at least one member is undocumented and undergoing deportation proceedings and the others are U.S. citizens, so if the law is enforced the family members would be split from each other. Also, the undocumented immigrants' cases would be ones that might strike ordinary citizens as unfair because of their otherwise exemplary records—for example, a man from Guatemala who came to the United States during the 1980s for political asylum but lost his case because he could not read a court letter that was sent to him only in English. Activists decided that, once they found families that fit these descriptions, they would ask them to go public with their cases to draw attention to the injustices of current immigration policy. In return, the emerging network of activists would offer them legal support in their immigration cases, spiritual support, and financial support or any other forms of radical accompaniment that they could.

Toward the end of 2006, Interfaith Worker Justice (IWJ) agreed to publicize the Los Angeles group's idea of reviving sanctuary, broadcasting it through their national network. Almost overnight, the LA group began receiving messages from people around the country saying they supported the idea of sanctuary and of starting a national network around it. Through her CLUE contacts, Rev. Salvatierra talked to several foundations and other groups about the idea of a new sanctuary movement and the need for startup funds. At least one liked it enough to commit a small amount of funding to the growing group during its initial phases.[36]

The funding enabled the LA group, along with some IWJ activists, to organize a national meeting for people interested in mobilizing sanctuary in different areas of the United States. Around 60 people from around the country attended the meeting in Washington, D.C., in January 2007. While not everyone had envisioned sanctuary as the way forward and the focus on sanctuary remained contested in some quarters, the new version of sanctuary resonated with people from many different places.[37] Within a couple of months, they had made plans to launch a New Sanctuary Movement around the country, using a reimagined form of sanctuary as their rallying cry and their main strategy for political and religious change, a strategy whose concrete tactics would be as wide and varied as those involved.[38] In particular, they focused on two tactics with special religious resonance and efficacy, which became key to the New Sanctuary Movement's practice of sanctuary: witnessing through *storytelling* and seeking direct experience with "the other" through *story-sharing*.

Religious Transformation and the Shape of Sanctuary

Like Joe and his wife, New York City sanctuary immigrant Jean had little use for traditional sanctuary. Armed with a green card, he migrated to New York from Haiti as a teenager to join the rest of his family, who had already migrated to the United States. Facing harsh structural realities as a black, working-class teen in New York, he was arrested on a drug charge during the War on Drugs and served time in prison. After his release, he became a business owner, husband, father, and community leader. But years later, Jean found himself facing deportation and being forced to report to immigration authorities several times a week. He was not yet forced to leave his home and seek shelter elsewhere, so he preferred to stay with his family and continue working in the midst of his deportation proceedings.

With the reimagined version of sanctuary as radical accompaniment, Jean was able to do just that. From the start of the New Sanctuary Movement, he was in a sanctuary partnership with Judson Church in New York, a relationship that provided an opportunity for largely white, native-born, middle-class Christians to become intimately acquainted with Jean's struggles. Over time, Jean and his family became members of Judson, regularly attending services there alongside long-term members. These members provided legal and financial support when needed, played with Jean's children during coalition meetings, and accompanied Jean to his check-ins and court appearances, as at this typical check-in in a Soho building back in 2008:

Accompanied by a group of six Judson members, Jean waits as the elevator rises to the third floor. When the doors open, Jean and his companions step out and turn left. At the end of the hall, they head through a wooden door with a sign beside it reading "BI Incorporated." BI Incorporated is a private corporation contracting with the U.S. government to run the U.S. Department of Homeland Security's Intensive Supervision Appearance Program. Known as ISAP, this program requires certain undocumented immigrants to check in with BI Incorporated case managers up to three times a week. Program participants must also wear an ankle bracelet so that BI Incorporated can track their every move, ensuring they do not leave town and that they keep the program's 7 p.m.–7 a.m. curfew by staying at home during those hours.

While some commentators lauded the early implementation of the ISAP program in 2003 as positive because it allowed immigrants already in detention to leave detention as part of the program, it is now being used on immigrants who would otherwise be unsupervised—by some accounts, an attempt to frustrate and dehumanize them to the point that they will leave the country on their own. As with other private governmental corrections contracts, BI Incorporated has a financial interest in keeping people like Jean in ISAP for as long as possible.

The BI office lobby is small and simple, with blue chairs lining the off-white walls. The walls are stark except for two posters in flimsy black frames, one depicting Niagara Falls and the other the Statue of Liberty—the latter especially ironic considering its history as a symbol of welcome to immigrants. The most unsettling part of the room is the door leading to an unseen back room, where unlucky immigrants who are detained at their check-ins must go in preparation for entering the U.S. detention system. To go through it, one must walk through a large metal detector, a formidable gateway to a place of no return.

Jean has been checking in with officials for years now. As physically, financially, and emotionally draining as the process has been, he has always been set free. On this day, he walks up to the bulletproof glass and talks with the immigration agent while the activists talk among themselves, occasionally glancing over at Jean to make sure things seem in order. Most of them had little to no interaction with immigrants undergoing deportation proceedings prior to their church's partnership with Jean. Today, many of them accompany Jean to his check-ins multiple times a week, talking with him about their respective families, their jobs, and their everyday lives. Their faces relax into smiles as Jean rejoins the group, saying he is free to go. The group leaves the BI office and heads for the diner next door, where one activist always treats Jean and the team to lunch.

Sanctuary's fitness for the New Sanctuary Movement's religious goals lay in its ability to involve people in both the hearing of *stories* and the sharing of *experiences*. Like many activist groups, New Sanctuary used storytelling to create empathy and to recruit participants.[39] Sanctuary immigrants attended most town hall meetings where congregations debated whether to join New Sanctuary, telling their stories in hope that the stories would humanize an often abstract issue. This act of witnessing and testimony sharing is common in many major religious traditions, such that its role in the lives of religious institutions may make it especially resonant for religious people.[40] In religious traditions, the purpose of witnessing, of sharing testimonies about the divine, is religious *conversion*.[41]

But as William James's classic work on religious experience suggests, the hearing of stories does not affect the same kind of conversion that direct religious experience does.[42] Sanctuary was a fitting strategy for New Sanctuary's religious goals precisely because it moved beyond storytelling to *story-sharing*, to direct, intimate experience with "the other." Judson Church members did not hear Jean's story and then never see him again, becoming activists that might sign the occasional petition or go on the occasional bus trip to Washington, D.C. Instead, through check-ins, church services, and other activities, they constantly interacted with Jean and his family, creating intimate relationships with people that were formerly community outsiders (Figure 3.1). Even churches like Judson with a long tradition of progressive religious activism had things to learn from people like Jean, since the community had long been primarily made up people who were Anglo and native-born.

The idea that conversion of religious communities and the individuals in them might be more likely through direct, intimate experience with undocumented immigrants is in line with sociological research on the importance of interpersonal contact in shaping perceptions of other social groups.[43] Having

FIGURE 3.1 Jean and his son relax with Rev. Donna Schaper during downtime at Judson Church. (Photo by Mizue Aizeki.)

close friends from other racial or national backgrounds makes a person's attitudes about members of those groups significantly more positive.[44] As sociologist Mark Warren's research shows, one of the ways white activists come to be invested in racial justice activism is through developing close relationships with people of color.[45] However, casual contact—such as hearing an immigrant tell his story at one's church—may have neutral or even negative effects on attitudes about the other. It is the sharing of *experiences* that comes through more prolonged, intimate contact that has greater potential to make people's attitudes more inclusive.[46]

Earlier in this chapter, I quoted a Good Shepherd member who stated that her involvement in the New Sanctuary Movement was the first time she "felt there was a purpose to being a Christian." This purpose stemmed in part from building a personal relationship with Joe, his wife, and their children, sharing the joys of worship and food and the fears of check-ins and court cases with them. As Rev. Salvatierra wrote in the 2007 *Sojourners* article quoted at length in Chapter 2, the root of sanctuary in the New Sanctuary Movement was meant to be sharing experience with the other: "One of the deepest roots of our connection is the common experience of God's mercy...Someone had compassion on us—literally 'com' (with) and 'passion' (feeling)—someone felt with us, felt our pain as if it was his pain, our hopes and dreams as if they were his hopes and dreams."

Many sanctuary congregation members, like those who accompanied Jean and Joe, did this in deep and prolonged ways, forming close relationships with sanctuary families that moved beyond sharing stories to sharing concrete lives and experiences. Indeed, the potential of sanctuary to create intimacy is so strong that social scientist Randy Lippert has critiqued the practice due to the potential for exploitation created by this intimacy, since sanctuary providers typically hold greater power over the relationship's future than people taking sanctuary.[47] Prior to their involvement in New Sanctuary, this intimacy with undocumented immigrants was largely lacking in most of New Sanctuary's majority-native-born congregations. Typically only the pastor or a lay leader had close relationships with undocumented immigrants prior to their involvement in New Sanctuary, so that native-born laypeople were potential converts through their relationships with sanctuary immigrants and with members of coalition immigrant congregations who were undocumented. For people like Good Shepherd's member, becoming closely involved with an undocumented immigrant enacted a shift in religious identity and practice that was so profound that it is best described as conversion.

In his classic work *I and Thou*, Jewish philosopher and theologian Martin Buber distinguishes between relationships with the other that treat the other as a "thou"—as a subject—versus an "it"—an object.[48] According to Buber, encountering the other person as a whole person rather than an objectified or abstract stereotype changes not only one's perception of the other but also one's self. The intimacy created through the use of sanctuary creates opportunities for this kind of deep transformation in relation to the other. Similarly, in some of my earlier research on the Catholic Worker movement, I found that the personal relationships formed through living in diverse intentional communities that cultivated close relationships with "the other" shaped Catholic Worker identity, allowing community members to perceive of themselves as inclusive despite the need to draw boundaries between their own community and outsiders.[49]

For many native-born religious individuals and communities, the transformations created through their relationships with sanctuary immigrants also changed other aspects of their religious lives. In an interview, an evangelical pastor described his interactions with Jean via the New Sanctuary Movement. He explained that even though many of his fellow evangelicals, who he believed had a more legalistic view of religion, might argue that Jean should be deported for his crimes, now that he knew Jean, "I would defend him until the end." He described how knowing Jean changed his views about how religious people should think about basic theological ideas:

I don't think that a lot of people from a conservative background are gonna stand for allowing [people like Jean] to be protected. They would say if they're a criminal, let's deport him...If a man commits a crime—he's an American citizen man and commits a crime—we put him in jail and break his family unity...But now here's where I don't necessarily even buy what I just said, and you can say that the New Sanctuary Movement has to stand separate from the political side. In other words, you could politically think about whether or not you'd be willing to keep criminally convicted people in America or not, and that could be a political issue that needs to be decided in the ballot box. But maybe us religious groups and religious leaders, we should stand more on the extreme side of saying forgiveness for all and we'll take anybody. We don't care if you've committed any crimes or not. We'll stand on the extreme side of grace and mercy. I think that's one which appeals to me.

His personal experience with Jean, hearing his story, and forming a relationship with him through ongoing work in the New Sanctuary Movement, helped move him from a theology focused on the need to obey the laws of the land to an emphasis on the theological concepts of grace and mercy, without regard for national and legal status or criminal history.

Beyond issues of religious right and left, the New Sanctuary Movement's practice of sanctuary had the potential to transform native-born religious congregations' understandings of who counts as their "brothers and sisters"—moving them from a focus on rules and borders to a form of religious inclusion and globalism that sees all people as deserving of compassion and rights by virtue of their humanity and their status as children of God. Through developing close relationships with sanctuary immigrants, congregations were better able to put a human face on undocumented immigrants, looking beyond an emphasis on the need to protect national identity to one that sees borders as irrelevant in the eyes of God.

As a strategy for religious change, sanctuary resonated with religious beliefs, practices, discourses, and identities on multiple levels. By putting the spotlight on undocumented immigrants and their stories, it provided a venue for witnessing as a route to religious conversion. But, more importantly, the sanctuary partnership between undocumented immigrants and native-born religious congregations gave nonimmigrants direct experiences with "the other," interactions that had the potential to open them up to different kinds of relationships, both in their congregations and in their everyday lives.

Conclusion

Whether the New Sanctuary Movement will ultimately be successful in creating religious conversion through the use of sanctuary is not yet known. But the strategic choice itself points to the religious goals of the group's leaders, and some initial data suggest that sanctuary does at least have the potential to achieve the kind of change early activists sought. For instance, while both Good Shepherd and Judson Church started out as progressive congregations, both theologically and politically, as majority white, native-born congregations, some members of these congregations had never had a close relationship with an undocumented immigrant. Perhaps as a result of this, some were more conservative about immigrant rights than they were about other issues, emphasizing the needs of their fellow Americans as more important and relevant than those of people from other countries. But after getting to know Jean, the views of many in the congregation shifted. By 2009, people went out of their way to accompany Jean to his immigration check-ins, treating him not as a recipient of charity but as a friend. Others argued that they would "do anything" to keep his family together.

Judson's pastor, Rev. Donna Schaper, often pointed to Jean as a source of religious conversion in her congregation. "Jean is now the primary spiritual mentor for 50 of my congregants. I mean everyone talks about mission in reverse, you know, that you may go to Guatemala and serve but you'll come back—you'll be the one who's changed." In the New Sanctuary Movement, sanctuary did not simply mean the church helping Jean. It also meant Jean helping the church by revealing the truth about immigrants as fellow children of God deserving of compassion and rights. Rev. Schaper believed that her mostly native-born, white congregation was moving from ambivalence about immigration to impassioned investment in religious hospitality. In other words, they had come to see immigration as a *religious* issue. As of 2009, a growing number of immigrants had started attending the church as well.

When recognizing the New Sanctuary Movement's goals of religious transformation as well as political change—its status as a multi-target social movement—the decision of early activists to use sanctuary as its moniker and main strategy becomes understandable. It no longer appears to be merely a nonrational or expressive decision. Instead, it was a rational, strategic attempt to create religious change through the building of relationships between undocumented immigrants and religious congregations.

Early activists' cultural repertoires provided them with the option of sanctuary: engagement with religious and political institutions, texts, history, and culture made activists familiar with sanctuary as a possible strategy for religious and political change.[50] Embeddedness in particular institutional contexts provides one with knowledge of the rules of the game in those contexts, knowledge that is necessary for change.[51] Multi-target social movements need crossover strategies—ones that are present in multiple institutions' cultural repertoires—to be resonant and effective. As a result, it may be more difficult for multi-target social movements to make decisions about strategy because of the relative rarity of true crossover strategies.

Sanctuary in its past forms was not a true crossover strategy, as it was a more efficacious strategy for religious than for political change. As a result, New Sanctuary activists sought to reimagine it, suggesting that multi-target social movements may have to engage in strategic adaptation more frequently than other types of collective actors, a process that is often fraught with difficulty but can also produce important strategic innovations.[52] In this case, this adaptation was only moderately successful in addressing sanctuary's political inadequacies, as I will show in later chapters. As the case of New Sanctuary also suggests, the relationship between religion and activism is much more complex than religion acting a resource for achieving activist goals, since religion can act as both resource and constraint *simultaneously* in multi-target social movements. In influencing and providing the choice of sanctuary, activists' religious repertoires were a resource for achieving New Sanctuary's religious goals, but they were simultaneously a constraint for achieving its political goals, since sanctuary was not a particularly good fit for helping people like Jean and Joe change policy or their own legal status. Compared to movements and movement organizations with a single target, in multi-target social movements, religion may be especially likely to both enable and limit goals at once.

4 FOCUSING ON FAMILIES

It is a miserable December evening in New York, the coldest so far this year. Rain pelts the ground and the wind whirs around buildings and through bodies, freezing the rain into ice pellets as the sky darkens. A crowd huddles in front of a large stone building. Nothing outside would indicate that this building on Varick Street in Soho would draw a crowd: no sign reads "ICE Detention Center." Yet its very invisibility draws the hundred or so people to this place, bundled up in their coats and scarves, hands stuffed in their pockets. They gather for a candlelight vigil sponsored by the New Sanctuary Coalition of New York City, organized for immigrants and their supporters to "come together as families during this holy season" and to "remember NYC families who are being separated by current immigration policy."[1]

Many of the usual New Sanctuary figures roam around behind the police barricades set up on the sidewalks in front of the detention center. Some less familiar faces dot the crowd as well, mostly immigrants gathering to protest the recent firing of several immigrant employees by a local grocery delivery chain. Members of the New Sanctuary Movement steering committee and staff talk together near a table, hunched over a small menorah and an electronic speaker with an attached microphone. As people rub their hands together for warmth, a man wearing a clergy collar tries to get the microphone system up and running. An activist passes around paper cups and small candles, instructing everyone to punch the candle through the bottom of the cup to create a barrier from the wind. Soon light starts breaking through the darkness, as people touch candle to candle, passing the flame (Figure 4.1). Toward the back of the crowd, a black man with dreadlocks and a boy of about 12 stand together, hugging each other for warmth.

Roxroy—the man with the dreadlocks—and his son Elijah are the only sanctuary immigrants at the vigil: the rest of the New Sanctuary members here are partners and supporters. Holding their candles, they look together at a sheet being passed around,

FIGURE 4.1 New Sanctuary leaders light a menorah at the 2008 vigil. (Photo by Felton Davis.)

a "Litany for the Detained." The microphone is finally working, and a white mainline Protestant pastor greets the crowd and begins reading the litany, which is structured as a call-and-response prayer. "From our fear of strangers and of those who dress and speak differently than we do," he begins, and the crowd responds: "Deliver us!" The litany continues for several minutes, concluding:

LEADER: To the desperation faced by those who have no place to go,
RESPONSE: Open our hearts.
LEADER: From the hopelessness that grows in the human soul within this place of Detention,
RESPONSE: Liberate them and let them breathe free!
LEADER: For the parents who are being separated from their families because of unjust immigration laws,
RESPONSE: We walk and work together to bring a better tomorrow.

Following the litany, the pastor begins to sing, gesturing that the crowd should join in. People start singing a well-known song with an upbeat tune, "This Little Light of Mine."

The version for tonight has several new verses, replacing "This little light of mine…" with "In the darkness of our times…" and "When people are forced to live in fear…" The song ends with the verse, "Where families are being torn apart, I'm gonna let it shine," and Roxroy and Elijah wave their candles in beat to the tune. As the crowd moves on to other songs, the wind picks up, blowing several candles out, and people struggle to relight them. Roxroy and Elijah sing quietly together, Elijah pointing out the darkened candles to his father. The two smile at each other, sharing a moment of amusement as they watch people struggling to relight the candles.

As the crowd sings the chorus of a South African hymn, "We are walking in the light of God," a group of five or six unfamiliar men and women approach the vigil, wearing camouflage and waving American flags as they blow whistles and shout. Several police officers, who until now have been monitoring the vigil, hurry over toward the other group, setting up barricades between their group and the New Sanctuary crowd. Turning themselves to directly face the New Sanctuary group, the white counterprotestors begin yelling into a bullhorn and whistling, scrunching up their faces as they scream, "Go away!" and "You have no rights!" (Figure 4.2).

The singing fades to barely a whisper as people adjust to the unexpected arrival of the newcomers. Some activists simply stare, unsure of what to do

FIGURE 4.2 Anti-sanctuary protestors attempt to disrupt the vigil. (Photo by Felton Davis.)

next. Others quietly ask those standing next to them, "How did they know about the vigil?" A few of the immigrants from the grocery store raid yell back at the counterprotestors. The pastor quickly asks the crowd to pray for the other group, not to engage with them in anger. Following his lead, none of the New Sanctuary regulars join in with the yelling. Instead, they turn back to their song sheets and begin throwing all of their energy into reviving their singing—now, the African American spiritual "Go Down, Moses"—which grows progressively louder: "When Israel was in Egypt's land—Let my people go!/ Oppressed so hard they could not stand—Let my people go!"

As they sing, the yells of the anti-sanctuary group become simpler and quicker, as they begin chanting, "Fuck you! Fuck you! Fuck you!" over and over at the New Sanctuary crowd, timing their chants with the waving of their flags. Roxroy concentrates on his song sheet, determined to ignore the yells directed at him and the other immigrants, though his hand shakes a little as he sings. But Elijah keeps stealing glances at the counterprotestors, his eyes wide and his mouth clamped shut, moving closer to his dad as he looks away.

By standing, singing, and praying outside of the Immigration and Customs Enforcement (ICE) Detention Center, the New Sanctuary Movement targeted the people inside. They sought to give hope to the detainees but also to influence the ICE agents inside by depicting undocumented immigrants as valued members of society. But the immigrants detained inside (and immigrants in the United States more generally) came from a plethora of backgrounds and had many different family situations, raising the question: why the emphasis specifically on families like Roxroy's—mixed-status families— for sanctuary? During the early years of New Sanctuary, fewer than half of the undocumented immigrants in the United States were members of mixed-status families.[2] Many undocumented immigrants were living alone in the United States, and they were arguably just as deserving as families. A strategy of focusing *only* on families may have contributed to the lack of immigrants at the vigil: Roxroy and Elijah were the only immigrants present who were involved with the New Sanctuary Movement. Restricting sanctuary to mixed-status families may have harmed New Sanctuary's political efforts by constraining its ability to recruit a large number of immigrants, but this strategy may have also been strategic for some of its political goals and *necessary* for its religious ones.

New Sanctuary organizers invited media to the vigil. Reporters and photographers surrounded the crowd, broadcasting images that contrasted the people praying for compassion and hospitality for immigrant families with the counterprotestors shouting words of exclusion and hostility. Through the wide circulation of these images, the New Sanctuary Movement hoped to change national discourse around immigration, both in the minds of policymakers and among religious communities, from legalistic hostility to prayerful welcome.[3] But as I will show in this chapter, to challenge the dominance of a religious vision that emphasized rules and laws and to replace it with a more inclusive religious vision, New Sanctuary activists needed to engage with the most familiar religious discourse of this era: that of family values.[4]

From Sanctuary for All to Sanctuary for Families

As the vigilers finish singing "Go Down Moses," New Sanctuary organizer Juan Carlos Ruiz steps to the microphone, thanking everyone for coming. He talks about the holiday season—Hanukkah and Christmas are coming soon. The holidays are usually a time of joy, a time of family, he says. But for the people in the detention center, it is a time of despair, as their families are being torn apart. Juan Carlos turns toward the door of the detention center and the ICE agents inside, chanting into the microphone, "Free your people! Free your people!" The crowd joins in, beginning to drown out the voices of the counterprotestors and their bullhorn. After a few moments, he changes the chant from "Free your people!" to "Free our people!"

In a reflection he circulated after the event, he wrote, "As I began shouting into the microphone, 'Free your people,' I realized that they are *my* people and thus changed my shouting into, 'Free our people.' Maybe the key is in those two phrases. In order to stop the madness we need to stop asking God to free his/her people and we need to realize that they are *our* people and we are the ones who are responsible for each other. Our collective body is suffering— from head to toe." After chanting "Free our people!" for a couple of minutes, Juan Carlos begins the chant: "No deportations! Support family values!" The crowd chimes in, including Roxroy, who nudges Elijah, coaxing him to join in the chant. "No deportations! Support family values! No deportations! Support family values!" The chant rings through the cold night air, gathering strength and volume despite the continuing whistles and yells nearby.

At the same time that activists were vigiling outside, inside, the Varick Street Detention Center was likely full of immigrants from all walks of life. In the mid-2000s, immigrants in detention and deportation processes came from around the world: Latin America, China, Africa, Central Europe. Each had his or her own migration story, and while some had been in the United States for years others had been around for only months. Many were initially drawn to the United States by the dazzling beacon of better economic opportunities, while others came to escape religious or political persecution or to reunite with family members. And while many had family in the United States, many were in the country alone, mostly men who were single or who came seeking jobs to support families back in their home country.[5]

But the great diversity of immigrants being detained and deported from the United States was not represented in the New Sanctuary Movement. Though it claimed to support the rights of *all* immigrants, New Sanctuary significantly changed the shape of sanctuary compared with its typical use during the Sanctuary Movement of the 1980s.[6] In the 1980s, sanctuary was open to most immigrants from Central America who identified as refugees in need of a place to stay on the journey across the Mexican border and, later, across the United States.[7] Sanctuary churches in Arizona and Southern California were often filled with immigrants, who slept on pews and even church floors for a few weeks before moving on to their next pit stop.[8]

Instead, the New Sanctuary Movement focused only on select immigrants: in particular, on mixed-status families. This restricted definition of sanctuary had its political uses, but it also created problems for New Sanctuary's political goals. In terms of benefits, many Americans find families more empathetic than lone individuals, so framing the New Sanctuary Movement as designed to help families broadened its political appeal in some ways. After the religious right's ascendance during the 1980s and 1990s, discourses of family values were adopted in more secular political arenas to an extent.[9] Tapping into these trends in cultural resonance as well as the strategic utility of emphasizing undocumented immigrants' family roots in the United States, some immigrant rights organizations chose to focus on the impact of deportations on family unity, such as La Familia Latina Unida (LFLU) in Chicago and Families for Freedom in New York City.[10] These organizations—the former with religious roots and the latter secular—viewed an emphasis on families as a strategy for achieving goals in the political realm.

However, the decision to highlight the stories of mixed-status families also created obstacles to New Sanctuary's political goals. It was much more difficult to find an entire family that was willing to go public with their case, especially since parents worried about the effect that the media attention and counterprotestors would have on their children. Perhaps more importantly, it made it appear as though the New Sanctuary Movement was concerned only about "model immigrants" who conformed to dominant cultural values, potentially leaving a bad taste in the mouths of many immigrants, who felt that the group did not speak on their behalf. This was one of the criticisms among early activists who disagreed with the strategic choice of sanctuary for mixed-status families, and scholars (including myself) have noted this difficulty as well.[11] Further, by excluding the large number of immigrants who were not members of mixed-status families, such as single people or members of undocumented families, New Sanctuary and similar organizations may have hindered their ability to mobilize the support of a broad base of immigrants and to advocate for their political rights.

Chapter 3 discussed how New Sanctuary activists reimagined sanctuary to make it more appropriate for the current political context. Sanctuary could have been further adapted in a way that better fit New Sanctuary's goals of changing immigration policy for all undocumented immigrants and of building a network of movement organizations that included more immigrants themselves. They could have made sanctuary open to any immigrant who wanted it, making it easier to find immigrants who were willing to go public with their cases and thereby increasing the number of sanctuary immigrants, building a larger coalition that could have attracted greater media attention.[12] As another alternative, they could have chosen a form of selective sanctuary to keep the numbers of immigrants in sanctuary under control, while selecting immigrants from a wide variety of backgrounds that more fully represented the diversity in the undocumented community. They could have also screened these applicants to focus on particularly "deserving" cases if they felt it was necessary.[13] Finally, they could have decided to give sanctuary only to the most vulnerable immigrants regardless of their circumstances, people whose cases were on their last leg and had nothing to lose by partnering with a faith community for a few weeks in hope of gaining some media attention and a last-minute reprieve. By moving away from a focus on *model immigrants*, the New Sanctuary Movement could have arguably better challenged the roots of immigration policy.

But many of these options would not have allowed for the formation of more long-term, intimate relationships between faith communities and sanctuary immigrants, the types of relationships that were necessary for meeting the New Sanctuary Movement's goals of religious change. Also, the other options did not have the same religious or cultural resonance that the symbol of the family did.[14] Family issues were so central to the religious identities of many Americans and to wider assumptions about religion in American culture that it may have been necessary to use discourses of family in seeking to reach a broad swath of people on a religious basis and to challenge the legitimacy of a restrictive conception of the family and of religion.[15] As with the choice of sanctuary more generally, the choice of focusing on sanctuary for immigrant *families* rather than sanctuary for *all* immigrants makes more sense when recognizing New Sanctuary's goals of changing not only political policy but also religion.

Focusing on Families as a Double-Edged Sword for Political Change

In a recent analysis of LFLU in Chicago, social scientists Amalia Pallares and Nilda Flores-González highlight the group's construction and deployment of a "family frame" in advocating for the rights of undocumented immigrants in the United States.[16] Started in 2002 and housed by the organization Centro Sin Fronteras, Elvira Arellano (the group's president and later, the first of the new sanctuary immigrants) and her son Saul made up one of the 35 families facing separation who joined together to launch the campaign. Though LFLU had religious ties, its primary target was the state. It sought to stop the deportation of its undocumented members, thereby keeping their mixed-status families intact. In other words, LFLU chose to focus on the family unit primarily for what they saw as its political utility. Pallares and Flores-González explain: "In the face of disempowerment and the almost impossibility of self-representation as individuals, members of LFLU have pursued stand-in representation through the focus on children."[17] Similar to LFLU, Families for Freedom in New York City—also founded in 2002—was made up largely of mixed-status immigrant families seeking political change that would keep their families together.[18] Partly following the lead of these organizations, some other immigrant rights groups also began stressing the issue of family separation to frame their own discourses around the need for immigration reform, including some participants in the 2006 immigrant mega-marches.[19]

The spread of the family frame suggests that many immigrant advocates believed it had political utility and that it would therefore have been a good strategic option for the New Sanctuary Movement's political goals. However, like many of the other organizations using this frame, New Sanctuary sought to do more politically than ending the separation of mixed-status families. Its political goals included reforming immigration policy to make it fairer for *all* undocumented immigrants, not just for those who have children who are U.S. citizens. As such, while the choice to focus on families had political utility, it also lay in direct contrast to some of the New Sanctuary Movement's political goals by emphasizing an exclusive subset of undocumented immigrants. In other work on New Sanctuary, I have highlighted the ways that focusing on model immigrants unintentionally creates a hierarchy of deservingness between different categories of undocumented immigrants.[20] Pallares and Flores-González also identify problems with the frame, writing that focusing on mixed-status families is "exclusionary insofar as it relies on a conventional model of the traditional family... What is critiqued is not the model itself but the fact that undocumented immigrants and their relatives are not included in the imagined community of these traditional families."[21]

Like the choice of sanctuary as strategy, the decision to focus on families makes sense in light of some of its political goals, but not others. Focusing on families is not an obviously strategic choice for its political goals. Instead, it is a complicated and confusing one. However, the reasonableness of New Sanctuary's choice to provide sanctuary only to mixed-status families becomes clearer when considering the utility of this frame not only for some of the group's political goals but also, and perhaps more particularly, for its religious ones.

Family Values and Public Religion in America

Discourses about the *ideal* family and the often different shapes of *actual* families have shifted over time in the United States.[22] After the 1960s, a decade that challenged women's subordinate position within the patriarchal family system, individuals and groups invested in what they called the "traditional family" began organizing to defend their vision of the ideal family.[23] Focus on the Family started in 1977 and rose to prominence in the 1980s, the same time that Jerry Falwell's Moral Majority also experienced major growth. Founded by Dr. James Dobson, an evangelical Christian psychologist, Focus on the Family started as a radio show promoting the nurturing of what many evangelicals saw as the divinely ordained model for the family: a married woman and man and their children, with the man as primary or even sole breadwinner. As its audience grew, Dobson became known nationwide, especially among evangelicals. Focus on the Family has long been admired for offering everyday parenting advice to families, emphasizing both enforcement of rules and frequent displays of loving kindness toward children. It became controversial due to its use of a framework of conservative gender roles during a time when women were making strides in challenging the hegemony of patriarchy in the family, the workplace, and the law. Only later did it emerge as one of the nation's leading "culture warriors," staunchly questioning the civil rights of gays and lesbians and a woman's right to choose abortion.[24]

One white evangelical New Sanctuary activist, who still identified as conservative, described his association with groups like Focus on the Family during his youth in the late 1970s and his growing discomfort with their politics despite a respect for much of their original family-centric agenda:

> Well, definitely the thing people don't understand about the rise of the religious right—people who don't like it—what they don't understand is that we come from a very sincere religious motivation. The religious people that want their children to grow up in a morally positive atmosphere: let's get rid of crime, let's get rid of pornography, let's get rid of these morally harmful social issues, so let's create this political movement of Christians who fight for these good and worthy causes...But there was something in me that was holding me back [from getting more involved]. And I think it was this future impulse, that something with it wasn't quite right.

The future impulse he spoke about had to do with the increasing emphasis among groups like Focus on the Family on gays and lesbians and abortion. As these groups—which collectively became known by names such as the religious right, the Christian right, and the New Christian Right[25]—increasingly became associated with Republican politicians, voting Republican became something of a litmus test for "genuine religiosity" as well.

Though Jimmy Carter was the first evangelical Christian elected to the highest office in the United States, his vision of what it meant to be an evangelical—indeed, of what it meant to be a Christian—differed in many ways from Focus on the Family's vision. While he identified as pro-family, he did not embrace the religious right's entire political platform, including its emphasis on America as the divine "city on the hill."[26] As a result, the Democratic president Carter never had the full support of organizations like the Moral Majority and Focus on the Family, despite their shared religious background. Of course, Carter's policies were widely criticized, not only by religious conservatives but also by the broader American public, as evidenced by his loss to Ronald Reagan in 1980. By contrast, Reagan succeeded not only in capturing the public's imagination but also in garnering the support of many groups on the religious right, whose organizational backing helped him secure the presidency.[27]

With eight years of presidential support during the Reagan era, the agendas of religious conservatives in America took a front seat in the national debate over all sorts of policy issues, including rising religious nationalism as part of the Cold War as well as several issues these organizations claimed were about family values.[28] During the same period, mainline Protestants, Catholics, and Jews struggled to redefine their public religious identities, as their numbers declined and the memory of the Civil Rights Movement faded.[29] Sociologists Robert Wuthnow and John Evans describe this period in depth in *The Quiet Hand of God*, arguing that mainline Protestants continued working on issues like peace and justice, but in an institutionalized and relatively uncontroversial way, hoping to keep negative attention away from their struggling denominations.[30]

With mainline Protestants and Catholics taking a backseat in public life and the religious right growing in public influence, it was not long before the public image of religion in the United States became largely equated with theological and political conservatism.[31] In media and political discourse, and therefore in the eyes of much of the country, to be religious meant to care about family values, and to value the family had two primary meanings in public discourse: to be against rights for gays and lesbians and against the right to choose an abortion.[32]

The combined presidential election of George W. Bush in 2000 and his reelection in 2004 was, in many ways, the zenith of the religious right's influence. An evangelical Christian was in the White House, and not one like Jimmy Carter—one who embodied the commitment of many white evangelicals to family values.[33] In 2000 and 2004, the media largely credited what it called *values voters*—people who cited issues of gay rights and abortion as the most important factors in their votes—with President Bush's election and reelection.[34]

The ascendancy of the religious right and its equation of religiosity with commitment to a patriarchal vision of the family was going strong in 2005,[35] when the Sensenbrenner Bill passed and groups like CLUE were beginning to search for a response.[36] For several years, religious people around the country had become increasingly frustrated by the dominance of the religious right, evidenced in the quick expansion of groups like Sojourners, a progressive Christian organization and magazine, whose circulation increased by 87% between 2002 and 2010.[37] Arguing that Americans needed to rethink what it means to be religious, Sojourners and similar groups called for increasing attention to values voters from a variety of religious traditions (including evangelicals, especially young evangelicals) whose votes were primarily driven by religious values other than those prioritized by the religious right, instead emphasizing poverty, peacemaking, and the environment.[38]

The New Sanctuary Movement was born in this context. Its activists often mentioned the need to show that loving God and being faithful does not have to mean being conservative—indeed, many activists contended that conservative stances were less faithful to God's vision. At a 2009 gathering, an activist asked to list New Sanctuary's strengths said, "Well, we're progressive and religious. Conservatives don't have a hold over what it means to be religious." At times, New Sanctuary Movement activists explicitly talked about the need to remind people that valuing the family was not an exclusive prerogative of the right. For many—especially those who argue that lesbian, gay, bisexual, and transgender (LGBT) families are blessings from God and that a woman's right to choose is central to a compassionate religious vision, though New Sanctuary activists disagreed about these issues—a truer form of caring about the family is not seeking to regulate the kinds of families that exist but celebrating and supporting the ones that actually do exist. And in the United States in the mid-2000s, the types of families that actually existed included a large number of mixed-status families threatened with separation by deportation.[39] At the 2007 vigil, when New Sanctuary activists yelled, "No deportations! Support family values!" they were speaking not only to the ICE agents in the detention center but also to the media, to religious people watching the coverage at home all over the country, and to their own religious communities, challenging the idea that being religious and caring about family was the sole province of religious conservatives.

Valuing Immigrant Families

Roxroy and his family shine a light on the complex lives of many families in the United States today and the challenges involved in supporting families who find themselves in oppressive situations. Roxroy came to the United States from Jamaica in 1977. At 21 years old, he accompanied his father to the United States, hoping to get an education and to start a career. While he did not have papers, this was less controversial at the time, as immigration to the United States was at a low point and laws were relatively flexible (see Chapter 1). But after a short time in Brooklyn, he was charged with minor drug offenses in 1979 and again in 1989. Though he maintained his innocence, and still does today, his lawyers advised him to plead guilty in both cases, since such minor offenses would require no jail time if he entered a guilty plea. After his brush with the law in 1989, he was determined to turn things around. He landed a job as a lead remover and started a family, having four children with his common-law wife, an American citizen. Elijah is his youngest child, though all four are U.S. citizens and depend on him for their livelihoods.

Almost fifteen years later, having made good on his efforts to start anew, Roxroy set out to make his relationship official with his home of 25 years. Roxroy's mother—a U.S. citizen—petitioned for legal residency status for Roxroy. Then, in 2007, he received a notice to appear in immigration court. Under the 1996 immigration law (IIRAIRA), which retroactively made criminal convictions for minor drug offenses reason for automatic deportation, Roxroy was now deportable. While he started appealing his case in court, according to the IIRAIRA, immigration judges are not allowed to consider the ways undocumented immigrants may have turned their lives around, might be integral members of their communities, or might have family members who depend on them. They are able to take into account only the crime, even if it happened long before the 1996 law was passed.

If Roxroy was deported to Jamaica, his wife and four children would be left without their husband and father. The "hopelessness of the human soul" mentioned in the vigil litany that opened this chapter afflicts not only those already detained but also people like Roxroy and Elijah, who had reason to fear that their time together as a family was swiftly coming to an end. Perhaps this was part of the reason that, every time I saw Roxroy at a New Sanctuary event, Elijah was by his side, just like at the vigil.

New Sanctuary activists argued that the vulnerability of Roxroy's family and millions of other families like his were religious and moral outrages. Not all New Sanctuary activists agreed that *all* families should be equally valued. A few participants from more conservative religious traditions agreed with the religious right on issues like same-sex marriage, for instance. But they all agreed that families play an important role in society and that the government and community members need to work to support them, perhaps especially vulnerable families like Roxroy's.

The New Sanctuary Movement's focus on families was particularly clear at the following event, five months after the vigil where Roxroy and Elijah huddled together in the rain: On May 8, 2008, the New Sanctuary Coalition of New York City is holding an event celebrating its first anniversary. The prior year, it had launched around Mother's Day to highlight the separation of immigrant families through deportation, and this event aims to do the same. The anniversary event is being held at the historic Riverside Church in Manhattan. Its limestone walls rise into the air, forming arches near the high ceilings, and gothic stone carvings wind throughout the building, lending an air of grandeur and mystery to the place. It is easy to get lost here. Take an elevator and you will end up in the education tower. Take a staircase and you will find yourself in the breathtaking sanctuary, its ceilings soaring and altar glowing as blue light from the stained glass windows bounces off figures carved in gray stone.

Yet another staircase leads to a small chapel. People crowd up the stairway and through a large doorway, marking the appropriate route for newcomers who might otherwise lose their way. Like the rest of the church, the chapel has limestone walls with intricate carvings at the front. Engraved above the altar are the biblical words: "The Truth Shall Make You Free." The wooden pews fill up with about 40 people; several have cameras swinging from their necks and notebooks jutting out of their pockets. As the event begins, a member of Riverside, a bald African American man in his 40s, stands behind a podium, welcoming everyone as cameras flash. Noting Riverside's history of commitment to oppressed groups, he prays, "Give us, Lord, churches and communities that will not remain silent," to which the crowd responds, "Amen."

Marsha,[40] a white woman in her 60s, approaches the podium next. Soon, her mainline Protestant church will be partnering with Roxroy as his sanctuary faith community. She begins reading "A Mother's Day Litany," speaking into the microphone: "Some of us are new mothers and some have been mothers for decades. Some of us are grandmothers. Some of us are adoptive mothers. Some are mothers-in-law and some are step-mothers. Some of us are single mothers." The crowd reads the written response together: "We ask for patience, support, guidance, and community as we try to be good-enough mothers to our children." She continues:

ONE: Some of us are mothers separated from our children by oceans and borders. Some of us have been or may be separated from our children by unjust laws and an inhospitable country.
ALL: We ask for strength and sanctuary as we press for safety and justice.
ONE: Some of us are mothering sanctuary, mothering dissent, mothering ourselves, and mothering our planet. Many of us are visionary mothers, who imagine a welcoming world for our children.
ALL: We ask for energy, creativity and spunk as we nurture our work in the world.

As she finishes reading the Mother's Day Litany, Marsha—a mother and grandmother—moves towards her seat, squeezing Jean's arm as he passes by her on his way to the podium. Reaching the microphone, Jean clears his throat and begins telling his story, as he does at most public coalition events. He talks about his family, about the children of immigrants, and concludes, "I hope we can stand together as people of faith."

The main part of today's service of renewal and commitment, as Rev. Schaper describes it later, is the public introduction of the coalition's two new sanctuary families, both of which include undocumented women undergoing deportation proceedings. Jean introduces Amina,[41] a Senegalese woman whose husband was recently deported. Now, she is trying to care for their six U.S. citizen children alone, despite speaking only a little English, as she navigates the terrain of her own immigration case. A tall, thin woman, wearing the hijab that is customary for many Muslim women, she speaks quietly into the microphone, "I don't want to go back to Senegal," she pleads as the cameras flash. "There is not food, or clean water, or doctors." Several of her children sit in the pews, watching and waiting for their mother to rejoin them. Sandy, a white woman in her 50s from a local Catholic parish that is partnering with Amina's family, says, "We will stand with our sister Amina," pledging to support her in her search for a job and better housing for her family.

After Amina returns to her children in the pews, a short white woman with glasses comes to the podium. Sister Rose,[42] a nun from the Sisters of Charity of New York, explains how her religious order has served immigrants throughout its history. Now they are partnering with a Guatemalan woman named Patricia, or "Patty." While she is not at the event, her husband, Jarrett, an American citizen, is here to represent her, and he joins Sister Rose at the podium. Looking at Jarrett as he stands beside her, Sister Rose says, "Jarrett and Patty's marriage is a sacrament blessed by God that the government is trying to break up. It's not right!" Jarrett, a white man in his late 20s, begins to speak, his voice shaking. He says that he and his family have been citizens all of their lives and that they never would have understood the difficulties immigrants face if he had not married Patty. "Most Americans don't comprehend our situation. By marrying me and applying for a green card, now she may be deported," he says, tears filling his eyes. He pauses, before continuing, "Sometimes policies aren't just. I'm powerless. I just want to be able to live a normal life."

By focusing on giving sanctuary to mixed-status immigrant families like Roxroy's, Amina's, and Patty's, the New Sanctuary Movement sought to demonstrate that family unity was a value that was not just important for religious conservatives. However, New Sanctuary's definition of acceptable families, and therefore of people whose families deserved protection and advocacy, was more expansive than that typically emphasized by the religious right, reflecting their inclusive religious vision more broadly. In the "Mother's Day Litany," mothering was not defined solely in terms of conservative gender roles: to mother is not just to nurture submissively; it is to lead, to dissent, to have spunk, to envision and work for a better world. Similarly, the litany began by recognizing and affirming the presence of many kinds of mothers, including stepmothers and single mothers alongside others mothers, refraining from creating a hierarchy of the morality or desirability of these various types of motherhood. Instead, all of the mothers were praying together for the same thing, that they would be made "good-enough mothers" for the tasks they faced.

Likewise, when asked about why she got involved in New Sanctuary rather than some other immigrant rights organization, a white, middle-aged, Jewish woman said:

> I think the family component. These people are coming to the country... and they just want to take care of their families, you know, they're not causing a problem, it's not hurting anybody. Like, you know, the gay rights movement: it doesn't hurt anyone if two people, you know, want to get married or be together, have kids, you know create a loving environment. How is that hurting anyone else, you know? So I don't know... it just makes me angry.

As in the Mother's Day Litany, this activist's religious vision of the family was different from the vision espoused by the religious right. But that is not to say that she did not value the family. She compared the struggles of immigrant families to the struggles facing LGBT families, seeing little distinction between the two. For her, valuing the family meant embracing and helping the diverse types of families that existed—people coming together to "create a loving environment," whether immigrant or native-born, gay or straight—rather than working to protect or promote a particular kind of family structure.

The religious right's tendency to downplay other family-related political issues compared with its focus on defending a particular version of the family by opposing LGBT rights and abortion may be one of the things that enabled New Sanctuary to reach out to evangelical and Pentecostal immigrants. Many of these immigrants have traditionally identified more with the religious right than with progressive religious activists like those in New

Sanctuary. As a Latina evangelical woman, one of the first New Sanctuary activists, explained:

> I know in terms of media, in terms of what has come forth publicly when folks hear of evangelical, they're thinking of the Jerry Falwells of the world, and Pat Robertson, who attempt to be these dominant voices but are definitely not—I want to emphasize—*not* representing all evangelicals…I would say the Spanish evangelical churches have been more aware and engaged with this issue, because it's very—it's close to home for us, with immigration specifically.Formerly, the Spanish evangelical churches have been supportive of the Republican platform—this is where the disconnect has happened—where they supported the Republican platform because of some other more conservative values. But when it comes to immigration, there's been a real kind of a breaking away. "They support these issues we're standing for, but what about what's happening in my community, and in my family? And what about my brother-in-law, and whomever? You know, why are you not speaking to that?"

While this activist considered herself a progressive evangelical, many of the Latino evangelicals in her congregation were more conservative. Still, as she suggested, they had begun questioning whether the religious right really valued families, since they felt it had largely ignored the plight of immigrant families being split up through deportation. Similarly, a white pastor of a mostly immigrant congregation in Los Angeles said: "Because we're a congregation of immigrants, even the conservative immigrants have been, you know, shifting their thinking a little bit. Because they've said, 'Now wait a minute, all these people that were talking about family values, they don't particularly care about *our* families, you know?'"

Showing that the religious right does not own the family not only allowed religious people who were not conservative to publicly frame themselves as legitimately religious but also enabled them to reopen the larger public conversation about what being religious actually *should* mean. For example, one New Sanctuary activist, a white Catholic man in his 50s, challenged the emphasis of Christians on issues of family and home life, arguing that families were not central to Jesus's teachings. In fact, he claimed, Jesus challenged the patriarchal family structure of his time because of the ways it oppressed people:

> So many Christians are so excited to espouse family values—which is interesting to me because Jesus doesn't say shit about it, or at least

nothing good. That's the primary power structure of his time, that's the first social organization. So when he says "daughter-in-law against mother-in-law," he's saying "disrupt the power structure."

While this activist was not arguing that families are unimportant to God, he believed that defending a particular family model—especially when it upholds certain power structures—was antithetical to Jesus's teachings. Another activist, a white mainline Protestant pastor in Los Angeles, articulated the values he saw as central to Christianity, ones illuminated by New Sanctuary's focus on keeping immigrant families together:

> Jesus's teachings and the themes of God's justice, love, and compassion are core values. So many churches are more about consumer spirituality or very narrow partisan politics—family values agendas and stuff that really isn't about love, justice, and compassion... In Jesus's prayer, he taught his disciples "on earth as it is in heaven." So I mean, if you're really looking long and hard at the state of our world, it's obvious that we're, you know, we've got a lot of work to do and the church needs to be engaged in that transformation.

New Sanctuary activists hoped not only to challenge the idea that only religious conservatives care about families but also to show that religion is not just about gender and the family. Rather, they argued, its core values are love, justice, and compassion both inside and outside of kinship bonds. Religious conservatives might argue that their religious and political agendas *are* about love and compassion—compassion for fetuses; love for children who might be "led astray" by the legalization of same-sex marriage; or "love for the sinner" that seeks to help him or her avoid the "sins" of having sex before marriage or with someone of the same sex. But for many Americans, both religious and secular, their agendas come across as attempts to maintain restrictive, unequal gender roles and to force their own visions of sexual morality on groups whose moral visions differ. In other words, these agendas are often experienced as unjust, oppressive, false, and hurtful rather than as loving and compassionate. As such, New Sanctuary activists sought to replace the dominant vision of public religion with what they saw as a more inclusive one, rooted in protecting "outsider" immigrant families from separation through deportation but also in creating an even broader vision of inclusive, loving family that is not restricted to ties of blood.

All People Are Children of God

The New Sanctuary Movement wanted to do more than offer an alternative to what they saw as the religious right's exclusive public religious vision by demonstrating that religious progressives, too, care about family values. It sought to go further with its emphasis on families, highlighting the need to care not only about immigrant families but also about the *family of God*. In this way, it moved beyond the family-centric strategies of organizations like LFLU that also focused on immigrant families. According to New Sanctuary's vision, if the mainline Protestant pastor in LA was right and the core of most religious traditions is love, justice, and compassion—"loving as we are loved," as another activist said—then religious people must be concerned about loving not only the families next door but also all people, just as they believed God loves all.

This, of course, is the vision of religious globalism.[43] It emphasizes not only fairness and compassion for one's fellow citizens but equally for all of the world's people, American or non-American, with or without papers. As one of the leading New Sanctuary activists in Los Angeles said, "We make visible people who are invisible as children of God." Another Los Angeles activist, a mainline Protestant pastor, described the religious vision shared by many in the New Sanctuary Movement, one they hoped to both embody and to spread:

> The church is called to be a community of folks who support one another and follow Jesus and embody Christ's presence. And being the body of Christ and understanding who Christ is, as the one who was anointed to preach good news to the poor. And so in order to be true to the one we claim as our redeemer, we need to walk with him in his walk with those that the world has marginalized and denied their rights as children of God, created in God's image to live to the fullness of life. And that's not just to be some kind of rhetoric or charity: it's supposed to be the kind of nature and identity and the work and daily bread of the community faith.

Recognizing the rights of all people as children of God, created in God's image, is not optional for Christians, he argued. Instead, it is supposed to be central to the religious identity and work of Christian congregations. But this view of true religiosity was not restricted to the Christian members of New Sanctuary. Jewish and Muslim activists repeated similar refrains. For instance, in a speech at a California mosque, an imam on the LA New Sanctuary steering committee proclaimed, "We are all God's creation."[44]

At the 2009 national New Sanctuary gathering, a rabbi reflected on similar themes, especially in reference to the New Sanctuary Movement's use of the word stranger. From the beginning, one of New Sanctuary's main slogans was "Welcome the Stranger." At first, it could be found all over its website, in brochures, and in its public pronouncements.[45] Jewish, Christian, and Muslim scriptures all include some form of this injunction. In the Torah, the Israelites are commanded to welcome members of other tribes and to treat them as one of their own. In the Christian Gospel of Matthew, Jesus instructs followers to welcome strangers, saying, "I was a stranger and you welcomed me."[46] Together, these teachings provided religious justifications for New Sanctuary's support for undocumented immigrants. Early New Sanctuary activists knew about this language and deemed it appropriate for their cause. But by the 2009 national gathering, things were changing, as this story demonstrates:

Jean walks up to a microphone in the center of a large room at Riverside Church. As the 70 activists gathered in the room look on, he stands with his wife and two of his children and begins speaking. "This movement is the best we have for immigrants facing deportation. We need your support. Families are being torn apart. It's time to stop this madness. Family unity is the most basic human right there is." Concluding, he introduces Rabbi Michael Feinberg, a member of the New York coalition's steering committee. Rabbi Feinberg comes to the microphone and stands with Jean, who remains beside him as he talks. "Shalom Aleichem," he says, a Hebrew greeting roughly meaning "Peace be with you." "This is what solidarity looks like," he continues, as he and Jean look at each other and smile. "I want to read a prooftext of immigrant rights," he says, opening a copy of the Hebrew Scriptures he holds in his hands. "In Leviticus 19, we read: 'When a stranger resides with you in your land, you shall not oppress the stranger. The stranger who resides with you shall be to you as the citizen among you; you shall love the stranger as yourself, for you were strangers in the land of Egypt.'"[47]

Closing the scriptures, he looks up. "We are commanded to love the stranger more than 30 times in Hebrew Scripture. In comparison, we are only commanded to love our neighbor once," he says. He pauses for a moment before continuing. "But, you know, I think we need to reject the concept of the stranger. Scripture tells us that every human being is created in the image of God. The picture it offers is a picture of humanity as common and undivided. Really, our work theologically is to undermine the very concept of the stranger." As he speaks, several people in the room nod, watching him attentively. He continues, "On the Jewish calendar, this is the month of Ellul. For the Jewish community, this is a time of communal reflection. We think and pray about how to rededicate ourselves to our highest ethical ideals." Looking at Jean and his family, he continues, "I hope this gathering can be a time of introspection for the national movement and that we can think about how we can better reject *all* borders, boundaries, and fences."

Around the room, people clap loudly at the end of his speech, continuing to applaud as Rabbi Feinberg, Jean, and his family walk to their seats. On the other side of the room, a white woman in her 20s makes her way to the podium. She says, "It truly is an honor to be among all of these voices. I'm United Methodist, so my scriptures are the Christian scriptures." She reads an excerpt from the 25th chapter of Matthew about welcoming the stranger, then pauses before saying that she really appreciates Rabbi Feinberg's point about New Sanctuary's language. She says, instead of strangers, "We really are brothers and sisters in this work. We need to keep working on how to do it with more love and more grace."

Rabbi Feinberg was not the first to make this point about the language of the stranger as rooted in "othering." New Sanctuary activists had used phrases like "children of God" and "brother and sister" since its earliest days. For instance, "An Invitation to Become a Part of the New Sanctuary Movement," a pamphlet circulated in the early days of New Sanctuary, described its work in the following way, combining the language of children of God with the language of stranger:

> What the New Sanctuary movement will do is to call attention to the false theology of the immigration system and to make visible the plight of the invisible and frightened. It will offer addresses of congregations so that enforcement officials have to see that some people care about what happens to the "strangers" in our midst. The Biblical warrant is full and complete: we are not to ignore the plight of the lowest, the least and the lost. They are Christ among us. They are hardly "illegals" or "undocumented," labels which sting and objectify; rather they are God's beloved children...[Our] primary purpose is to awaken the imagination of the city's congregations to the plight of immigrants.

From the beginning, New Sanctuary activists hoped to "awaken the imagination of congregations," transforming them from a religious nationalist perspective to a religious global perspective, from seeing undocumented immigrants as "illegals" to seeing them as "God's beloved children." So even though references to immigrants as strangers had been part of New Sanctuary's ongoing discourse, so had references to immigrants as part of God's family, as brothers and sisters.

But Rabbi Feinberg's speech at the 2009 national gathering was part of a changing trend in some quarters and offered a wake-up call to those who had not yet started thinking about the problems associated with using the language of "welcome the stranger." The New Sanctuary Movement was trying to better embody and encourage a religious global perspective, replacing the use of stranger with the language of brother and sister in many of its materials and practices. Most importantly, the New Sanctuary Movement's slogan had been slowly shifting from "Welcome the Stranger" to "Radical Welcome." At the 2009 national gathering, New York activists handed out pins that included a logo designed by Sandra,[48] one of the NYC sanctuary immigrants. The logo included two hands clasped around a heart, with the words "New Sanctuary Movement—Radical Welcome" encircling it. The program for the gathering and its website all used the language of *radical welcome* rather than *welcome the stranger*. In 2009, the New Sanctuary Movement's new website included the new logo and the radical welcome language and used no stranger language.[49]

By intentionally moving from the language of stranger to the language of brother and sister in describing undocumented immigrants, the New Sanctuary Movement was searching for a way to emphasize their status as children of God, worthy of the same justice, love, and compassion as American citizens. They hoped that stressing this divine brotherhood and sisterhood would not only get the attention of politicians and ICE agents but would also move the hearts of religious people around the country, challenging them to see their religiosity in a new, less bounded, way.

By focusing on families, the New Sanctuary Movement both tapped into a religious discourse with a great deal of resonance in the United States and subverted that discourse, replacing the religious right's more narrow vision of the ideal family as a married heterosexual couple with children with a broad vision of family as the presence of loving relationships, a more expansive definition—even all-inclusive when taking religious globalism into account. In this discourse, family values came to mean supporting people's ability to create and sustain intimate, loving, *present* relationships with significant others, perhaps especially across lines of difference. By directly comparing itself to the religious right through the use of a pro-family frame[50] and then offering its own religious ideas about the family, New Sanctuary attempted to replace the dominant public image of religiosity as focused on rules about personal morality and family structure with an image of religiosity as focused on inclusive acts of love and mutual care without condition.

According to religion scholar James Wellman's book on evangelical and liberal Protestants in the Pacific Northwest,[51] these distinctions map onto the basic differences between conservative and progressive religious traditions more generally, at least as far as Protestantism is concerned. Wellman argues that both religious traditions have a core moral worldview, which informs their rituals, projects, and all aspects of their organizational life. For liberal Protestants, this worldview focuses on "loyalty to the image of Jesus as the one who includes all and is hospitable toward all" by following Jesus's example, while for evangelicals it emphasizes "a relationship to Jesus Christ…all things, whether family life, education, missions work, ritual experience, or the moral life, start with this relationship."[52] In other words, liberal Protestants are not necessarily less devout than more conservative Christians—they are *differently* religious.

This is not to suggest that conservative Christians are not welcoming or loving people, or that some do not already welcome immigrants and see them as brothers and sisters. There is a great deal of diversity within conservative Protestantism, particularly evangelicalism, and many evangelicals support welcoming immigrants, though recent data do suggest that white, native-born evangelicals are more likely to hold Christian nationalist views and anti-immigrant attitudes compared to members of other religious traditions.[53] But the primary difference is one of emphasis: on average, conservative Protestants are more likely to emphasize a relationship with Christ over inclusion and justice as central to what it means to be Christian.

Wellman's research on evangelicals and liberals suggests that the New Sanctuary Movement's decision to highlight a liberal or progressive religious vision of the family may even be necessary for contesting the religious right's dominance. He writes that the issue of defining the family, particularly the battle over same-sex marriage, "is one of the main pistons of the clash of cultures between these churches—two models of family life and worldviews that construct different norms and behaviors, each based on a powerful moral worldview that is judged sancrosanct and absolute."[54] Same-sex marriage and abortion may be less central to the religious concerns of ordinary conservative evangelicals than everyday issues like loving and caring for people in need. These two issues have arguably been overemphasized by conservative evangelical religious leaders, enterprising conservative politicians, and the media, who have typically ignored progressive evangelicals' expressions of support for same-sex marriage and even abortion under certain circumstances.[55] But for many evangelicals, a more inclusive vision of the family is nonetheless threatening because it undermines "a core plank of their moral worldview."[56] For many liberal Protestants, a restrictive vision of the family challenges their vision of an inclusive God who celebrates the diversity and freedom of creation rather than seeking obedience and conformity.[57] To a certain degree, to battle over what it means to be religious in the United States in the early 21st century, religious activists *must* engage with discourses of the family. The New Sanctuary Movement's innovation was that they connected family values to the image of the divine family, expanding the circle of religious concern to include immigrant families, as the following story demonstrates:

At the 2009 national gathering, several hours after Rabbi Feinberg called for the use of language that would better embody the group's commitment to religious globalism, his vision is coming to life not only in words but also in bodies. Around 60 people gather at the front of the room where the day's meetings have been held, excited murmurs filling the space as people watch a band setting up its equipment. While they are mostly known for children's music, the popular band Dan Zanes and Friends won a Grammy Award in 2007, so New Sanctuary activists are abuzz about having celebrities in their midst. To combat what they see as a hostile and unwelcoming culture, the band members recently recorded a Spanish language CD, and they are committing the profits from the sale of their most recent CD—called *The Welcome Table*—to the New Sanctuary Movement.[58]

Dan Zanes is a tall, skinny white man whose huge gray Afro merely calls greater attention to the thinness of his frame. He straps on an acoustic guitar and pulls the microphone closer to him as people applaud and call out in excitement. He starts by telling the crowd about the band and its commitment to New Sanctuary, saying how thankful they are for the group's work. "Today we are going to perform some songs from our newest CD, The Welcome Table," he says. "They are loosely based on some old gospel tunes. We hope you like 'em." Turning and facing the other members of the band—another tall skinny white guy with an accordion, an eight-months-pregnant white woman balancing a huge wooden bass, and a Latina woman in her twenties with long, dark hair and a mandolin—he nods three times to cue the start of the song.

"I'm workin' on a building for my Lord," he sings, and the Latina woman sings harmony with him. The tune is fun and upbeat, and the music is a down-home, gospel style. Some of the activists have their children with them, and the kids run back and forth in front of the band, dancing and laughing. After a long, emotional day of reflection and planning, the faces of the New Sanctuary activists have relaxed into smiles as people clap, wave their hands in the air, and tap their feet to the music. The band member with the accordion dances around as he plays, and the other band members grin at each other. Around the room, immigrants and native-born, documented and undocumented laugh together, some twirling each other around as they dance to the music. The band moves on to another song, singing:

> When all God's children gather under the sun
> When all God's children gather under the sun
> Look out of the window see a new day has begun
> When all God's children gather under the sun
>
> So get your brush and colors and paint it now
> So get your brush and colors and paint it now
> Maybe you can't see it but just make it anyhow
> Get your brush and colors and paint it now

As people laugh, twist, twirl, and shake, the band slows down, looking at each other and strumming their instruments with exaggerated arm movements, signaling the end of the song: "Dancing all together won't it be fine, When all God's children gather won't it be fine!"

A Family Divided

Despite the jubilant vision they were dancing into being that night, earlier that same day several New Sanctuary members had struggled to hold back tears, finding it hard to imagine the day "when all God's children will gather" and all will be fine. Just a month earlier, in August 2009, Roxroy Salmon had received his final order of deportation. His appeals exhausted, the only hope for his case was prosecutorial discretion, which enables local agents to decide not to enforce a deportation order when they so choose. For months, the New Sanctuary Coalition of NYC, Families for Freedom, and other allies had collected signatures of support, petitioning local ICE agents to use their lawful right to discretion in Roxroy's case, allowing him to stay with his son Elijah and the rest of his family. His sanctuary partners at a local mainline Protestant church organized a vigil on his behalf, meeting in front of the ICE office at 26 Federal Plaza in New York to call for compassion and love. They also organized a four-month-long fast, with at least one individual or allied organization fasting each day from March 8 to July 7, a plea for mercy from the state and an effort to transform themselves spiritually, to maintain solidarity even when things seemed hopeless.

Not everyone at the Presbyterian church that partnered with Roxroy and his family was on board with New Sanctuary in the beginning. They were uncertain about whether undocumented immigrants like Roxroy deserved the same rights as Americans. They pointed to national law, and they worried that their own church might be placed on some kind of national watchlist if they partnered with an immigrant like Roxroy. After months of conversation with New Sanctuary activists, especially immigrant families, they decided to officially join the New Sanctuary Movement, partnering with Roxroy in 2008. This was not the decision of a handful of people. In the Presbyterian polity, a large group of members called elders must approve a decision like this one, and the clergy do not have the right to vote. Soon, Roxroy and his family—especially his son Elijah—were regular fixtures at the church, becoming intimately acquainted with a church of mostly white, middle-class, native-born people, many of whom had never known or interacted with an undocumented immigrant.

Marsha, the woman who read the Mother's Day Litany at the 2008 anniversary event, spearheaded much of the work. In 2009, she helped start a blog to publicize Roxroy's case after he received what is known as a bag and baggage letter: an order to report to ICE for deportation once all appeals have been exhausted (the name referring to instructions in the letter about the size of luggage allowable on one's departing flight). To respond to the letter by showing up would result in his deportation; to refuse to show up would turn his case over to ICE's fugitive unit, meaning that he could be forcibly detained and deported at any time, including at his home in front of his family. One can only imagine the pain that Elijah, Roxroy's wife, and Roxroy himself must have felt in making the decision about whether he should "self-deport." But members of First Presbyterian also mourned. Despite the importance of national identity in many American religious communities, Roxroy had come to feel like one of their own, a fellow member of God's family, their church family, and their own extended families. On August 16, two days before Roxroy's deadline for reporting to the ICE office, Marsha wrote on the blog:

Tomorrow is the day when we will learn whether our elected representatives have been successful in averting Roxroy's deportation scheduled for Tuesday, Aug. 18th. Since Roxroy received his order to appear for deportation just 10 days ago, I've had a ball of fear in the pit of my stomach while anger and prayer vie for supremacy. It seems unbelievable to me that such a loving husband, father and grandfather, could be separated from his children in 2 days... Tomorrow we will know...

I repeat over and over: "I lift my eyes to the hills. From whence does my help come? My help comes from the Lord, who made heaven and earth... The Lord will keep you from all evil; he will keep your life. The Lord will keep your going out and your coming in from this time forth and for evermore."

In her desperate prayer with the Psalmist, Marsha begged for God to "keep her from all evil," to keep her life. The prayer does not distinguish between needing help for Roxroy and needing help for herself: the bond goes deeper than that. She concluded the blog post with a message to a man she now saw as her brother, knowing that whether he showed up for his deportation or not, it might be a very long time before she saw him again: "May God be with you, Roxroy. We love you."

Conclusion

The New Sanctuary Movement's decision to focus on families was unnecessary and, in some ways, unfitting for some of its political goals. Even though its religious goals required a strategy like sanctuary, designed to create intimacy between native-born religious people and undocumented immigrants, sanctuary did not have to be restricted to mixed-status families. While the family frame has cultural resonance beyond religious groups, if New Sanctuary had included single people and members of undocumented families as well as mixed-status families as sanctuary recipients, it could have represented a broader swath of the undocumented population for whom it claimed to advocate. This would have helped its political goals in two ways. By opening sanctuary up to a wider pool of people, it would have made it easier to find immigrants willing to go public with their cases, something New Sanctuary struggled with throughout its existence. Also, it would have shown the undocumented community that the New Sanctuary Movement sought to care for and advocate on behalf of all immigrants rather than only a select few.

But these options would not have had the same public religious resonance as an emphasis on families. Framing itself as pro-family, both in discourse and practice, allowed the New Sanctuary Movement to engage the imagined religious community of the American religious public,[59] tapping into existing public assumptions about what it means to be religious while simultaneously challenging those assumptions. Though somewhat puzzling when New Sanctuary is viewed as a network with solely political targets, the reasoning behind both the group's choice of sanctuary and its choice to give sanctuary to immigrant families rather than all immigrants becomes clearer when recognizing New Sanctuary's religious targets.

As both this chapter and the last have shown, the strategic decisions of multi-target social movements can be misinterpreted—attributed to a misreading of the political needs of constituents or a lack of imagination—if they are viewed only through the dominant theoretical lens of single-target social movements focused solely on changing the state. For activists like Marsha and her fellow church members, participation in the New Sanctuary Movement certainly involved political advocacy on Roxroy's behalf. But their sanctuary partnership with Roxroy changed them as well, cultivating a new level of spiritual and relational intimacy with former strangers, thereby strengthening and affirming a religious vision of an inclusive, loving God who promises to care for undocumented immigrant families and the entire human family.

The case of New Sanctuary also demonstrates how combining religious and political targets can produce strategic and tactical innovation. By drawing on both religiously and politically resonant discourses, New Sanctuary shifted the meaning of family values, expanding religious frames while also offering an innovative discourse for pro-immigrant activism rooted in collective claims (the human and divine family) rather than individual claims (human rights). Given criticism among some scholars of the use of the discourse of human rights for pro-immigrant activism because of its emphasis on the individual,[60] New Sanctuary's innovation suggests that multi-target social movements may be positioned to provide important strategic innovations due to their combination of institutional targets and accompanying discourses.

5 THE ART OF BALANCE

Activists mill around the wood-paneled basement of a Los Angeles church as the second day of the 2007 national gathering draws to a close. People around the room yawn as they talk quietly, their bodies sapped of the energy and enthusiasm they displayed this morning, prior to a full day of meetings and workshops. Along the room's walls, organizers have taped large sheets of butcher-block paper from earlier in the day, words scrawled across them describing the local coalitions and everyone's assessments of the New Sanctuary Movement's strengths and weaknesses. Rev. Maria,[1] the pastor facilitating the evening's events, calls the group to attention, asking them to start the evening by walking quietly around the room, reading the sheets and reflecting on what stands out to them from the day's activities. Silence spreads as people begin wandering from sheet to sheet, slowly soaking in the insights before continuing to their seats.

After the folding chairs fill up with bodies, a woman named Jacqueline[2] leads the crowd in a song inspired by an old spiritual, replacing images of the devil with the image of Immigration and Customs Enforcement (ICE) agents. She smiles as she sings out, her voice clear and jubilant:

> Victory is mine,
> Victory is mine
> I tell ICE, get thee behind
> 'Cause victory today is mine

Laughter trickles around the room as people register the new version of the song. An imam near the back of the room leans over his shoulder and whispers loudly to the person next to him, "The next verse should be, 'I'll tell ICE to kiss my behind,'" and five or six people near him chuckle. Still smiling, Jacqueline gestures for everyone to join her, and the group begins singing. For the first time this evening, people exude energy, laughing and singing with gusto.

After the singing, Rev. Maria asks everyone to offer their thoughts on the New Sanctuary Movement's current state, keeping in mind what they have discussed throughout the day. Jacqueline speaks up, saying, "I'm a labor organizer, and when there's no conversation about an issue it's not good. No one is talking about immigration on a national scale. We have to make this a national movement if we're going to win this, but if you ask your average person they've never heard of it." Around the room, several people nod their heads in agreement. She continues, "It's only going to be won if we take it to the streets. We know that from history." She mentions the 2008 elections, saying that as they get closer, "the New Sanctuary Movement needs to become more visible and think about a national campaign to get some exposure."

Rev. Candace,[3] a Protestant minister, speaks up, arguing that while she understands people's desire to do more political activism, "one of the best things about this movement is that we are keeping our language religious." She continues, "Religious activists need to reinvent movements—what they are, how they work, and what they do," she argues. She recommends combining religion and politics in new ways. "We could contact the faith-based campaign directors of all of the presidential candidates and do what we do best. We need to insert ourselves above politics, morally."

As she talks, Dan,[4] a layperson with limited religious activist experience, grows red in the face, rolling his eyes and furrowing his brow. He shoots his hand into the air and shifts back and forth in his chair, eliciting glances from those sitting nearby as he visually registers his disagreement with her proposed direction for social movements in general and sanctuary in particular. When Dan's turn to speak finally comes, he says, "I take issue with what Rev. Candace said. The 1970s and 1980s were incredibly important! What Martin Luther King did was groundbreaking! Other people in the streets stopped a war! You can make progress politically, but I don't like the idea of contacting the faith-based director of the campaigns." Instead, he suggests getting 5,000 people to march in each coalition city around the issue of immigration: "It will show our numbers and force politicians to listen." During his speech, Rev. Candace's face grows bright red, but she purses her lips and remains silent.

Sensing growing tension, Rev. Maria rises from her chair. "I'm a preacher so I do better standing up," she says. "Right now, we need to focus on changing hearts and minds. We have done a lot that doesn't work in past movements. I'm getting older. I need to use my energy more strategically." She continues, saying she wants to stress sharing stories, focusing on the stories of immigrant families—who are "victims and prophets at the same time"—to create spiritual change across the country. She speaks slowly and warmly yet firmly, commanding the attention of the room. Even Dan watches silently, nodding as if acquiescing to the power of her charisma, even though her message shares more in common with Rev. Candace's approach than with his own.

While at first glance the foregoing debate seems like a simple struggle over differences in tactics—whether people should contact the faith-based directors of campaigns or whether they should organize more conventional street protests—the struggle was a deeper one. Both of the pastors were clergy with long histories of engagement in struggles over the public definition of religion through progressive religious activism. The other two people—Jacqueline and Dan—were not clergy, had little experience with religious activism, and were more devoted specifically to changing immigration policy than to religious change. As such, they were operating within different institutional positions—with different sets of commitments, material interests, and cultural repertoires—that structured their investment in challenging multiple targets simultaneously (or the lack thereof).

Before and directly after New Sanctuary's launch, it was made up almost entirely of *crossover actors*—people committed to changing multiple institutional targets and whose positions at the intersections of these institutions gave them expertise on each. But as this vignette suggests, as the New Sanctuary Movement grew it became more diverse. Multi-target social movements must recruit some actors who are institutional specialists, who have a deeper knowledge about each institution's terrain than crossover actors—with their more divided affiliations—often obtain.

Increasingly over the course of its first two years, the New Sanctuary Movement included activists who were not crossover actors but instead were *single-institutional actors* with extensive knowledge about and commitment to only one of New Sanctuary's targets of change. As multi-target social movements like the New Sanctuary Movement grow, how do they maintain commitment to multiple targets? What obstacles exist, and what are the consequences of falling prey to those obstacles? Though all social movement organizations face some degree of internal conflict and other obstacles in the creation of strategic capacity,[5] this chapter suggests that these challenges are magnified in multi-target social movements because of the need for a delicate balance of diverse participants with different contacts, cultural referents, expertise, and commitments.

From Dominance of Crossover Actors to Increasing Activist Diversity

When it was forming prelaunch in late 2006 and early 2007, the New Sanctuary Movement's early activists consisted almost solely of clergy with histories of progressive religious activism, like the clergy in this chapter's opening vignette. Because they told the story of New Sanctuary's emergence and initial strategic and tactical choices, the prior chapters of this book have told what is largely *their* story. They sought a religious response to the growing immigration crisis and the dominance of the religious right, worked to build a network of movement organizations with political and religious goals, and chose sanctuary and family values as the religious-political tools around which to organize the New Sanctuary Movement's moniker, identity, discourses, and strategy.

Their lives existed at the intersection of the institutions they sought to change. They were mostly both clergy and participants in the U.S. immigration system, either as long-standing advocates for immigrants or as immigrants themselves. Most stood committed to changing both institutions. But just as important, they had knowledge about how these institutions worked, expertise in the "rules of the game"[6] that enable challengers to develop the strategic capacity necessary for changing those institutions.[7] As such, I call them *crossover actors*, a term highlighting their position as key actors in multiple, at times overlapping, institutions (Figure 5.1).[8]

But after the launch, as New Sanctuary began to grow, its membership became more diverse, increasingly including more single-institutional actors such as laypeople with less expertise about and investment in religious institutions, people with little experience with religious activism, and secular immigrant rights activists. As this chapter will show, these activists were embedded in different institutional settings compared to the early activists, resulting in increased conflict over the New Sanctuary Movement's commitment to changing multiple targets. To manage this *target conflict*, which encompassed conflict not only about strategies and goals but also about things as central as the name, identity, and activist base of the network, New Sanctuary needed to cultivate balance by retaining a core group of crossover actors while also recruiting a relatively equal number of single-institutional religious activists and single-institutional immigration activists.

When I conducted activist interviews in 2008, approximately one year after the launch, crossover activists remained dominant in both the New York and Los Angeles coalitions. However, both coalitions contained an increasing

FIGURE 5.1 A group including several crossover activists blocks traffic near the Varick Street Immigrant Detention Center in NYC, protesting the breakup of families through detention and deportation. (Photo by Mizue Aizeki.)

number of single-institutional actors as well, leading to more diversity in the institutional positions and expertise of New Sanctuary Movement participants. My interviews revealed that these differing positions often translated into different ways of thinking and speaking about the relationship between religion and politics and the desirability of working on them simultaneously. In other words, the increasing diversity of the institutional locations of activists created more diversity in their commitments to one or both of New Sanctuary's targets for change.

In seeking to better understand how having multiple targets might shape movements and movement organizations in distinct ways, activists' discourses about their participation can provide an important piece of the puzzle. In his study of religious people's discourses about reproductive genetic technologies, sociologist John Evans argues that examining how people talk is important when studying public issues, as "a person's language about their thoughts, rather than solely their thoughts, influences others in the public sphere."[9] Discourses are a central part of people's cultural tool kits and they reflect their institutional locations.[10] In fact, "talk conveys meaning because it is culturally patterned."[11] Someone that has been part of a religious group for years will talk about it differently compared with someone who has had a recent conversion experience.[12] Further, those who participate regularly in an institution, consistently shaping it and being shaped by it, will talk about that institution differently compared to an outsider, whose knowledge of the institution is necessarily more limited and whose investment in its well-being may be nonexistent. In examining how participants talked about religion and activism, I adopt a cultural perspective that interprets their statements as discourses shaped by their institutional locations rather than as reflections of their deeply held beliefs about the topic, though these discourses may indeed represent their beliefs and values.[13]

These interviews reveal that New Sanctuary activists and potential recruits talked about the relationship between religion and political activism in two primary ways: by using discourses of integration and distinction.[14] The *integration discourses* construct an image of religion and activism as integrated entities with overlapping beliefs, institutions, and practices, whereas the *distinction discourses* portray religion and political activism as distinct phenomena. Overall, activists described religious institutions as inherently rooted in public battles over power and authority. Of those I interviewed in 2008, 61% described religion and politics as integrated, 20% described them as distinct, and 19% talked about them as both distinct and integrated, moving between discourses during the interview.[15]

Discourses of Religious-Political Integration

The first set of religious-political discourses stresses the integration of religion and politics. This way of talking about religion and politics stresses how the purposes, institutions, symbols, and rituals of religion often overlap with those of politics. According to this discourse, seeking change in one would go hand in hand with seeking change in the other. Even in 2008, a year after the launch, the majority of activists I interviewed (61%) talked about the relationship between religion and political activism using this discourse. In other words, most remained committed to the group's religious-political vision.

The largest portion of my interview respondents contended not only that religious commitments motivated their activism but also that their political activism was a form of religious practice for them. I call this religious-political discourse the *overlap* discourse. Recall from Chapter 2 that Rev. Donna Schaper, an early New Sanctuary leader, explained her views on the relationship between religion and politics in this way:

> People don't understand this about people on the left like me. This
> is really religion, not politics for me. Now does that mean that my

religion is the equivalent of my politics? No. Not at all. I mean I'm a great fan of Oscar Romero who as a Roman Catholic bishop in El Salvador always said, "Never let your religion be as small as your politics." Always keep a transcendent place where you can judge your own politics, those of the state, and especially those if you have a victory. That God is larger than any one point of view. And I really believe that, very powerfully. Having said that, I read scripture as totally saying that God is found in the stranger and the outsider… Jesus in Matthew says, "When I was outside, you let me in." It's very clear. It could say, "When I was an immigrant, you let me in."

Rev. Schaper argued that politics and religion are intertwined, concerns that must be addressed together. Her politics were not the totality of her religion, but they were an important part of living out her Christianity (Figure 5.2).

In another instance of using the overlap discourse to describe the relationship between religion and politics, a rabbi in the New Sanctuary Movement described his experiences with activism over the years:

I would say it [activism] is the most profound practice of my faith. I'm not the most observant Jew ritualistically in terms of keeping kosher or the Sabbath or what have you. Rather, I think that the justice work

FIGURE 5.2 Rev. Donna Schaper is arrested for blocking traffic near the Varick Street Immigrant Detention Center in NYC. (Photo by Mizue Aizeki.)

for me is the expression of my Judaism. I don't knock the work of ritual performance, I find a lot of it quite beautiful and moving… You
know everyone has a—the balance goes one way or another, mine is
more on the justice organizing side than the ritual observant side. It
was Heschel who said, when he was marching in Selma, he felt like
his feet were praying, his legs were praying. I guess I have that feeling.
The most profound religious moments for me have been in political
engagement. So I really see the power of transformation happening,
I've seen that.

Activism was central to his Judaism, whether he was participating in an
explicitly religious activist cause or not. He had been spiritually transformed
through his political work, and vice versa. He even quoted Abraham Joshua
Heschel, the Jewish philosopher and theologian who marched in the Civil
Rights Movement with Martin Luther King Jr., saying that he was "praying
with his feet." In other words, he was not just doing politics—he was not
participating in something that was qualitatively different from his religion.
Instead, the overlap discourse holds that political activism can be a source of
religious transformation and a central aspect of what it means to be religious.
Multiple respondents mentioned this quote by Heschel in their interviews
when explaining why they got involved in the New Sanctuary Movement and
how they understood the relationship between religion and political activism.

A few of my respondents went even further by arguing not only that religion and politics overlapped but also that they were necessary for each other.
According to this discourse, political activism is a central religious practice,
one required for faithfulness and the source of genuine religious conversion.
Whether the cost is inconvenience or even one's life, when injustice exists, a
religious person must stand up against it, practicing her faith by participating in an activist cause. I call this religious-political discourse the *duty* discourse, as it sees activism not only as religious practice but also as religious
duty. A New Sanctuary Movement activist, a white male in his 30s who was
ordained but not currently serving as a pastor, said:

Well it's the gospel message, and my understanding of the gospel is that
Jesus was on the side of the poor and engaged in nonviolent resistance
against systems of domination. And so in following Jesus I have to do
that, I have to engage in nonviolent resistance against systems of domination. And he talked a lot in hyperbole, that the first will be last and
the last will be first. But he was talking about the leveling out of society.

And that is a huge part of the kingdom of God, it's economic, it's social, these are spiritual issues. Economic issues are spiritual issues, issues of war and peace are spiritual issues. And this is where Jesus engaged and that's what it means, I think. To be saved is to engage in these things with Christ and to give your life for others.

This respondent described political activism, saying that salvation happens through participation in challenging injustice. While this respondent came from an evangelical Christian background, his conception of salvation differed from the more typical evangelical notion of salvation as being saved from eternal damnation through professing faith in Jesus Christ. Instead, his concept of salvation as following Jesus's example aligned with what James Wellman identifies as the liberal Protestant worldview, a reminder that the boundaries between evangelical and liberal Protestantism are more porous than is often assumed, including on issues related to personal salvation.[16] Another respondent, a white male pastor, even went so far as to say about the participation of religious people in politics, "We are condemned to that; we have no choice." According to this discourse, as a religious person, engaging in the fight for justice might be difficult, but it is not optional. It is something one must do to experience religious transformation and to fulfill religious duties.

Discourses of Religious-Political Distinction

In contrast, the second set of discourses stresses the differences between religion and politics and their distinction from one another. According to this perspective, the purposes, institutions, symbols, and rituals of religion are different from those of politics, and while they might sometimes interact with each other or influence each other this does not mean they do or should overlap. The distinction discourses are widely known and used by politicians, pundits, and other public figures in debates about the appropriate relationship between religion and politics, and many religious groups also affirm discourses of distinction.[17] While a small number had always done so, by 2008 New Sanctuary was diverse enough to include a sizeable minority of activists who spoke about religion and politics in this way, even though it emerged as an explicitly religious-political movement organization. Close to half of my interview respondents at least occasionally talked about religion and politics as distinct concerns, with 20% speaking of them solely in this way and another 19% describing them as both distinct and integrated as the interview progressed, suggesting their knowledge of both discourses.

Some activists argued that religion and politics were separate concerns that should not be combined, what I call the *separation* discourse. The First Amendment of the U.S. Constitution has two clauses, one guaranteeing freedom of religious expression and another prohibiting state sponsorship of religion. Many have interpreted this to mean that, for the good of both institutions, religion and politics should have nothing to do with each other. In this view, religion is a private matter that individuals can choose to participate in or to ignore, but it should not influence politics. Another way of thinking about this perspective is that religion is simply not *about* politics—it is about personal salvation and holiness. As others have argued, this was one of the distinguishing features of fundamentalist Christianity in the United States prior to the rise of the evangelical movement and to the rise of the religious right.[18]

People regularly use this discourse in the media and public debates, referencing the constitution and arguing that religion has no place in politics. Groups like Americans United for Separation of Church and State argue that religious groups should keep out of political deliberation. When New York State lawmakers voted down a bill that would give same-sex couples the right to marry, Eric Adams, a Democratic state senator from Brooklyn, asked people to set aside any religious beliefs that might interfere with the civil rights of gay people. "When I walk through these doors, my Bible stays out," Adams told his fellow lawmakers.[19] In religious groups, some leaders tell their members not to be "of this world," or laypeople get angry with their pastors for talking about "politics," implying that religion and politics are and should be separate.[20]

As the New Sanctuary Movement grew and attracted a more diverse set of activists, more of those activists expressed belief in the separation of religion and politics. New Sanctuary activist Carver,[21] a white, native-born layperson in a mainline Protestant church with some experience with secular political activism but little prior experience with religious activism, said:

> I struggle with this 'cause I hear [my pastor] say from the pulpit that you really can't divorce the two. And I think that I do. I think I kind of keep them separate. For a period of time this year in the Lenten period I just went through a practice, sort of a morning devotion, which I don't normally do, that involved saying a series of prayers every morning, reciting a psalm, going through a list of prayers for people that I have on a little white board in my kitchen. And I feel like that's the heart and soul of religious experience to me... But in terms

of large-scale action where that political action becomes separated in some ways from any particular person you know: that's just not who I am... So I think I see more of a distinction than a lot of people at my church including our pastor, but everybody knows that.

According to Carver, there was a disconnect between religion and politics, and this was as it should be.

Others argued that religion and politics were distinct institutions and endeavors but that religious beliefs might inspire one to participate in political activism. Though this discourse depicts religious salvation and change as occurring through religious institutional channels, it recognizes that religion provides guiding rules for everyday life as well. According to this discourse, people's religious beliefs help guide their understanding of the public good whether they like it or not. This *inspiration* discourse is common in public conversations, religious groups, and among sociologists, and its use by my respondents was more common than their use of the separation discourse. One activist, a Latino Catholic layperson with little prior experience with religious activism, used the discourse to describe his understanding of the relationship between religion and politics:

> I really believe that my faith calls for justice, so in a way what I'm doing is because of my beliefs, my religious beliefs... All the teachings of our religion call for justice. Calls to help the needy. Calls to help the migrant. That's what inspired me, basically. Those kinds of readings and teachings are my belief.

This activist argued that his religious beliefs inspired him to get involved in political advocacy for immigrants as part of New Sanctuary. However, in opposition to integration discourses, in the inspiration discourse, political activism is not considered religious. Rather, it is an activity that is motivated by religion but nonetheless remains distinct from it. I had the following interaction with another layperson, a white mainline Protestant woman in her 60s who told me that her church attendance as a young child led her to activism as an adult. When I followed up by asking her whether religion was an inspiration for her work in New Sanctuary specifically, she responded:

> Oh, yes. Often, absolutely. You know, it's not like praying and all that exactly, but just, you know, I think there's a way we're supposed to live, and I don't think there's anybody that knows for sure exactly what that

is, but I think a lot of the—a lot of the Christian faith, and most faiths for that matter, are struggling to understand as much as we can about how best to live.

This activist argued that Christianity and other faiths offered insight into "how to live" that might inspire activism, but she was also clear that her activism was "not like praying and all that." According to this discourse, people might join movement organizations because of their religious beliefs, but political activism is not religious in the sense that something like praying is religious. Rather, institutionally based religious activity is the source of religious conversion, not political advocacy.

Institutional Location and the Use of Religious-Political Discourses

Though the New Sanctuary Movement started out with a core group of crossover activists committed to both religious and political change, the foregoing activist discourses on the relationship between religion and politics suggest that by 2008 the activists involved had a more diverse set of commitments. While a majority continued to see religious and political concerns as deeply intertwined, making it easier for them to maintain a commitment to both religious and political targets of change, a sizeable minority described religious and political concerns as distinct from each other. The popularity of integration discourses among these largely progressive religious activists suggests that religious conservatives are not the only ones for whom religion and politics are deeply connected. Instead, perhaps when religious progressives avoid explicitly religious language in some of their activism it is for other reasons, such as attempting to be religiously inclusive by using secular language, focusing on secular language because of the dictates of funding, or avoiding using religious language as justification because "that's what fundamentalists do."[22]

As might be expected, the use of these discourses and the commitments they reflected were not random. Rather, they varied according to people's relationships to religious and political institutions, as Table 5.1 demonstrates. Those who solely drew on integration discourses and those who did not were distinguished by their status as clergy versus laity, with clergy more likely to describe religion and politics as integrated than laypeople.[23] As the heads of religious institutions, clergy are more invested in how religion gets defined and who holds public religious authority than laypeople are, and they are more rooted in the institution's culture as well.[24] While only half of the

Table 5.1 Use of Religious-Political Discourses by Institutional Location

Religious-Political Discourses	High Experience	Low Experience	Total	Clergy	Lay	Total
Distinction	4 (11%)	10 (30%)	14	5 (14%)	9 (26%)	14
Integration	30 (83%)	13 (38%)	43	26 (72%)	17 (50%)	43
Both	2 (6%)	11 (32%)	13	5 (14%)	8 (24%)	13
Total	36	34	70	36	34	70

laypeople used integration discourses to describe religion and politics, almost three-fourths of the clergy drew on discourses of integration.

In addition, those who drew solely on integration discourses and those who did not differed in the amount of their prior experience with religious activism. Over four-fifths of respondents with religious activist experience drew solely on integration discourses (83%). Many of these activists were more invested in a progressive religious identity and would therefore have more to gain from this image of religion gaining greater public legitimacy and power. In contrast, respondents who had little experience with religious activism were about evenly split in terms of who used integration discourses, who drew on distinction discourses, and who used both.

To summarize, activists with closer relationships to religious institutions— clergy and experienced religious activists—were more likely to talk about religion and politics as integrated compared to laypeople and activists with little prior experience with religious activism. According to institutional theories of culture, these differences are likely due to two factors, both of which are related to the different institutional locations of these groups.[25] First, people with strong connections to religious institutions have a greater material interest in creating religious change, as their livelihoods depend on the ability of their own religious identities and religious institutions to survive and thrive. In the case of progressive religious leaders and experienced progressive religious activists, challenging religion's public association with political conservatism was important to establishing their own view of religion as legitimate and powerful, as they were more embedded in these cultural patterns and had the most to gain materially by increasing progressive religion's public legitimacy and power.

Second, people with strong connections to religious institutions are more embedded in their *institutional logics*—"the socially constructed, historical pattern of material practices, assumptions, values, beliefs, and rules by which individuals produce and reproduce their material subsistence, organize time and space, and provide meaning to their social reality."[26] In other words, their discourses are shaped by their ongoing participation in institutional settings that encourage people to view and to talk about religion and politics as intertwined.[27]

This variation in use of religious-political discourses suggests that, while New Sanctuary started out with a small group of activists mostly committed to both religious and political change, increasingly some activists were more committed to one target than the other. One's level of commitment to multiple targets appears to be related in part to one's institutional location. As New Sanctuary began to include more single-institutional actors like laypeople and people with little experience with religious activism, activists' commitments were not the only things that changed. Their knowledge and expertise regarding how to change these institutions also shifted, since biographical factors influence strategic capacity.[28] However, growing differences in commitment to and knowledge about multiple targets of change did not manifest themselves solely in talk about religion and activism. Perhaps more importantly, these differences emerged as significant in other New Sanctuary practices as well.

Balancing Religion and Politics: Sanctuary and the ICE out of Rikers Campaign

In its early days, the New Sanctuary Movement focused on sanctuary as a religious strategy centered on radical accompaniment, involving the partnering of religious communities with mixed-status families. In "An Invitation to Join the New Sanctuary Movement," the original website (created in 2007) described this mission:

> As an act of public witness, the New Sanctuary Movement will enable congregations to publicly provide hospitality and protection to a limited number of immigrant families whose legal cases clearly reveal the contradictions and moral injustice of our current immigration system while working to support legislation that would change their situation.[29]

As this early statement suggests, New Sanctuary's initial focus was building relationships between congregations and immigrants, a vision that fit well with its goal of transforming religious communities. The website did not mention other strategies or tactics that might also be definitive of the New Sanctuary Movement and its activities. If one used the website only to assess its activities, one would assume that several years after its launch its sole emphasis remained the sanctuary relationship.

But visiting the more recently created websites of local coalitions provides a different picture of New Sanctuary in actual practice. While the first five coalitions—Chicago, Los Angeles, New York, San Diego, and Seattle—were all committed to various degrees to sanctuary as strategy as well as moniker, as the network grew these coalitions and others diversified the strategies and tactics being considered and used by activists. In the story from the November 2007 national gathering that opened this chapter, activists were fighting over this very issue. Many clergy and experienced religious activists continued to advocate for the use of sanctuary as the group's central strategy, though they were also willing to entertain other strategies and tactics that might combine religious and political change, such as the proposal to engage with presidential candidates' faith-based campaign offices in a way that might challenge prevailing assumptions about both politics and religion.[30] Increasingly, other activists were primarily invested in either religious or political change and were therefore less committed to sanctuary and other religious-political strategies.

The discord between those invested in a more religious vision and those committed to more political tactics and targets happened not only on the national level but on the local level as well. In the New Sanctuary Coalition of NYC, these struggles took shape around the issue of whether to emphasize the family–congregation partnerships or to focus on solely political campaigns. Prior to the coalition's launch in May 2007, there was some debate as to how involved the New Sanctuary Movement should be in tactics other than sanctuary partnerships between congregations and immigrants. For example, in NYC, Families for Freedom (FFF) had long focused on campaigning for the passage of a piece of legislation called the Child Citizen Protection Act (CCPA), which would allow immigration judges to consider an undocumented immigrant's family situation in deciding his or her case. However, following the New Sanctuary launch, this conflict between sanctuary and other strategies and tactics continued and even strengthened. During most steering committee meetings for the first couple of years, debates would occur around whether to focus their limited energy on supporting the families taking sanctuary in the coalition or whether to work with Families for Freedom on a political campaign that became known as ICE out of Rikers.[31]

From the beginning, a couple of activists in the New York coalition were committed to working with Families for Freedom on this and other political campaigns. As secular immigrant rights activists, they had less interest in and experience with issues of religious change, and they pushed New Sanctuary to consider partnering with other local immigrant rights organizations in political campaigns. However, for the first year, the New Sanctuary Coalition of NYC primarily focused on its strategy of sanctuary, working to recruit new congregations and new sanctuary immigrants to build on its initial model of partnership for both political and religious change. This is not to say that New Sanctuary activists were opposed to these more explicitly political campaigns: some activists were very supportive. But the initial emphasis on sanctuary and the recruitment of congregations meant that crossover actors often outnumbered those wanting to focus more energy on political campaigns like ICE out of Rikers.

Rikers Island lies in the East River between the New York City boroughs of Queens and the Bronx, just several hundred feet from LaGuardia International Airport. The small island is home to NYC's main jail complex, where arrested New Yorkers that cannot afford or obtain bail await trial, ending in either release or conviction and transfer to one of the state prisons. In 2007, the year of the New Sanctuary Movement's launch, the average daily inmate population was approximately 14,000.[32] Since Rikers inmates included as-yet-unconvicted criminals awaiting their hearings and convicts serving sentences of less than a year, a large portion of these 14,000 people posed minimal threats to the safety of their communities compared to prison inmates. And while the majority of Rikers inmates were citizens or legal immigrants, the population also included undocumented immigrants.

As of 2007, the NYC Department of Correction (DOC) had been partnering with ICE for several years by allowing ICE agents to access inmates at Rikers Island, to question inmates to ascertain which were deportable under immigration law, and to place detainers on them so they could be detained and deported from the United States immediately after their release from the jail. To accomplish these tasks, ICE had a field office on Rikers Island. This was unnecessary, since local law enforcement officers were not legally obligated to participate in federal enforcement. It also potentially contradicted city law, which made NYC a *sanctuary city*—one of multiple cities around the country whose local ordinances prohibited local law enforcement officers from asking about a person's immigration status in their course of duty.[33] Nonetheless, as a 2005 directive from the DOC indicated, these ICE officers possessed the same rights to question inmates without providing their credentials as New York city and state law enforcement officers.[34] Thus, an undocumented immigrant who was arrested and charged for a crime he did not commit could still be deported from the country, often without any contact with family members, lawyers, or other advocates who might be able to launch a defense of his right to remain in the country.

In late 2007, lawyers working with New York University Law School's Immigrant Rights Clinic visited a NYC coalition meeting to share stories they had been hearing of ICE officers entering Rikers jail to question suspected undocumented immigrants, failing to identify themselves to inmates as ICE agents, to inform them of their right to remain silent, or to explain any documents they asked them to sign. As a result, undocumented immigrants were reportedly responding to questions about their nationality without realizing that this information would be used to place detainers on them so they would be deportable when released.[35] This meeting represented an important shift in the New Sanctuary Coalition of NYC toward consideration of political campaigns in addition to the focus on sanctuary:

A crowd of 20 people gathers in the tower of Riverside Church, the highest church tower in the United States. New Sanctuary organizer Angad Bhalla—an activist with a good deal of experience with secular immigrant rights activism—is facilitating the meeting. A Canadian immigrant with Indian ancestry, the twenty-something has his long black hair pulled into a ponytail. As usual, the meeting begins with the sanctuary families and their partner congregations providing updates on their cases. One coalition member, the pastor of a local United Church of Christ church, tells the story of a new coalition family, a Chinese couple named Sam and Sandra.[36] "Their landlord wanted them to move out of their apartment, so he falsely accused them of terrorism," he explains. Because they were reported to the authorities, both Sam and Sandra are now required to report regularly to immigration authorities, with the potential for detention or deportation. After the pastor finishes relaying the story, Angad reminds everyone that Sam has an immigration check-in the following day and requests that "everyone keep Sam in their prayers tomorrow."

Following these updates, Angad introduces three people from the NYU Law School's Immigrant Rights Clinic. He explains that he has been working with them to find out more about the cooperation between local law enforcement and ICE as well as how to stop this cooperation. The lawyers pass around a detention fact sheet as they begin a story about an immigrant they are working with and his encounter with ICE. "A California man calls the police for protection from an assailant. When they arrive, he lies about his immigration status and is arrested because of this lie. Within two days, he is picked up by ICE." They ask, "Will immigrants stop calling the police, who are supposed to be there to protect everyone from criminals, because they are afraid it will somehow result in their deportation?" They describe current practices in Rikers Island jail, arguing that the Department of Correction is allowing ICE to conduct covert interviews to elicit confessions from inmates they believe are in the United States without authorization. "And immigrants who are detained after their release from Rikers are often moved to far-away places like Texas. Then it's very hard for them to mount any defense to delay their deportation."

After they finish speaking, Angad draws a connection between New Sanctuary's work and NYC's status as a sanctuary city,[37] asking coalition members, "What does being a sanctuary city even mean? It doesn't mean this!" Jean, a sanctuary immigrant who has spent time in jail, speaks up: "Most people there have never been in jail, so they don't know they should complain and defend themselves. Can't we at least keep them from sending people to places like Texas? Maybe through a lawsuit?" While Jean's face is filled with frustration and anger, some around the room appear less engaged in this part of the discussion. The head of the law clinic responds that litigation has not been effective but that they are counting on the coalition to raise awareness about the issue.

Angad asks, "So what do we think? Can we take this issue on?" One activist asks, "Is there already a campaign around this issue?" The NYU lawyer responds, "We *are* that campaign." People begin tossing around ideas, such as requesting a meeting with DOC to discuss the issue or a teach-in with congregations to spread awareness. Jean, still frustrated, says, "Yeah, but we need *legal* change. That's the only way that things will really change for immigrants." One pastor agrees, blurting out, "I'm flabbergasted and pissed off! If we do legal epidemiology, why is this happening? If I have to write letters, I'll do it, but I'm like Jean. I want to stop this."

After the discussion, Jean passes around a flyer about an upcoming fundraiser for Families for Freedom. "They are the number one organization stopping deportations and helping families," he says, encouraging people to attend: a reminder that many New Sanctuary activists do not know about the coalition's affiliation with FFF. Angad adds, "And Families for Freedom is a coalition member, so it's not like some other group is holding a fundraiser." While the flyers circulate, activists discuss the time and date of the next meeting. Angad thanks everyone for attending, expressing special gratitude to the NYU guests. Jean breaks in, urging the lawyers one last time: "We really need legal support to stop the madness. We are getting spiritual support, but we need help!"

Following this meeting, Angad continued to push the coalition to work with NYU on the collaboration between DOC and ICE, dedicating himself to learning more about what was happening and how they might stop practices they saw as harmful. The ICE out of Rikers campaign[38] launched formally in August 2009, a partnership between the coalition and two secular immigrant rights groups in NYC. They began calling for NYC's DOC commissioner Dora Schriro to reign in ICE's practices, requiring them to inform inmates of their rights prior to questioning and ultimately demanding that DOC end its cooperation with ICE.

Throughout the period of 2007 to 2009, the NYC coalition dealt with conflict over the extent to which they should focus on political campaigns like ICE out of Rikers, since these campaigns took time, energy, and resources away from their focus on sanctuary. As the vignette demonstrates, while some activists knew about FFF's political campaigns, many did not and were less focused on these issues than on sanctuary and on families. Jean's plea for more legal advocacy in addition to the spiritual support he was receiving highlights this tension. While most activists agreed that the sanctuary partnerships were central to the coalition's work—if only because they had already committed to working with the coalition's sanctuary families—some were more supportive of expanding its focus to include political campaigns than others.

Before the launch, most activists were committed to sanctuary above other campaigns. As mentioned before, these activists were mostly clergy and people with a history of religious activism. However, a couple of early activists, and some of those who joined later, were more interested in political campaigns than in sanctuary, reflecting their position as laypeople or people with more experience in secular political activism than religious activism. One early activist, a layperson with a history of progressive religious activism, expressed her concern about the conflicts between sanctuary and the more political campaigns:

> There have been times where I've felt the campaigns like where we talk about DOC/ICE or whatever, have kind of taken precedence over the real…taken precedence over the families and I think we're still trying to learn where the balance is with all this because certainly it shouldn't just be the families because we all know that it's bigger than us, it's bigger than the families…So don't get me wrong. I think the campaigns are key but there have been times where I have felt like our time and our

energy have been spent more there and less with the families…I guess like when I first started to explore the New Sanctuary Movement I imagined it very differently. I imagined it being totally about working with the families and just kind of didn't anticipate all these other things that pull from different directions…And I'm sorting this out because [another coalition member] doesn't see why the family support is so essential and vice versa. I sometimes don't want to really give much priority to the campaigns. I see them as extras, so there's been this tension.

This person saw the DOC/ICE campaign and other more exclusively political campaigns as "extras," less central than the sanctuary partnerships. This view was shared by many early activists, particularly clergy and people with long histories of religious activism. While they typically supported the political campaigns, they argued that these should not take precedence over the coalition's commitment to sanctuary. However, by late 2009, because of support from more single-institutional political actors and other changes I discuss in the book's concluding chapter, the ICE out of Rikers campaign became more central to the coalition's work, as indicated by its headlining on the coalition's website.[39]

The Delicate Balance of Multi-target Social Movements

As the New York coalition grew, its activist base began to shift. Early activists were largely clergy and experienced religious activists, people interested in religious as well as political change. Their commitment to religion as a target for change makes sense in light of their institutional locations. Their capacity to work toward that change was enabled by their familiarity with the religious institutional field. They understood religious language, had connections to religious groups, and had the institutional knowledge required to navigate systems in service of change.

On the other hand, as more people joined, the number of laypeople and people with primarily secular rather than religious activist experience also grew. While activists' institutional locations did not map exactly onto their commitments to targets of change, as the differences in discourses and campaign support here suggest, a relationship between institutional locations and target commitments did exist. To summarize, actors will differ in their commitment to targets of change and in their capacities to change them based in part on their relationships to those targets.[40]

To balance commitment to multiple targets of change, multi-target social movements must recruit activists even more strategically than other movements and movement organizations, as they need to cultivate different characteristics, though it is necessarily difficult to intentionally recruit large groups of people from any background to a movement organization. In discussing strategic capacity, sociologist James Jasper writes, "Some resources and skills...are specific to an arena" and that "general capacities provide flexibility, while specific ones yield efficiency."[41] To maintain commitment to multiple targets of change, multi-target social movements will ideally have and cultivate a core group of crossover actors, who can provide greater flexibility due to their embeddedness in multiple institutional arenas. It is likely that any multi-target social movement will begin with such a group of actors, but it is especially important that the participation and leadership of these actors is nurtured and sustained.

But because they also need people with a deep level of expertise about and commitment to changing each institution (and therefore greater efficiency), multi-target movements must also recruit single-institutional actors. They must balance the number of those with investment and expertise in one target with activists with investment and expertise in the other target. If multi-target social movements are unable to recruit participation from both groups, they will have difficulty balancing commitment to both targets.

The ease with which this task is accomplished—and therefore of maintaining commitment to multiple targets of change—likely varies according to the institutions being targeted. When the institutions already overlap to a large degree,[42] it will be simpler to recruit actors that are familiar with and invested in both, making it easier to maintain a core group of crossover actors despite problems like activist burnout.[43] But when institutions in society are widely portrayed and perceived as distinct rather than integrated, it will likely be more difficult to recruit a core group of crossover actors, forcing a multi-target movement to rely even more on a careful balance of single-institutional actors with different institutional locations. This situation is likely to lead to far more *target conflict* and to the problem of *target domination,* a condition that can lead either to the rebalancing of targets or to the eventual transformation of a multi-target movement into a single-target movement.

Conclusion

Before the New Sanctuary Movement's launch in 2007, activists debated the extent to which they should focus on sanctuary versus other less religious and more political campaigns. But most of these early activists were crossover activists. Their positions as both clergy and as immigrants or experienced advocates for immigrants placed them at the intersections of religion and the immigration system, giving them investment and expertise in both. These activists tended to talk about the institutions of religion and politics as integrated, as concerns that can be pursued in conjunction with one another and indeed perhaps cannot be addressed apart from each other.

Following the launch, as New Sanctuary sought to grow by recruiting new activists, it increasingly needed single-institutional actors with experience with and expertise in changing one target more than the other. Disagreement over the centrality of sanctuary partnerships versus political campaigns like ICE out of Rikers demonstrates the ways not only disputes about tactics but also quarrels about targets might manifest themselves in multi-target social movements. This target conflict can be managed, but it is difficult since it requires a delicately balanced activist base.

Whereas many movements and movement organizations are primarily concerned with recruiting as many supportive activists as possible, leaders of multi-target movements must be especially cognizant of how the commitments of people joining might shift energy and capacity around different targets, potentially leading to target domination and transformation into a single-target movement. While future research may show that this is the eventual fate of all multi-target social movements, since to maintain target balance in the long run may prove prohibitively difficult, in the short run activists may be able to respond to potential target domination through learning and a creative shift in strategies and tactics.

This is precisely what happened in the New Sanctuary Movement. In the following chapter, I demonstrate how crossover strategies made it difficult for New Sanctuary to attract an essential group of single-institutional actors: immigrants themselves. However, Chapter 7 shows how a committed group of crossover activists engaged in processes of learning and creativity to increase strategic capacity for attracting religious and ethnic minorities, the type of innovation that can help multi-target social movements maintain commitment to multiple targets.

6 AN IMMIGRANT RIGHTS ORGANIZATION WITHOUT IMMIGRANTS?

Juan Carlos Ruiz is no stranger to immigrant congregations. Before signing on as head organizer for the New Sanctuary Coalition of New York City, he forged relationships between immigrant churches as a coordinator for a local community-based organization. As a community organizer, he moved in and out of the Mexican Catholic community in New York, connecting churches and training them to fight for their shared interests using symbols of their faith, like Mexico's beloved Virgin of Guadalupe. But even with his experience, Ruiz struggled to get immigrant faith communities involved in New Sanctuary. "To organize communities who are affected directly is just really difficult," he explained over coffee in 2008. "Because they are under the guns. I'm sorry to use such a violent term, but that's what it is."

When I first met Ruiz back in 2005, he had just moved into a row house in the Bronx, a Catholic priest starting a house of hospitality in the tradition of the Catholic Worker movement. Shaped by Latin American liberation theology's focus on the blessedness of the poor and oppressed, he hoped the house would serve as a way station for new immigrants seeking a place to stay until they got on their feet. As a researcher studying the Catholic Worker movement, I was an unexpected guest at the meal and mass celebrating the opening of the house, but he welcomed me as an old friend, kissing my cheek as I entered the house. In candlelight, we slurped hearty bowls of bread soup before Daniel Berrigan, a legendary radical priest, preached the homily at the mass. After we sang a song called "The Lord Hears the Cry of the Poor," Ruiz walked through the house with a bowl of holy water, sprinkling the walls and the icons adorning them while worshippers murmured blessings on the house's future immigrant inhabitants.

Years before, Ruiz himself migrated from Mexico to the United States, and his past still bubbles up inside him when he hears stories of immigrants in trouble. He knows how it feels to be an immigrant and to be scared. He knows what it means to be Mexican and to be devoutly Catholic. This shared knowledge and experience build a necessary bridge of trust in communities that are understandably suspicious of outsiders given the hostility toward Latinos in the United States today.[1]

So if anyone was ever prepared for the work of immigrant organizing, Juan Carlos Ruiz was. "I see myself like a snail with his house on his back and with this weight," he explained to me. "I think we need to really, all of us, leave these kind of sticky, moistened traces everywhere, you know? We need to leave our marks behind." But while—like a snail—his goal was slow-moving but measurable progress, through the early years of New Sanctuary, even gradual success in recruiting immigrant congregations to New Sanctuary eluded him. Day after day, he chased down pastors, priests, imams, and rabbis—not just in the Bronx but all over the city—selling the New Sanctuary Movement and hoping they would buy in. Few were persuaded to even sign a letter of support, let alone to get involved in the regular work of the New Sanctuary Movement. To the disappointment of Ruiz and his fellow New Sanctuary Coalition of NYC leaders, he was one of only a handful of immigrants regularly involved in the coalition. Instead, during its first two years, the immigrant-native coalition they hoped to form turned out to be mostly white, both in the NYC coalition and in many other coalitions around the country.

This was no small problem for Ruiz and his fellow New Sanctuary activists. From the beginning, New Sanctuary activists had little interest in simply creating a native-born organization that "helps" immigrants—what social movement scholars typically call a solidarity movement. Instead, they insisted on immigrants forming a central part of their network, on immigrants as prophets and leaders with a distinct, divinely inspired message that the world—including native-born religious communities—needed to hear. Committed to an inclusive religious vision grounded in liberation theology, many believed God has a special relationship with the marginalized. But beyond theological reasons, early activists had strategic reasons for building an immigrant–native coalition, reasons related to both their political and their religious goals. Without immigrants, their ability to effectively and legitimately target immigration policy would dwindle, but their capacity for religious change through sanctuary partnerships would disappear as well. Their difficulty attracting new sanctuary families and immigrant congregations was more than a minor disappointment.

Armed with theological and strategic commitment to immigrant participation and leadership, Juan Carlos Ruiz and a small group of leaders marketed the coalition to immigrant and nonimmigrant religious communities in the early, prelaunch days of New Sanctuary. At the launch of the NYC coalition in May 2007, an ethnically diverse group of congregations and religious leaders stood side by side in the Church of St. Francis.[2] Of the five congregations partnering with immigrant sanctuary families, two were Spanish-speaking immigrant churches. Half of the coalition's steering committee members were immigrants as well, their social networks encompassing huge numbers of immigrant congregations in the city. As immigrants and nonimmigrants joined hands in front of the altar at the launch, they had high hopes that their existing relationships with immigrant congregations would grease the wheels in creating an immigrant–native coalition. Certainly Ruiz hoped his phone calls, emails, and conversations with leaders of immigrant congregations would produce more fruit. Why did a national activist network that initially included immigrants as leaders—whose first leader, undocumented immigrant Elvira Arellano, provided the inspiration for sanctuary—later have so much trouble attracting more immigrants? What can this teach us about multi-target social movements? In what follows, I demonstrate how New Sanctuary's multiple targets and the related choice of sanctuary as crossover strategy limited its ability to attract immigrant participation.

The Need for Immigrants

The core tenet of liberation theology is that God lives in oppressed and marginalized people in a special way, so they deserve honor from other people as well. If "comfortable" people want to know what God wants, they need to hear the cry of the poor—to work alongside them, listen to their stories, share their experiences, and learn from them. By focusing on God's love for those typically marginalized by society, liberation theology complements liberal Protestantism's inclusive religious vision in many ways, though each has a distinct genealogy and theology.[3]

Liberation theology had shaped the life, beliefs, and aims of Juan Carlos Ruiz. But it also pervaded the worldviews of the native-born, white leaders of New Sanctuary. In interviews and press conferences, they quoted heroes of the Latin American liberation theology movement, like Oscar Romero, a Salvadoran archbishop who was assassinated by right-wing death squads during the 1980s for his support for poor people's movements there. As they joined together in 2006 and early 2007, seeking a way to respond to the political and religious crises around immigration, a shared commitment to liberation theology guided many early activists toward a vision of an activist network that would include immigrant participation as central for political and religious transformation.

Activists' beliefs and values shaped internal New Sanctuary goals, such as a commitment to immigrant participation.[4] But New Sanctuary's need for immigrants went beyond the values-oriented theological commitments of its activists. Immigrant participation was necessary for reaching both the New Sanctuary Movement's political and religious goals. To build the knowledge and legitimacy necessary for navigating and changing the immigration system, they needed immigrants whose direct experience with the system gave them this expertise. Crossover actors, who had more limited knowledge of any one institution, were not enough. Single-institutional actors with deeper experience with the immigration system, particularly immigrants themselves, were essential to political change. Also, New Sanctuary's chosen strategy—sanctuary, defined as a relationship of accompaniment joining undocumented immigrants and immigrant congregations with majority-native-born congregations—depended on immigrant participation at its core. Without immigrants, religious conversion could not happen.

New Sanctuary activists had reasons related to both their political and religious goals for seeking immigrant involvement. Dividing their attention and commitment between these two targets made strategic choice and adaptation more difficult. If their only concern was changing the state, they might have focused all of their attention on forging alliances with other immigrant rights groups, building their legitimacy in immigrant communities, gaining knowledge about the cultural repertoires common in immigrant rights activism, and attracting larger numbers of immigrants. Instead, New Sanctuary's dual emphasis on changing policy and transforming religious communities guided them to the choice of sanctuary as moniker, strategy, and even recruitment model. The adoption of this crossover strategy required that they forge alliances with native-born religious communities, build legitimacy with these groups, and tap into religious symbols and styles that would attract their participation.

Despite an initially diverse network which made building an immigrant–native coalition seem possible—in Los Angeles in particular, where several congregations housing sanctuary families were primarily immigrant congregations—New Sanctuary's commitment to changing multiple targets led to problems with recruiting more immigrants over time. As I will show, this was partly because the crossover strategy of sanctuary created a cultural disconnect with some immigrants, becoming an obstacle to involvement. Likewise, the emphasis on developing a single, religious global network inclusive of native-born Americans, immigrants from a variety of ethnic backgrounds, and a diverse group of religious people stood in contrast to most types of immigrant-led efforts that existed, ones often bounded by ethnic or denominational identity. Finally, the lack of immigrants in New Sanctuary resulted in an inability to recognize the costs and benefits involved for immigrants and a related slowness to adapt to the political and cultural realities of immigrant communities by replacing sanctuary with a strategy that might have appealed more to immigrants.

The Cultural Disconnect: Sanctuary's Religious Legacies

One hundred fifty miles north of the Mexican border, sandwiched between desert to the west and lush green land to the east, San Antonio's skyscrapers shine next to buildings with red-tiled roofs. In the midst of the city, the Mexican American Cultural Center stands as an oasis for the exploding population of Mexican American Catholics in and around San Antonio.[5] Offering courses and workshops on working with Mexican American religious communities, the center draws organizers from around the country for education and networking. Asked to serve on an ad hoc board about immigration curriculum for the Catholic Church, Juan Carlos Ruiz flew to San Antonio for a meeting in October 2006. At the conference, he met Rev. Alexia Salvatierra.

Like Ruiz, Rev. Salvatierra had Mexican ancestry. Like Ruiz, she had sojourned in Catholic Worker communities and liberation theology circles. And like Ruiz, she was an experienced progressive religious activist. With all of their commonalities, the two became fast friends at the San Antonio conference. "We had some pretty remarkable conversations about the sense of what the religious community needed to be about at that moment," she told me in 2008, "that we needed to be about something that was truly radical in the sense of something that was a sacrificial response." The response that emerged from their conversation was the strategy of sanctuary.

In San Antonio, Ruiz and Rev. Salvatierra talked about the current political and religious landscapes and sanctuary's place in them. "We had to recognize that we couldn't protect people," she said. Instead, sanctuary would become a strategy and tactic for helping immigrants to the degree they could, for drawing media attention, for training immigrant leaders, and for the conversion of religious communities through accompaniment. Because of the 1980s Sanctuary Movement, sanctuary had connections to cultural legacies of both charity and justice, so New Sanctuary activists mobilized sanctuary to perform both humanitarian and political functions.[6]

But its association with social movement and social justice traditions, which Ruiz and Salvatierra found meaningful because of their familiarity with the 1980s Sanctuary Movement, was more common in native-born, white religious communities than in new immigrant ones, despite the fact that the first public new sanctuary congregation was a Latino congregation, Adalberto United Methodist Church (UMC) in Chicago. This was due to different levels of exposure to sanctuary as movement strategy during the 1980s. Many recent immigrants were not yet living in the United States at that time and were therefore unfamiliar with the 1980s Sanctuary Movement. There were some exceptions to this general rule. In both the Los Angeles and New York City coalitions, several Latino congregations played a central role in launching New Sanctuary. But while the initial coalitions in both places were diverse, they struggled to elicit regular participation from additional immigrant congregations.

Sanctuary as a Religious Strategy for Social Justice

In the wake of the widely successful fundamentalist book series *Left Behind* by Tim LaHaye and Jerry B. Jenkins, popular conceptions of prophecy conjured up images of people predicting ominous, even apocalyptic futures. Instead, much of Jewish, Christian, and Muslim tradition portrays a prophet as a person who speaks the truth about injustice and points the way toward change.[7] The 1980s Sanctuary Movement built on this biblical legacy of prophecy, using the religious tradition of sanctuary as a strategy for witnessing to the injustice of U.S. foreign policy, calling for a more just form of engagement with Latin American nations.

But while sanctuary has a long history, this form of sanctuary as prophetic activism[8]—in which it serves as a *social movement strategy and tactic* for seeking broad political and religious change—is a more recent incarnation, one that has been present but less common outside of the United States.[9] The most important exceptions to this are Nicaragua and El Salvador. During the 1980s Sanctuary Movement, religious activists in these countries partnered with U.S. congregations to better assist refugees from their civil wars, making sanctuary a resonant movement strategy for some natives of those countries.[10] However, knowledge about sanctuary in these countries was often restricted to activist communities who directly participated in the process, knowledge that did not necessarily become widespread enough to make it familiar to people who would migrate to the United States in later decades. Even in places like Canada, where there have been many instances of sanctuary for immigrants in recent decades, sanctuary has largely been an act of individual religious communities and secular organizations rather than a nationally organized movement strategy seeking broader political change.[11] With a few exceptions, the 1980s Sanctuary Movement was not large enough to spread internationally, meaning that the legacy of sanctuary as a movement strategy was less known abroad than sanctuary as charitable aid.[12]

In the mid-2000s, the people with whom sanctuary resonated most as a political strategy were people like Father Michael Rosario.[13] A second-generation Mexican immigrant from East LA, Rosario presided over mass for close to 10,000 immigrants a week at one of Los Angeles's largest immigrant churches. "My second assignment as a priest, I came here," he told me as we talked in his church office. Coming from a background in community organizing, including working with Cesar Chavez and the United Farm Workers, he hoped to use his skills to organize immigrants at the church. "The church is very important in developing leadership," he explained.

A few years after his arrival, the civil wars in Central America started heating up, and the Sanctuary Movement in Arizona started looking for partners in other areas of the country. He remembered, "It took about one year to study, and to really fully understand, the complex meaning of sanctuary—what it really means and what might happen to a church that defies the law." He and his fellow priests decided to declare their church a sanctuary for Central American refugees. People poured into the enormous church, as did press and Hollywood supporters. But by the 1990s things cooled down. Ronald Reagan's presidential terms were over, foreign policy changed, the civil wars ended, and legal status was granted to many of the Central American refugees that had fled to the United States for their lives in the 1980s.

As a second-generation immigrant, Father Rosario's experience with the 1980s Sanctuary Movement gave him more in common religiously with his fellow progressive religious activists—most of whom were native-born whites—than with many recent immigrants from Mexico. He may have counted the Virgin of Guadalupe among the cultural symbols that resonated with him religiously, but just as important were the cultural symbols of U.S. progressive religious activism: Martin Luther King Jr.; farm workers striking in the fields; and images of the 1980s Sanctuary Movement, of immigrants with their faces covered by bandanas as they told the press their stories from inside a church building. These were the symbols New Sanctuary capitalized on when it advertised sanctuary as prophetic witness, as a movement strategy for widespread change.[14] And this brief legacy of sanctuary was less familiar and therefore held less meaning for many recent immigrants compared with native-born religious activists like Rosario. Instead, many immigrants associated sanctuary with its more historic and widespread meaning: the offer of refuge in a religious building, a form of charitable aid.

Early New Sanctuary organizers were slow to realize this in part because the inspiration for building a *new* sanctuary movement came from the decision of an undocumented immigrant—Elvira Arellano—to adopt sanctuary as a strategy for changing immigration policy by moving into her Chicago church. Since sanctuary as a religious strategy for social justice resonated with Elvira and Adalberto United Methodist Church, many activists thought it might similarly resonate with other immigrants.

Sanctuary as Charitable Aid

When Immigration and Customs Enforcement (ICE) agents came knocking, Yolanda—an undocumented immigrant from Guatemala—knew her options for staying in LA with her U.S. citizen daughter were limited. Determined to stay together, they devised a plan. Stuffing suitcases with their most treasured belongings, they closed the front door of their family home behind them and moved into their church as part of the New Sanctuary Movement. Two years later, they still lived in the same converted Sunday School room in Trinity Church,[15] the church they had attended for years.

The fact that the room her fellow church members provided her was in the church building they all shared meant that ICE would have a harder time apprehending her than if she had stayed in her own home because of the informal yet special status of religion in the United States.[16] That was precisely why she joined New Sanctuary: she believed it would protect her for the time being and might eventually help her get papers. New Sanctuary activists tried to make it clear to immigrant families taking sanctuary that they could not promise legalization or keep them from ultimately being deported if ICE decided to enter their churches. But offering legal and moral support to families—and building their power to resist unjust situations—gave some immigrants the impression that sanctuary was in the direct aid business. A member of the congregation described some church members' initial expectations regarding Yolanda's well-being and the church's partnership with the New Sanctuary Movement:

> In the early days after they moved into the church there was all this talk about "there's this lawyer." There was a lot of talk about her case and

how he was gonna be involved and how there were conference calls and it all sounded like this was gonna be just as much about providing really hard-hitting legal representation…She may have thought that there was—that this was gonna have a more direct impact on her legal situation than it has. And she now finds herself likely in the uncomfortable position of being like, "What do I do? I'm not gonna live in this church forever."

New Sanctuary activists were aware of these difficulties with sanctuary. Though the New Sanctuary Movement had the potential to be in immigrants' interests in the long term, it could provide little concrete aid in the short run. Still, the cultural legacy of sanctuary as protection and help was strong.

The assumption that sanctuary was a form of charity for those in need, especially for immigrants, was not just a misunderstanding on the part of some of Yolanda's church members. As I showed in Chapter 3, for most of its long history sanctuary *did* mean a form of direct aid to people in desperate need. People fleeing the authorities for a variety of reasons could take refuge in a church, temporarily finding protection and perhaps eventually a change in their situation that would enable them to leave the church freely. Even aside from these traditions of sanctuary in religious buildings, in international law the concept of sanctuary has long been associated with asylum, a type of legal aid enabling those fleeing violence and persecution in one nation to seek the protection and aid of another country in the form of legal immigration status.[17]

For some recent immigrants, these traditions of sanctuary, which had a much longer history and had been more widely practiced internationally, were more culturally resonant than the symbol of sanctuary as a religious movement strategy. When recent immigrants thought of social movements or revolutions, they thought of other strategies and tactics, ones that were more common in their countries of origin and were therefore more central to their cultural tool kits.[18]

New Sanctuary activists hit this obstacle in seeking immigrant involvement, as my interviews with immigrants who did not join and with immigrant pastors trying to recruit immigrants demonstrated. Many times, in reaching out to recent immigrants, people encountered the view that the New Sanctuary Movement's primary goal was to provide protection and charitable aid to specific undocumented immigrants rather than seeing sanctuary as a strategy to draw attention to the political and religious problems associated with Americans' treatment of immigrants more broadly. A Latino pastor described impressions among his congregation members, most of whom were recent immigrants, who raised opposition to joining New Sanctuary:

> That's where the tension lies with people who might say, "Well, you know, I've been here all my life and nobody helped me, and here you are helping someone who just came." And it's that kind of conflict that sometimes arises. You have poor who are here a long time but they're citizens... and so again, the fight for resources.

His immigrant congregants viewed sanctuary as "helping someone who just came," as a form of aid to undocumented immigrants rather than a sacrificial act that sought change in broader political and religious structures governing the lives of all immigrants, including themselves. Likewise, a white, native-born activist recounted his conversation about New Sanctuary with a fellow congregation member, a legal immigrant from India:

> I asked her what were her feelings about this whole situation. She said, "Oh, I think it's really great that we're doing this. I think it's really important," and you can say that she was kind of towing the party line. But when I sort of dug a little bit more it turns out that, for example, this woman had been arrested several years ago on what apparently were some false charges... She felt, "When I was going through this legal situation people at the church didn't step up for me the way they're stepping up for her," so there was definitely some resentment there.

Despite New Sanctuary's attempts to highlight sanctuary as a movement strategy seeking widespread political and religious change, many of the people they tried to recruit viewed it as "stepping up" for only certain immigrants, as helping them—as a form of charity.[19] New Sanctuary congregations were seen as protectors, privileged and empowered to give aid to needy individuals rather than as challengers of the system as a whole.

Even once inside U.S. borders, recent immigrants had greater cause to associate sanctuary with aid and safety than with prophetic witness, if they had heard of it at all. The 1980s Sanctuary Movement's heyday ended before many of today's immigrants arrived. In contrast, controversy around U.S. sanctuary cities made national headlines several times leading up to the 2008 presidential election.[20] For instance, as part of that election cycle, Republican candidate Mitt Romney decried NYC as "the poster child for sanctuary cities in the country," criticizing it for being a "zone of protection" for undocumented immigrants.[21] Again, sanctuary was synonymous with protection, safety, and help rather than with prophetic movements and movement organizations.

To Ruiz and Rev. Salvatierra, sanctuary seemed like a good strategy for their political and religious goals. It allowed immigrants to speak for themselves, making them visible and empowering them to tell their stories in their own voices. It was provocative, possessing the potential to attract media attention for the purposes of broader political and religious change. It offered an opportunity for native-born religious communities to engage directly with immigrants, creating intimate relationships with the potential for religious conversion. But as progressive religious activists with ties to the 1980s Sanctuary Movement, they were blinded by their own religious repertoires.[22]

Put another way, different groups possess varying types of cultural and institutional knowledge, so the same practice can have very different meanings depending on the group at hand. Because of the dominance of sanctuary as movement strategy in their own religious tool kits, early New Sanctuary activists viewed it as a crossover strategy appropriate for both political and religious change. However, for many recent immigrants, sanctuary was not culturally resonant as a social movement strategy for changing immigration policy and enforcement. As mentioned earlier in the book, many immigrant religious groups were quite political. Their lack of interest in sanctuary was due not to an apolitical orientation but to greater familiarity with and preference for other movement strategies and tactics. Instead, while there were certainly exceptions to this general rule (including Adalberto UMC), its primary resonance as a movement strategy lay with native-born and long-time U.S. residents, progressive religious activists whose familiarity with and respect for the 1980s Sanctuary Movement inspired them to get involved in this newest incarnation of sanctuary.

A Second Cultural Disconnect: Religious Group Styles

The disconnect with immigrants went beyond different understandings of sanctuary. While initial coalitions included immigrants, they also included a significant number of native-born, white, middle-class Protestants. Theories of white dominance and white privilege would lead one to expect that the religious group styles of primarily white congregations—and of multiethnic congregations, which often unintentionally preserve white dominance[23]—would come to dominate in a multiethnic religious setting like New Sanctuary.[24] Indeed, cultural disconnects became embedded in the cultures of religion and activism in New Sanctuary, with the religious cultures of Anglo groups more often dominating in the group's meetings and events.

Sociologists Paul Lichterman and Nina Eliasoph argue that group customs shape what particular groups can and cannot accomplish together, calling these customs *group styles* and suggesting that different groups have distinct, often unspoken rules governing their ways of speaking and acting together.[25] Though Lichterman examines faith-based community organizations (FBCOs) made up of congregations, he focuses on how those FBCOs' group styles influence their ability to partner with other community organizations rather than exploring where those group styles came from in the first place (including from the member congregations).[26] But the religious groups making up congregation-based activist coalitions have their own preexisting styles—sociologist Penny Edgell Becker calls them cultural models—that embody their missions and shape conflict within congregations.[27] The mostly white, middle-class congregations she studies share a consensus-based style common among the U.S. middle class. But she also notes that other types of congregations—immigrant religious groups, for instance—may have very different cultural models.[28] In the New Sanctuary Movement, the *religious group styles* of the initially dominant congregations shaped the group style of the network as a whole, inadvertently creating obstacles to immigrant involvement (Figure 6.1).

FIGURE 6.1 Gatherings of primarily white activists were common, as were Anglo musical styles and other religious practices. (Photo by Tom N. Martinez.)

In the New Sanctuary Coalition of NYC, the most dominant congregation in the beginning was Judson Church. A church with a congregationalist
polity, a white, middle-class membership, and an antiauthoritarian tradition,
Judson Church's decision-making was largely consensus-based even though
its decisions were influenced by the pastor. Several of the church members
participated in New Sanctuary activities from its earliest days. In contrast, the
immigrant religious leaders in the coalition at the time of the launch included
two leaders who were not associated with congregations at all and two leaders
of immigrant congregations whose decision-making styles were more pastor
driven, with few laypeople regularly involved in New Sanctuary. So while the
coalition's steering committee included both immigrants and nonimmigrants
at the time of the launch, the religious group styles of native-born congregations became more dominant than those of immigrant congregations in part
because a larger number of initial activists came from these groups.

This type of imbalance created problems for attracting immigrants for several reasons. First, religious people who are used to more hierarchical forms
of decision-making may become frustrated by a consensus-based model since
it requires that a movement organization move more slowly. In Lichterman's
research on community organizations, people from working-class backgrounds often clashed with those from more middle-class backgrounds
precisely over this issue of hierarchical versus consensus-based decision-making.[29] In the case of the New Sanctuary Movement, several immigrants whose
congregations engaged in more hierarchical styles of decision-making showed
impatience with the consensus model, sometimes voicing the view that every
movement needs leaders. Of course, many immigrant religious communities
do not engage in hierarchical or pastor-driven forms of decision-making, but
several of the ones who helped start New Sanctuary largely did.

Second, many immigrants may simply feel less comfortable in this type of
activist environment. For instance, every New York coalition meeting started
with a ritual of personal introductions, where activists sat in a circle, went
around the room, and introduced themselves and talked about what brought
them to the meeting. Sociologist Betsy Leondar-Wright argues that working-
class members of social movements populated by middle-class people are
sometimes uncomfortable with practices like personal introductions or talking about "why we are here," since this emphasis on the individual is less common in working-class culture.[30]

This is particularly true when one considers a third reason that differences
between the group styles of native-born and immigrant religious communities might create problems: often they literally speak different languages. Since

most New Sanctuary local coalition meetings and national gatherings were held primarily in English and the translators typically available were fluent only in English and Spanish, immigrants who wanted to participate would run into this important obstacle. To have a coalition meeting that included the greatest number of people possible, perhaps it was necessary to hold the meetings in English. But the lack of available translators for people speaking languages other than Spanish and the uncertainty about consistent availability of even Spanish translation made the New Sanctuary Movement feel more like a group for native-born religious activists than a group for immigrant religious activists. This was reinforced by the fact that many of the immigrants who did take leadership positions, including many sanctuary families, were ones who had mastered or were committed to mastering English.

Not only did the New Sanctuary Coalition of NYC hold its meetings in English, but its website and much of its printed materials were in English as well. Though portions of the website and some of its materials were also available in Spanish, this was not universal, and none of the website or materials were available in other languages. Activists recognized this weakness, but they did not have a strategy for addressing it, as a brief story demonstrates:

At a November 2008 steering committee meeting in New York, the coalition has just finished creating a new website. People talk about how excited they are to have this new resource, but they are still trying to figure out how to make the site more useful for immigrants. Some people express frustration that the website is only in English, arguing that the most important people—immigrants themselves—might not be able to read it. The person leading the meeting says, "Well, I think English only is better than just doing Spanish and English while not including other languages. That's what we usually do, but that makes it seem like we are a movement only for Latino immigrants." Another activist speaks up, saying, "Even if it's just Spanish, it gets us away from the idea that everybody should speak English." Other people around the room nod, seeming to agree. "Is anyone willing to do the translation?" the meeting leader asks, looking around the room. One of the activists, a Latino Spanish speaker who often ends up doing translations for the organization, sighs and says, "I'm really too busy to do it, but I guess I can do it if no one else can."

Thanking him, the leader asks, "Does anyone know any other languages at all? It would be really great if we could have the website in Chinese, especially since several of our families are Chinese." But when no one raises their hand, he moves on, finally agreeing that they can have a page on the website in Spanish that includes contacts especially for Spanish speakers. The website itself will primarily be in English, with one page in Spanish and no pages in other languages.

As this vignette suggests, the group style in the New Sanctuary Coalition of NYC was consensus-based, emphasized individual motivations and contributions, and primarily operated in English. These were not problems specific to New York. They were also characteristic of the style used in the national New Sanctuary gatherings, and the lack of multilingual communication was a problem on the national website as well.[31] While these were common customs in the religious group styles of native-born, white, middle-class congregations like Judson, they were less common in the immigrant religious communities involved. In contrast, some members of immigrant religious communities were frustrated by consensus-based decision-making, seeing it as wasting precious time and not recognizing the need for leaders. They were less comfortable with doing personal introductions and focusing on individual motivations and contributions, both because these practices were less common in their religious groups and because they were often less confident speaking English in front of a crowd. And perhaps most importantly, many immigrant religious communities conducted services in the language that the majority of their members spoke as their first language. When that language was not English, this meant they would feel less comfortable participating in a group where the dominant language was English. If they did not speak any English, they may have had no choice but to decline to participate.

The disconnect between the New Sanctuary Movement's group styles and the religious group styles of its members and potential members was another instance of sanctuary ultimately making it difficult for New Sanctuary to recruit immigrants. If initial activists had been solely invested in changing immigration policy, they would have selected a strategy more resonant with immigrants, enabling them to build a coalition including a greater number of immigrant individuals and religious communities, including ones with diverse types of religious group styles and ones with speakers of languages other than English and Spanish.

However, the New Sanctuary Movement's religious goals also created a need to make native-born, middle-class religious communities comfortable in order to make the process of religious conversion possible. As in many movement organizations that seek to build coalitions across lines of race and class, where the cultural styles of the more dominant groups often end up dominating in the coalition itself,[32] the New Sanctuary Movement's group style resembled those of native-born religious groups to a much greater extent than those of immigrant religious groups, creating an obstacle to immigrant participation.

An Institutional Disconnect: The Problem with
Religious Globalism

Early New Sanctuary activists sought to move religious people from religious nationalism to religious globalism. Because of this, it was important that the network include people from a variety of ethnic and religious backgrounds, creating a group that embodied and modeled the religious globalism for which they were working. However, as the last section showed, cultural disconnects, both in ideas about sanctuary and religious group styles, created immense obstacles to forming this type of interethnic and interfaith coalition.

But cultural disconnects were not the only problem. Perhaps more importantly, institutional disconnects made it difficult to create the kind of coalition that early New Sanctuary activists hoped for. Immigrants often join religious groups whose members share their ethnic identity and retain at least some ties to their country of origin. These immigrant faith communities often organize on the local level, at times joining with religious groups from other ethnic and faith backgrounds as part of faith-based community organizing efforts.[33] Some of these immigrant religious groups also began organizing on a national level following the passage of the Sensenbrenner Bill, concerned for many of the same reasons that early New Sanctuary activists were. But like their individual congregations, these national coalitions tended to be organized along denominational and ethnic lines.

Three of the best known of these groups were La Familia Latina Unida (LFLU), the Catholic Justice for Immigrants (JFI) campaign, and the evangelical Hispanic Coalition for Comprehensive Immigration Reform (HCFCIR). The LFLU was a campaign within the Mexican American organization Centro Sin Fronteras with a Latina Christian identity. JFI was restricted to Catholics and, while focused on immigrants from a variety of ethnic backgrounds, had roots in working to improve relations between the U.S. and Mexican Catholic churches. Finally, as its name suggests, the HCFCIR focused on Hispanic immigrants, and its membership included evangelical Christian pastors and laypeople.

As these examples show, on the national level religious immigrant rights coalitions were primarily institutionalized along ethnic and denominational lines, a type of institutionalization that reflected the character of many local immigrant religious communities, which were also often ethnically homogeneous. In other words, the institutional contexts of many religious immigrant rights organizations reflected the institutional contexts of the local religious groups from which they drew their members. In contrast, partly due to its commitment to religious globalism, the New Sanctuary Movement sought to build a coalition of people from multiple faith and ethnic backgrounds, a model that required institutional shifts from local faith communities that they may have found undesirable or even impossible.

The New Sanctuary Movement had to compete with other religious immigrant rights organizations for religious immigrant members, making it much more difficult to attract new immigrants. Together, the cultural disconnect of sanctuary and the dominance of white, native-born religious group styles made the New Sanctuary Movement a less attractive choice for many immigrants, regardless of how many immigrants were involved at the time of its launch. But even further, New Sanctuary's focus not only on political change but also on religious globalism—and its related interethnic, interfaith organizing model—created additional obstacles for immigrants who would have been forced to form new religiously and ethnically diverse coalitions rather than simply working within their own existing institutions.

Sanctuary: Refuge or Risk?

From the buzzing streets of one of New York's busiest thoroughfares, the glory of the exotic painted-tile dome of St. Mary's[34] transports sightseers to the coast of the Mediterranean. Step inside its auxiliary buildings, and the spell is broken. Here, 1970s interior design, complete with wood paneling, plants your feet firmly on U.S. soil. In a large meeting room, New Sanctuary leaders and potential recruits congregate around coffee pots, sticking nametags to their shirts and shaking hands with newcomers. The New Sanctuary Coalition of NYC's first annual retreat appears successful so far—the room is filling up, despite the fact that it is a weekday in September, a busy time of year.

After formal presentations by the organizers, people split up into small groups so they can ask questions about New Sanctuary. Shaykh T.A. Bashir, a tall African American imam and a leader in the coalition, takes charge of one group. One by one, people go around the circle and introduce themselves. But Shaykh himself introduces the man sitting beside him. Ibrahim[35] is a black imam from Brooklyn, and the mostly Christian activists around the circle smile and welcome him, excited about the presence of a newcomer, especially another Muslim leader.

A white activist from a local church asks, "So what exactly is the movement trying to do?" Shaykh Bashir hunts through his retreat folder and retrieves a flyer about New Sanctuary's campaign to pass the Child Citizen Protection

Act, legislation that would allow immigration judges to consider undocumented immigrants' family situations in making deportation decisions. "But our main goal right now is to care for the families," another organizer adds.

While people jump in and ask questions, Imam Ibrahim sits silently, looking at the ground as he listens to the conversation. A feisty, gray-haired Unitarian woman finally asks, "So when are we going to go pour blood on ICE documents?" (referencing acts of civil disobedience committed by radical Catholic activists in the Vietnam era, who resisted the war by pouring blood on draft cards). A few people laugh, but Imam Ibrahim shifts in his chair uncomfortably, looking up at her momentarily before gazing again at the floor. Shaykh Bashir brushes aside the joke, saying, "Oh no, we don't want to do that!"

Amanda,[36] a white employee of a mainline Protestant denomination, picks up on the theme of danger. "We are having our attorney come talk to us about the risks of getting involved. Not that risks are a bad thing," she says, "but we need to think through the risks of harboring immigrants." Smiling as though he has addressed the issue of harboring before, Shaykh Bashir says, "Most people aren't doing that [harboring]. We don't want ICE coming into our houses of worship." He tells a story about how several years ago, gun-toting officers entered a mosque during a police chase, angering both Muslims and Christians in the community. "We don't want ICE in our mosques and churches," he reiterates. "But you know, ICE is probably listening to everything we are saying right now anyway," he jokes, referring to the possibility of covert government surveillance and letting out a low chuckle.

Two weeks later, as September 2007 draws to a close, the coalition holds a follow-up meeting for people who attended the retreat. A lot of familiar faces from the retreat populate the room, but Imam Ibrahim is nowhere in sight. As we wait for the meeting to start, I chat with a pastor of a historic Brooklyn church and a rabbi who works with a local faith-based community organization. They are old friends, so I introduce myself, saying I used to live near the pastor's church in Brooklyn. "You used to be a union organizer, right?" I ask. The two men glance at each other. One says, "Do you work for the FBI? You read his file?" We all laugh, but just in case, I do some damage control, sticking in mentions of what I think will be credentials that establish my trustworthiness in these circles—my participation in the graduate student union strike at New York University, my research on the Catholic Worker movement. After a few more minutes of conversation, I sense that any suspicion is dispelled, as they tell me details about the coalition's work. But I learned my lesson about appearing to know too much in a group that distrusts outsiders. As we wrap up our conversation, people begin sitting down in folding chairs and the meeting starts. I look around—still no Imam Ibrahim.

The Risks of Sanctuary for Immigrant Congregations

This talk of infiltration by the Federal Bureau of Investigation (FBI) is not irrational paranoia. FBI agents infiltrated the 1980s Sanctuary Movement, spying on the everyday activities of its congregations and leaders. Tucson's Southside Presbyterian, the birthplace and center of the movement's activities, was open about its legal violations in the beginning, even sending a letter to Immigration and Naturalization Service (INS) officials explaining what they were doing and why they felt compelled by their faith to do it. But by 1983 over 45 churches and synagogues around the country had become sanctuaries, many secretly transporting undocumented immigrants from church to church until they reached waiting family or friends or, for many, the safe haven of Canada. It was these actions, revealed through FBI infiltration, that led to the eventual arrests and convictions of Fife, Corbett, and several other sanctuary activists in 1986.[37]

By 2007 the legal context was even more treacherous. With immigration enforcement housed in the U.S. Department of Homeland Security after 9/11, immigration shifted from a civil issue to an issue of national security, heightening the legal ramifications of aiding undocumented immigrants.[38] For any congregation, sanctuary activism involved genuine risk. At first glance, sitting in a meeting in a church basement may not seem like risky activity, but if you are in that basement strategizing about secretly transporting an undocumented immigrant from one place to another and an FBI agent is listening, you could be charged with aiding and abetting.

For immigrant congregations specifically, the risks were more frightening. Many immigrant congregations included undocumented members, so even signing a pledge of support for a controversial group like New Sanctuary could place the congregation on a government watchlist, bringing unwanted attention to any undocumented members. Several members of immigrant congregations told me that this danger was one of the things that kept their congregations from getting involved or at least kept them from joining more quickly. And the few immigrant congregations who were regularly involved recognized the depth of the risk they were taking yet chose to do it anyway. For instance, the pastor of an immigrant church in Los Angeles had a family member who was seeking a change in his immigration status with the authorities. The pastor worried that his involvement in New Sanctuary would negatively affect his family member's case, yet he also felt it was necessary to "carry that cross." Many immigrant congregations disagreed. Too many other types of immigrant rights activism existed, ones that carried fewer risks and greater short-term benefits, to make sanctuary worthwhile.

The real danger was not that gun-toting ICE agents would kick down the doors of a church where an immigrant was living. In the mid-2000s, U.S. immigration enforcement was as bureaucratic as it was physical. To enforce immigration law (i.e., to discover undocumented immigrants and apprehend them), officers first had to turn bodies into names on lists as part of a bureaucratic procedure. The jobs of ICE agents became much easier if they could find an institution they suspected of including undocumented immigrants, an organization that already had lists of members, donations, and attendees.

Social theorist Michel Foucault called this the *trap of visibility*.[39] As the controversy surrounding the Patriot Act reminds us, modern technologies like the Internet allow for increasingly individualized forms of surveillance, providing the knowledge and power that government institutions need to track individuals. Like a panopticon, it is this constant *possibility* of observation rather than surveillance itself that disciplines individuals, keeping them from stepping out of line. The fear that even voicing your mosque's support of New Sanctuary—let alone actually publicly partnering with an undocumented immigrant family—could endanger your own undocumented members was part of what kept people like Imam Ibrahim from coming back to New Sanctuary meetings.

Perceptions of risk matter for movement recruitment. Both New Sanctuary leaders and potential recruits believed that sanctuary was high-risk activism, even if leaders downplayed these risks to persuade congregations to join. But not all risks were subjective—in New Sanctuary, there were objective risks involved. Congregation members could potentially be fined or arrested. And immigrant congregations could unwittingly draw government attention to their undocumented members, leading to their discovery, detention, and deportation. In their study of the 1980s Sanctuary Movement, social movement scholars Gregory Wiltfang and Doug McAdam point out that different types of social movement activism carry different levels of risk.[40] While this is true, New Sanctuary serves as a reminder that the level of risk associated with a particular organizational action varies based on the *status* of the person engaging in that action. Signing a pledge of support for New Sanctuary might be relatively low-risk for a white, native-born congregation. But for an immigrant congregation, this action could be incredibly risky, restricting not only their involvement in New Sanctuary but their public support for it as well.

Immigrants recognized the risk of visibility in the existing legal context. In 2007, more than half of all Hispanic adults in the United States, regardless of their own status, reported worrying that they, a family member, or a close friend could be deported.[41] Many undocumented immigrants felt they were under constant scrutiny from both law enforcement and their fellow community members.[42] All immigrants without papers had reason to fear repression if they joined the New Sanctuary Movement, especially in the context of widespread anti-immigrant sentiment among the public and policymakers. Some believed that ICE ramped up its raids and deportations in 2006 and 2007 partly in response to the immigrant rights mega-marches in those years.[43] However, as Imam Ibrahim's behavior reflects, Muslim immigrants had dual concerns in this regard—not only were some undocumented, but they were also members of a group that faced increased discrimination from the government after 9/11, compounding the risks they faced.[44]

While a handful of immigrant congregations officially signed on to the New Sanctuary Movement in New York and Los Angeles, few with multiple undocumented members actually maintained regular involvement. Instead, they considered their act of signing the New Sanctuary pledge to be a show of solidarity and support but a risk beyond which they could not go because of the potential dangers to their congregation members. One immigrant who was part of New Sanctuary explained, "[They feel] yeah, this is a good thing, but never putting a face with that because they're afraid about their status, their immigration status, they're afraid of going forward further. It's like this is a good thing, but this is not my calling." Another immigrant, a Latina woman who was a member of a local coalition of immigrant religious leaders and had played a major role in seeking involvement from immigrant religious communities, said:

> I think, there's still, you know, suspicion—and I think fear, too—of being in a public situation and then paying the price for that. Given the Gestapo-like tactics that are being used. So, you have churches and leaders and faiths and different groups that feel like, "I have a lot of undocumented folk here." Right? "If we go public and support this, will this create more tension for my congregation, and will I create a worse situation for them?" Which is a legitimate question. So I think folks are stuck with that dilemma. "I want to participate. It's a real need. I don't want to jeopardize my congregation. And what if ICE just shows up?"

This activist and other immigrant activists involved in New Sanctuary from its early days had hoped to use their social networks in immigrant communities to recruit more immigrants. But they found that many immigrants were afraid of the repression they would face if they joined the New Sanctuary Movement. While the activists who were most centrally involved were taking certain risks in the New Sanctuary Movement by aiding undocumented immigrants, as U.S. citizens or immigrants with legal status they were taking fewer risks than those they were asking undocumented immigrants to take by getting involved in the New Sanctuary Movement, a situation that troubled potential recruits from a variety of backgrounds.

A brief comparison with campaigns to pass the DREAM Act, which had greater success in mobilizing undocumented immigrants, helps to better illuminate some of the challenges associated with sanctuary. As part of the movement around the DREAM Act taking place primarily between 2010 and 2011, many immigrant students "came out" as undocumented: a courageous, risky stand given their status. But the context of that movement differed from New Sanctuary's situation in two important ways. First, DREAM Act immigrants were "model" immigrants—they were college students, high achievers, and believers in the American Dream, irresponsible for their parents' sin of residing in the United States without papers. Their sympathy-inducing status, coupled with a specific piece of legislation on the horizon that might guarantee their legalization, made the very difficult act of coming out a bit easier for these students. In contrast, the undocumented immigrants in congregations recruited by New Sanctuary were not necessarily sympathetic at all, nor did they have any concrete hope for change in their statuses in the near future.

Second, the decision to go public as undocumented is one that *individual* students freely made for themselves. In New Sanctuary, whole *congregations* signed on for involvement in or support of the network. Though it was rare that more than a few congregation members were actually involved in its activities, the names of entire congregations were associated with New Sanctuary rather than of individuals alone. Many pastors, priests, rabbis, and imams were unwilling to make the decision to "come out" on behalf of their undocumented members. Unless all of those members agreed to the decision, religious leaders worried they would be forcing visibility on them rather than making going public an empowering personal choice, as it was for many DREAMers.

Most scholars of religion and social movements see congregations as good for social movements and movement organizations.[45] Religious institutions already possess many of the resources that growing movement organizations need to access, giving them an important boost in the early stages of organizing. Burgeoning activist groups can meet in their buildings; use their phones, computers, and copy machines for flyers; and peruse their membership lists to recruit new activists.[46] In the long run, religious institutions lend stability to movements and movement organizations and keep them grounded in the grassroots concerns of the constituents they typically claim to represent. The explosion of studies on faith-based community organizing, a model whose success is typically attributed to having the local religious congregation as the site for activism, is further evidence of the dominance of this view.[47] And while the congregation-based model helped New Sanctuary in some of the expected ways—like providing meeting space and members—it hurt its efforts to recruit immigrant participants. Because whole congregations needed to sign on, members of immigrant congregations were less likely to become involved due to the need to protect their undocumented members. In this case, an individual membership model may have been more effective for recruiting immigrants. But perhaps the associated dangers would have been deemed worth the risk if sanctuary had offered clear benefits for immigrants, as in the case of the DREAM Act campaigns, which had the potential to create immediate and widespread changes in constituents' lives.

The Lack of Benefits of Sanctuary for Immigrant Congregations

Our Lady of Guadalupe[48] is a Catholic church in LA with a neighborhood feel. Outside of the church in a small plaza, there is a bright yellow sign that says "Legalize LA," similar to signs posted around Los Angeles as part of local immigrant rights campaigns. In the front of the church, behind the altar, a brightly colored cross with farm and village motifs—a style common in Latin America—hangs on the wall. Murals of Our Lady of Guadalupe cover the walls in different parts of the church's small sanctuary. Otherwise, the walls are white, and simple wooden pews with kneelers fill the room. In the 1980s, Our Lady of Guadalupe was one of the centers of the Sanctuary Movement in Los Angeles. Hundreds of immigrants would sleep on the pews as they passed on to other more permanent places. But despite its history with sanctuary, or perhaps because of it, the church has chosen not to join the New Sanctuary Movement.

Tonight, Our Lady of Guadalupe is the site for an immigration forum. At the entrance to the sanctuary, a table displays several handouts for people attending the program: a "know your rights" packet and flyers with contact information for the sponsoring organizations. The handouts are in both English and Spanish. There are two speakers, both Latina women from local immigrant rights organizations, one that is a Latino-based organization and the other a coalition of multiple immigrant groups. Of the 40 or so people sitting in the pews, all but 2 or 3 are Latino. One man wears a T-shirt displaying the words "Who Would Jesus deport?"

The event, held mostly in Spanish, begins with a discussion led by church members of Jesus as an immigrant, a gospel reading, and a discussion of the Good Samaritan story.[49] After a few minutes of theological discussion, the two guest speakers begin talking about immigration law. The first speaker discusses the need for legal reform, saying her organization was against the comprehensive reform bill in 2007 because it did not go far enough in meeting the needs of immigrants. She directs a question to the crowd, asking how long people have been here and why they came. But rather than going around the room, making each person feel as though he or she has to participate, she poses the question to everyone so that anyone who is comfortable can shout out his or her response. Several people raise their hands or shout things out, seeming comfortable enough to be honest in this environment. She warns people that the government is targeting people who do not show up for their hearings in immigration court. She also explains some of the trends in recent policy changes: localities and states passing harsh laws since there is no federal reform; ICE and local police collaborating to identify undocumented people; and programs like ISAP focused on pressuring immigrants to voluntarily leave the country.

After describing the basics of recent policy and enforcement practices, she runs through the "know your rights" handout, making sure people know what they should do if they encounter immigration authorities. She cautions them to use discretion: that Miranda Laws protect immigrant rights and they should not open their doors or give their names if ICE does not have a warrant. She says that ICE often pressures and threatens people to get them to talk and to give away their status, so she warns people not to give into the pressure. The second speaker hits on similar themes, telling stories about the work her organization does in Los Angeles neighborhoods to forge unity between immigrant and African American communities.

When the speakers finish their prepared comments, a church member who is facilitating the event opens the floor for questions from the audience. One man asks, "Why are they arresting us when we are just looking for work?" The speakers advise him to join together with other workers, to try to organize for workers' rights. Another tells a small part of his story, explaining that he has been in the United States for 15 years. "Can I naturalize now?" he asks. The speakers respond that while each case is different, and they are trying to expand paths to legalization, things look bad right now for people in his situation. Another audience member asks how to address the problem of police asking them about their immigration status, since local law prohibits this practice (like NYC, LA is a sanctuary city). The speakers instruct them to get the police officer's badge number and to record it if at all possible, since police often argue that it never happened once a complaint has been made.

Several others ask questions about their specific immigration cases, and the speakers do their best to offer advice while also directing them to their organizations' legal resources. After 10 or so questions and answers, the pastor thanks everyone for coming. He closes the meeting by praying, asking God to help them not to lose hope as a church and as people. After he finishes the prayer, people "pass the peace" to one another, a ritual that is typically part of the Catholic mass and many other Christian services. For several minutes, people walk up to those standing near them, shaking each other's hands and saying "La Paz." As the crowd begins to leave, a chant starts up, and soon almost everyone in the room is chanting "Si, se puede!"

In the mid- to late 2000s, many immigrant rights organizations held "know your rights" workshops like this one, designed to provide immigrants with urgent, practical information that could keep them from being detained or deported. This tactic was especially common after the failure of comprehensive immigration reform in 2007, which might have provided legalization for some undocumented immigrants, and after the dramatic rise in raids, detentions, and deportations in 2007.[50] These forums were typically designed in such a way that immigrants would feel comfortable there: they were held in immigrant congregations, put no pressure on anyone present to speak or to share information about themselves, and were held in the immigrants' first language. Not only might immigrants feel safer and more comfortable in this type of environment, but they also arguably received more short-term benefits from their involvement compared to participation in a group like New Sanctuary, where most tangible benefits were on a national scale and were likely a long way away.[51] In other words, many individual immigrants, immigrant congregations, and immigrant rights organizations quite simply did not see sanctuary as a viable strategy for making a difference in immigrants' lives, especially after the failure of CIR in 2007.

But while other immigrant rights groups moved on to other strategies and tactics, such as know your rights campaigns, much of New Sanctuary's efforts remained focused on the strategy of sanctuary. This made it an isolated campaign with questionable legitimacy in some immigrant communities. Many undocumented immigrants appreciated New Sanctuary's efforts to raise awareness about raids, detentions, and deportations. But the potential negative repercussions associated with getting involved with a very public, controversial strategy were too great given the lack of clear benefits to immigrant participants.

Also, while immigrants and nonimmigrants shared an ignorance about the complex details of immigration policy (as the need for "know your rights" campaigns suggests), there was a vast difference between them in another type of knowledge: unlike nonimmigrants, immigrants already knew other people's migration stories and typically already saw other migrants as brothers and sisters. In other words, many immigrants were already converted to a religious global perspective.[52] Unlike native-born religious people, New Sanctuary's immigrant recruits had less need to engage in the immigrant–native relationships that sanctuary encouraged to meet the goal of religious transformation. As a result, they were less invested in the religious goals of the New Sanctuary Movement, and while they may have appreciated its political goals, these uncertain benefits were not typically enough to outweigh the risks and cultural disconnect associated with sanctuary.

The family-centric strategy of the New Sanctuary Movement was more resonant with immigrants than sanctuary was, given the universality of families, the use of the family frame by some other immigrant rights groups, and more conservative social values among immigrants.[53] But as newcomers, these communities were less invested in the battles between U.S. conservative and progressive religious activists in which the family frame was engaged. And even though they intersected with issues of the family, the moniker and many of the practices of New Sanctuary were still primarily organized around sanctuary.

Over time, some New Sanctuary coalitions recognized these problems and adapted their overall strategy, disengaging from sanctuary and from New Sanctuary itself, as I discuss in the book's conclusion. But during the first couple of years, the problem of the lack of immigrant participants became so serious that the New Sanctuary Coalition of NYC was unable or unwilling to find an immigrant organizer to lead the coalition when Juan Carlos Ruiz stepped down to pursue other work, as the following story relates. For many in the coalition, this was a wake-up call demanding that they adapt somehow to better appeal to immigrants and their needs:

Twelve people recline (as much as possible) in metal folding chairs, arranged in a circle in a meeting room at Judson Church. One person has his eyes closed, another stares at the floor—it is rare that steering committee meetings are a time of celebration. Like other meetings, the November 2008 meeting will focus on recent reports of raids and family separations and what to do about them. A couple of people talk with excitement about the recent election of Barack Obama as president, but others jump into their discussion, doubtful that the change in administration will translate into any real improvement in immigrant welfare.

But tonight's meeting will be different from most. Juan Carlos Ruiz has stepped down as head organizer for the coalition to take a position as a community organizer for a largely immigrant-based organization in the Bronx, and they must vote on a replacement. As usual, the meeting starts late, with those present waiting for others to arrive. Rev. Tim Ford,[54] who is leading the meeting, says, "In the Old South, people used to fill the back pews first so that anyone who was late would have to walk to the front of the church and be seen by everyone." People laugh, sitting up a little higher in their chairs. As the chuckles die down, Ford says, "Let's have a time of prayer." Grabbing the hands of the people to his left and right, he says in a soft voice, "Take the hands of the people next to you, and take a couple of minutes and make eye contact with every person in the room. Really see them."

People stand up, take each other's hands, and look around the room. Some smirk when catching each other's eyes, a little uncomfortable. Once everyone has had plenty of time to make eye contact with the other people in the circle, he says, "Now repeat a few lines after me: I will respect you." "I will respect you," they respond, looking around at others as they say it. "I will respect this space." "I will respect this space," their voices ring in unison. "I will respect our time together." "I will respect our time together," they repeat. "Amen," Ford concludes, squeezing the hands of the people next to him before letting them go. Several echo "Amen!" before settling back into their seats.

"Why don't we go around and introduce ourselves, just in case someone doesn't know someone else?" Though most of the people here have been through this introduction ritual more times than they can count, a couple of people are present who do not typically come to steering committee meetings. Of the 14 people at the meeting, only 4 are immigrants—the rest are native-born, white, and middle-class. Among the four immigrants, only one represents the affected population of undocumented immigrants. One after the other, each person in the circle says his or her name, the congregation or organization they represent, and why they are here.

For most of the meeting, the discussion revolves around strategies for recruiting more congregations, the potential for pushing through new legislative campaigns once president-elect Obama takes office in January, ways to better support the coalition's sanctuary families, and fundraising dilemmas. A couple of hours later, as the discussions finally draw to a close, it is time for the vote. A subcommittee has decided to offer the position to Melissa,[55] a native-born, white progressive religious activist who has worked as a coalition volunteer for over a year. She leaves the room while the broader committee discusses her candidacy and votes.

Ruiz says, "I love Melissa and have already talked to her about my concerns, but I would like this kind of job to go to someone more directly affected by the crisis," he says. The chair of the subcommittee, also native-born and white, says, "Well, we did do an open search, but we couldn't find anyone else who was qualified." Rev. Ford speaks up: "You know, Melissa is worried about the same thing Juan Carlos is. She only agreed to take the job on a temporary basis, until we can find someone who is more directly affected." "Yeah, maybe it's a good thing that she's been so hesitant," the subcommittee chair says. "She seems to understand the complexities of the situation."

They take a vote by acclamation, and everyone agrees Melissa should have the job. Several people smile and nod at each other, happy with the results. Melissa has done a lot of thankless work with the coalition and is well liked. When she reenters the room, everyone bursts into applause, including Juan Carlos. As people pick up their bags and briefcases, they hug Melissa, congratulate her, and bid each other good night. Juan Carlos and Melissa embrace, whispering something to each other, outside of the earshot of those standing nearby. She smiles and nods, looking him in the eye as they share a moment of understanding. As she turns to the next person waiting to hug her and talk with her, Juan Carlos pulls his bag over his shoulder, leaving the room alone.

Conclusion

As a multi-target social movement, the New Sanctuary Movement faced special challenges in meeting its internal goal of attracting immigrants and, as this last story shows, in cultivating immigrant leadership, goals that were directly related to reaching its external political and religious goals. Having multiple targets divided activists' attention and strategic focus between attracting immigrant religious communities and attracting native-born religious communities. Because of the sanctuary model, they mostly focused on attracting whole congregations rather than individual activists. The choice of sanctuary was a much better fit for native-born groups than immigrant ones for cultural, institutional, and political reasons, leading to a dearth of immigrant involvement in the first years of New Sanctuary.

The absence of immigrants in the New Sanctuary Movement hurt its capacity to reach its political goals, which immigrants were often more invested in and knowledgeable about, but it hurt its religious goals as well. Without immigrants, the vision of changing the hearts and minds of members of native-born religious communities through intimate relationships with undocumented immigrants became practically impossible, making it much more difficult for activists to achieve their religious goal of moving toward religious globalism.

In the last chapter, I argued that multi-target social movements must cultivate a carefully balanced activist base to maintain commitment to and capacity for the challenging of multiple targets. This chapter has shown how the use of crossover strategies can pose difficulties in recruiting the single-institutional actors a multi-target social movement needs, challenging its ability to create and nurture that necessary balance. Crossover strategies may not entirely resonate with members of either institution that a multi-target movement seeks to change, constraining its ability to recruit the participants it needs. But as the next chapter shows, a committed core group of crossover activists can sometimes mitigate this problem.

7 WHO RULES IN THE KINGDOM OF GOD?

On an early October evening in 2007, leaves dust the doorstep into Judson Church, where the New Sanctuary Coalition of New York City is meeting to vote on the members who will serve on its long-term steering committee. Before the meeting begins, two clergy members—a rabbi and a Protestant minister—argue quietly near the circle of chairs set up for the meeting's participants, discussing a conference call among coalition members earlier in the week. "You can't do calls like that on holidays. I can't make it on calls when it's a Jewish holiday," the rabbi says emphatically. Rev. Candace,[1] the pastor, nods, but since others are coming into the room they go their separate ways toward the chairs, waiting until later to finish their conversation.

The rabbi, Rabbi Jacob,[2] opens the meeting with a reflection. "The Jewish community just finished celebrating Sukkot," he tells everyone, looking down at the ground now and then as he talks, almost as though he is frustrated to have to explain this. "People go into tents, drink, and eat together. It's all about fragile structures, really," he says. "The tent is just like New Sanctuary: it's a sanctuary that is fragile, but one we can be secure in." Rev. Candace looks at Rabbi Jacob and catches his eye, maintaining eye contact as she says, "I agree, it is fragile. I'm sorry I offended you," she says.

The meeting turns to business, which includes strategizing about which faith communities to reach out to and why. A Muslim imam says he can focus on reaching out to African American religious communities. He says, "The work we're doing is opposed to the system. If you believe in God, whatever your religious tradition, you need to see things the way they are. It's a war against poor people. The Muslim community is underground because of 9/11. And Fox News is trying to make it seem like there is all this conflict between immigrants and blacks. But it's the power elite and the capitalists that are giving this message. If you really want to commit to the work, it has to be a way of life! Not just immigration, but everything it's connected to." Several people burst into applause as he finishes speaking, inspired by his comments. Rev. Candace says, "In our tradition, Baptists have the 'altar call,' where we respond to a message by taking action. After this good preaching, let's think about saying yes, about voting in a holy way."

Everyone agrees that members of a more long-term local steering committee should commit to serving for three years and that they should meet once a week, if not in person then over the phone. Rabbi Jacob says, "That's fine. But we need to keep religious holidays in mind, and not hold meetings on holidays. And we need to meet in person at least once a month." Yet after the vote the new committee is no more religiously diverse—no more able to recognize its religious blind spots—than the previous committee that scheduled an important conference call on a Jewish holiday.

Rev. Tim Ford,[3] a mainline Protestant minister, closes the meeting in prayer. "Please grab the hands of the people standing next to you," he says, and people begin moving closer together, tightening the circle as they join hands. "I want to thank Rabbi Jacob for educating me tonight on many things. And now, with my eyes opened, I want to ask all of us to pray with our eyes open, recognizing the presence of everyone else in the room." Looking around at everyone, he speaks in a calm, clear voice, speaking about birthing: God giving birth to us, God giving birth to justice through this movement. He references God, Allah, and Yahweh, citing them all as different names for the same reality. He says, "Before all of our divisions, there was God." As he continues praying, he says, "We need to throw out words like alien. They just seek to further divide people. But I don't even like the word *immigrant*. We are all children of God, brother and sister." As he finishes the prayer, many of those present say "Amen!" in a loud voice, squeezing each other's hands before letting go.

Since its beginning, the New Sanctuary Movement identified as and sought to be interfaith. To accomplish its religious goals of moving toward public dominance of an inclusive religious vision, New Sanctuary itself wanted to embody this inclusion. Additionally, its efforts to nurture religious globalism required participation from people from a variety of religious backgrounds, particularly those common outside of the United States, such as Islam and non-Western forms of Christianity.[4] As this story shows, the New Sanctuary Movement included an element of religious diversity from the start, giving activists hope that they might attract a diverse group of religious congregations. But as the narrative also suggests, they struggled to create a truly inclusive, global atmosphere, with religious minorities often marginalized by the larger numbers of mainline Protestant and Catholic activists.

In Chapter 5, I argued that multi-target social movements need to recruit a balance of single-institutional actors with deep expertise in the institutions they seek to change. The last chapter showed how crossover strategies can make it difficult to recruit single-institutional actors, since they may have trouble connecting to a movement or movement organization that is not completely focused on institutions in which they are invested and about which they are knowledgeable. In the case of the New Sanctuary Movement, immigrants and their congregations did not see sanctuary as a good fit for their needs and their knowledge, leading to difficulties in recruiting them.

As the introductory vignette of this chapter suggests, New Sanctuary also struggled to recruit a diversity of single-institutional religious actors, who would provide the necessary deep expertise to pose legitimate challenges to the dominance of certain religious views in the United States in the early 21st century. The network's problems with recruiting immigrants overlapped with its difficulties cultivating religious diversity, since in the United States immigrant congregations were the source of much religious diversity.[5] In what follows, I chronicle New Sanctuary's attempts to work toward an internally inclusive religious culture and their eventual partial progress in doing so.

How were New Sanctuary activists able to remain committed to religious change given the lack of actual religious diversity during much of the first two years? This chapter shows how by 2009 the New Sanctuary Movement was able to maintain and even build on its commitment to religious diversity through a core group of committed crossover activists engaging in two processes that sociologist Marshall Ganz argues are essential to strategic capacity: learning and creativity.[6] In working toward religious diversity, their actions kept New Sanctuary from giving up on pursuing both its political and religious goals, further demonstrating the centrality of crossover activists in maintaining commitment to multiple targets.

The Need for Religious Diversity

The United States has become increasingly religiously diverse over the last century, though the growth in religions aside from Judaism and Christianity has primarily occurred during the last several decades. The Hart-Cellar Act of 1965 eliminated national immigration quotas, opening the doors to immigration to the United States from countries in Asia, the Middle East, Africa, and other areas of the world where religions other than Christianity predominate.[7] In 2008, 26% of Americans were evangelical Protestants, 24% were Catholics, 18% were mainline Protestants, 7% were members of historically black Protestant churches, 2% were Jewish, 1.7% were Mormon 0.7% were Buddhist, 0.6% were Muslim, and 0.4% were Hindu.[8] A full 16% of Americans claimed no affiliation with any religious tradition, a large increase from recent years.[9] While this breakdown may seem to still reflect the reality that sociologist and Jewish theologian Will Herberg wrote about in his classic *Protestant-Catholic-Jew*, which depicted the nation being dominated by these three religious groups, in several ways today's reality is quite different from the one that existed when his book was published over 50 years ago.[10]

In the 1950s, while there was no officially established state religion, mainline Protestant denominations in particular held great sway over the nation's culture and resources.[11] Protestant Christians ran many of the nation's most elite universities and held most top political offices (including all of the nation's presidencies up to that point). However, in the years since that time, what some have called a disestablishment has occurred in the United States.[12] Rising secularization has been the trend of the last few decades, as mainline Protestants lost their hold on many of the nation's important institutions as well as their majority in terms of individual religious affiliation.[13]

Increasing immigration from areas of the world populated primarily with Muslims, Hindus, Buddhists, and members of other religions has produced a broadening of U.S. religious culture. With constitutional separation of church and state, these new religions posed a challenge to mainline Protestantism's power in the public sphere. In *American Mythos*, sociologist Robert Wuthnow writes, "As a proportion of the religiously active population, Muslims and Hindus or Buddhists and Jains are still arguably little more than a token presence... The cultural impact of this new religious diversity is far greater than the numbers of adherents would suggest, however."[14] Adherents of these new religions have been simultaneously carving out space for themselves in the public and private spheres while also challenging Protestantism's hegemony.[15]

At the same time, immigration has been changing the face of American Christianity. Both Catholicism and Protestantism in the United States have been transformed by the large numbers of Latino Catholics, Latino Pentecostals, and Asian Catholics and Protestants who have moved to the United States in recent years.[16] Even Protestant denominations with traditionally white populations, like the United Methodist Church and the Evangelical Lutheran Church in America, have been founding Spanish-language ministries at a relatively high rate.[17] Immigrants are transforming American Christianity in more ways than just changing the languages in which services are conducted, though. They bring their own theologies, celebrations, rituals, and worship styles with them, thereby transforming these elements of U.S. Christianity to some extent. For instance, Mexican Day of the Dead celebrations and Las Posadas are becoming increasingly common elements in U.S. religion,[18] as are Korean American cultural practices in U.S. evangelicalism.[19]

One of the most important differences between the religious immigrant rights activists that others have studied and the ones in the New Sanctuary Movement is one of geography. Prior studies have focused almost exclusively on local or regional efforts, especially ones centered along the U.S.–Mexico border.[20] These efforts have less need for religious diversity. Emphasizing relationships between Americans living near the border and Mexican immigrants, they can focus on the relationships between Protestants and Catholics and still largely represent the people for whom they claim to speak. So when sociologist Pierrette Hondagneu-Sotelo writes that "most movements for social change rely on a shared culture of beliefs and practice" and points to religion as a source for that shared culture for religious immigrant rights activists, the underlying assumption is that these activists will share a religious tradition similar enough that their preexisting beliefs and practices largely overlap.[21]

As of the first decade of the 21st century, partnerships between Protestants and Catholics were no longer enough for a national network of activists in the United States, one hoping to advocate for the political claims of a wide variety of immigrant groups and seeking to shift the national religious vision from religious nationalism to religious globalism. In addition to seeking to usher in an era of religious globalism, New Sanctuary activists hoped to build a strong religious voice—a coalition of people of faith—that could combat the religious right as the dominant religious voice in the United States (Figure 7.1). But the people who had typically been involved in past progressive religious efforts (mainline Protestants, liberal Catholics, and Reform Jews) were not numerous enough to accomplish that alone. Instead, activists from these traditionally progressive religious traditions recognized that they must build a broader religious coalition to challenge the religious right's hold on the national religious imagination, drawing participants from evangelical Christian, conservative and orthodox Jewish, Muslim, and other religious circles.

During an interview, a member of one of the New Sanctuary Movement's original congregations shared some of his notes from his church's first meeting about the New Sanctuary Movement. According to his notes, they talked about how "the New Sanctuary Movement intends to bring together leaders of many faiths and ethnic backgrounds to speak with one voice" and how "this kind of coalition is essential for future action around many issues including torture, war, and poverty." From the beginning, activists recognized the

FIGURE 7.1 Activists display a banner highlighting the New Sanctuary Movement's interfaith identity at a 2008 immigrant rights march in NYC. (Photo by Mizue Aizeki.)

utility of forming interfaith relationships for strengthening the impact of progressive religion in the public sphere. To transform religious communities and challenge broader religious culture, moving them toward inclusiveness and globalism, a group like New Sanctuary needed members from a wide variety of religious traditions. Religious diversity was necessary both for theological and practical reasons, as changing a variety of religious communities requires deep knowledge of those varied institutions. For all of these reasons, early New Sanctuary activists saw a broad coalition of faith traditions as necessary for achieving their goals of political and religious change. But they also thought it was possible, a key point to understanding their continuing commitment.

Commitment to Religious Diversity and Inclusive Religion

In *Working the Roots*, Matt Weiner—a former director of an interfaith organization in NYC—chronicles his organization's struggles as it moved from one model of interfaith activism to a different model, hoping to more fully include groups that have traditionally shunned participation in any group that brings together people of different faiths.[22] According to Weiner, more traditional forms of interfaith activism, like the one initially characterizing his organization, brought people together under the auspices of learning more about each other's religious traditions to cultivate greater tolerance, respect, and peace between religions.

While many would consider this an admirable goal, it inadvertently excluded more conservative members of most religious traditions since they worried that participation in these groups would require them to check some of their religious beliefs at the door—specifically, beliefs about their own religion's exclusive claims to the truth and the means of salvation. As a result, this type of interfaith activism did not live up to its name. It included members of certain traditions while excluding others, even if unintentionally. Eventually his organization adopted a different type of interfaith activism, bringing together people from a variety of faith traditions to work on shared problems facing members of their religious communities. Instead of emphasizing religious goals of mutual tolerance and respect for each other's traditions, they focused on political ones, hoping to attract more participation from evangelical Christians, orthodox Jews, and conservative Muslims.

The core group of crossover activists who started the New Sanctuary Movement retained the hope of combining these two types of interfaith activism. They wanted to attract members of religious groups that were often absent from progressive faith-based coalitions or were at least sorely underrepresented. There were several reasons they saw this as necessary for reaching both their political and religious goals. First, it was necessary because they sought to build a national coalition that included the faith communities of immigrants from all over the world, not just Latin America. Of course, this would need to include Muslim faith communities, and ideally Sikh, Buddhist, and Hindu communities as well. In trying to change immigration policy for all immigrants, New Sanctuary needed to have legitimacy as a voice for a variety of different groups. And to have any legitimacy in speaking on behalf of the interests of those groups, New Sanctuary would need to include members from their communities. The broader the religious coalition, the more clout they would have.

Interpretations of the New Sanctuary Movement framed by state-centered approaches to social movements would stop there in explaining commitment to interfaith activism, but for New Sanctuary activists doing interfaith work was about more than creating a representative coalition of religious groups for the purposes of political change. Instead, they wanted as broad a coalition of faith traditions as possible partly because interacting with people of different faiths was necessary to achieve the shift from religious nationalism to religious globalism. To see all people as children of God, it was important to break down not only the borders between people of different nationalities and ethnicities but also some (though not all) of the barriers between people from different religious traditions, humanizing members of traditions that had often been seen as enemies.

But they also believed it was *possible* for them to create a religiously diverse coalition. Many had experience working in interfaith coalitions, and their experiences had shaped their views not only of what was desirable but also of what was possible. When conversations began among future New Sanctuary activists in Los Angeles, New York, and Chicago in late 2006, they took place among individuals and groups that were already involved in interfaith activism. Their roots in multiple institutional contexts as well as their experiences with interfaith activism are important to understanding why crossover actors might be especially able to engage in the processes of learning and creativity I discuss later in this chapter. In his book *The Art of Moral Protest*, sociologist James Jasper argues that "we are so deeply embedded in cultural traditions that, even as we transform and attack them, we cannot escape them" and that "to understand artfulness...we need to pay attention to the biographical sources of individual variation, for these are the seedbed for innovations."[23] Because of their embeddedness in multiple institutional locations and their experiences with difference, crossover actors may be especially equipped to move beyond the boundaries of their own cultural traditions in artful, creative ways.

In Los Angeles, Clergy and Laity United for Economic Justice (CLUE) was the setting for much of the initial deliberation over a proper response to the Sensenbrenner Bill. Clergy from a variety of faith traditions were involved in CLUE, with Jews, Muslims, Catholics, mainline Protestants, and black Protestants on its board of directors, though its membership was primarily mainline Protestant and Catholic. Similarly, Interfaith Worker Justice (IWJ) in Chicago was a coalition of people from several different religions, with its board of directors including Catholics, mainline Protestants, black Protestants, Jews, and Muslims, again with the majority being Catholics and mainline Protestants. In New York, both Rev. Donna Schaper and Juan Carlos Ruiz had a good deal of experience with interfaith activism. As a result, they counted people from a variety of faith traditions as part of their religious activist networks.

Similarly, New York activist Rabbi Michael Feinberg was the director of the Greater New York Labor-Religion Coalition, an interfaith organization advocating for workers' rights. During college, he got involved in anti-apartheid organizing on campus; after graduation, he was an intern at the Martin Luther King Jr. Center in Atlanta. In all of this, he interacted with people from a variety of faiths, all of whom were working to bring a vision of religious justice into being. Describing his experiences, he said, "I've had very good models for what it means to be a Jew, a rabbi, a clergy person. And interestingly not all of them have been Jews, those models. I would say—I sometimes say—that I wouldn't be a rabbi if Dan Berrigan hadn't been the priest that he is or the human being that he is. And there's a lot of truth to that. I was very influenced by radical Catholic pacifists, by people from other faith traditions, Protestant, you know, prophetic-type figures. That really informed what I thought might be possible as a rabbi."

This experience working with people of other faiths did not lead to dilution of his own religious identity and commitment, however. The distinctiveness of the Jewish tradition, and his deep knowledge of its culture and institutions, remained very important to him. Rabbi Feinberg was ordained in the Reconstructionist Jewish tradition, one that is liberal theologically in many of the same ways as Reform Judaism but that also reclaims many traditional Jewish practices, incorporating them as an important part of being Jewish. As such, Rabbi Feinberg wore a yarmulke each day and observed most of the Jewish holidays. So, while maintaining the distinctiveness of Judaism was an essential part of his religious identity, he was nonetheless committed to moving toward a sort of religious globalism that respected differences while embracing people in other faith traditions:

> I feel my real community to be among progressive minded people. That's not defined within the boundaries of any faith community or ethnic community—it's cosmopolitan, if you want to say, or internationalist... Really I would say the biggest defining issue among religion now is not Jew, Catholic, Protestant, it's fundamentalist religion or, what I would say, a status quo hierarchical vision of religion versus progressive, nonhierarchical, non-fundamentalist. The differences are the most profound between those two camps, not between Jews and Muslims or Muslims and Christians. I can sit in a room with progressive religionists from whatever faith and feel like I'm perfectly at home with them because we share that common view of what religion should be. Whereas I could sit in a room with all other Jews who read the Torah literally, and you know out of that have an anti-gay perspective—just to pick one example—I would feel I would have very little in common with them theologically or certainly politically. So these become really complicated issues because unfortunately the fundamentalist version is the one that you see in the headlines.

Many Jews, Christians, and Muslims in New Sanctuary felt the same way— that a more exclusive, fundamentalist form of religion dominated the public sphere in the United States. They sought a more inclusive religious culture while also remaining embedded within their own distinctive institutions and traditions, maintaining a level of expertise in their own religious cultures that was unavailable to outsiders. This is why the presence of religious minorities in New Sanctuary was so essential: they provided expertise that could not be easily replicated.

Like Rabbi Feinberg, many early New Sanctuary activists were experienced with interfaith activism and were committed to changing immigration policy and to building a more globally inclusive religious vision. A mainline Protestant pastor who was involved in a lot of interfaith work told me the story of his travels to India almost 20 years before, relaying how his experiences there led to his commitment to an interfaith vision:

> This was a Copernican moment for me because I was still rather heavily Christocentric and…saw Christianity in the center of the circle and Hinduism and Buddhism and Judaism was everything out on this circle around us…But then, when I go to India, I found villages, multiple villages of people that I spent time with who loved God, loved their neighbor as themselves more fully and more completely than any Christians I'd ever seen in my life—and they were all Hindus. So, then, I'm starting to think, my God's too small, my God construct is too small, and I've got to find another way to understand the Christ event. In my theology, in my tradition, I've got to find another way. And so, what happens is—when I say my "Copernican revolution"—that I moved out to the circle with everybody else. And what's in the middle of the circle is the Divine mystery. Not Christianity, but the Divine mystery's in the middle, and we're all out here trying to somehow—in our finite way, bound by special and temporal language—trying to describe something that's mysterious.

After his experiences changed his ideas about the relation of Christianity to other religions, he came back to the United States and began to get involved in a variety of community activities that included partnerships with people from other faith traditions.

In addition to having experience with interfaith activism, which shaped their ideas of what was desirable and what was possible, New Sanctuary activists also built an early coalition of diverse religious leaders. Building on their networks from past interfaith work, people like Rev. Schaper, Juan Carlos Ruiz, and Rev. Salvatierra were able to create initial steering committees and coalitions that moved beyond the traditional groupings in progressive religious activism of mainline Protestants, Catholics, and Reform Jews. For example, the initial steering committee of the New Sanctuary Coalition of NYC included mainline Protestants, Catholics, Jews, Muslims, white evangelicals, and Latino evangelicals. Similarly, from an early stage, the Los Angeles coalition included Catholics, mainline Protestants, Jews, Muslims, and Latino evangelicals. Having begun with these diverse coalitions, they thought members of religious groups that had not traditionally participated in progressive religious activism—for instance, conservative and orthodox Jews, evangelical Protestants, conservative Catholics, and Muslims—would be able to reach out to fellow members of their religious traditions, continuing to draw participation from these quarters. But in spite of their beliefs in the possibility of creating an inclusive religious culture through the recruitment of a diverse group of single-institutional religious actors, particularly religious minorities, New Sanctuary was initially unsuccessful in doing so.

The Lack of Religious Diversity in the New Sanctuary Movement

When Shaykh T.A. Bashir enters a room, you notice. Standing at over six feet tall, his broad shoulders jut out like a linebacker's—no doubt an advantage when he fought in the Vietnam War. Glasses frame his face and a beard covers his chin. While his physical stature and his shyness made him seem serious and intimidating, drawn out of his shell, he was the first to make jokes during a boring steering committee meeting, keeping everyone laughing. An African American raised in a Muslim family, Shaykh Bashir was one of many imams serving the large African American Muslim community in New York. What distinguished him from some of his colleagues was his willingness to partner with people of other faiths, even when it meant feeling insulted at times by his interactions with members of dominant U.S. religious traditions.

Shaykh Bashir was the founder and chief executive officer of a nonprofit organization that provided social services to the Islamic community in a predominantly African American neighborhood in Brooklyn. The organization offered Islamic pastoral counseling, especially marital and youth counseling, to community members as well as workshops on domestic violence for people of all faiths. However, its mission to improve the surrounding community often required working with members of other religious traditions.

To address the common issues African Americans face, his organization joined the Brooklyn chapter of the Southern Christian Leadership Conference (SCLC), despite the fact that Martin Luther King Jr.'s former organization was still primarily a Christian one. His organization also became a member of the Interfaith Community of NYC. Confronted with the challenges facing fellow Muslims—immigrants whose families were being split up through deportation—it also signed on to the New Sanctuary Movement in 2007. Shaykh Bashir was a founding member of the New York City coalition, and for a year he even served as the NYC representative on New Sanctuary's national steering committee.

But as much as he hoped to convince other Muslims to join the New Sanctuary Movement, he had little luck. Just as New Sanctuary had trouble attracting immigrant faith communities because of fears of the government among the undocumented and their allies, in 2007 many Muslim communities still experienced a lot of fear, both of the government and of ordinary Americans.[24] After the September 11 attacks and the resulting government surveillance of and public animosity toward Muslims, many imams and mosques were hesitant to take the risk of public, controversial action.[25] I often heard him make tongue-in-cheek jokes about "the FBI watching us," suggesting an acute awareness of the government's power to secretly monitor communities it considers potentially dangerous, opening Muslim communities up to vulnerabilities that other immigrant communities did not face to the same degree.

"It's a very tricky situation with Muslims, as you know," Shaykh Bashir explained to me one afternoon as we sat talking in his office. "The Africans, they are in...they have the sword of Damocles over them, because they have so many people in their congregation that may have questionable status. So what happens is they really don't want to draw authorities to their mosque." The increased risks Muslim communities faced were coupled with the usual obstacles to mobilization among both poor and immigrant communities: the need to focus on the survival of their own families and communities.[26] "Most of the people I know in the African community work from sun up to sun down. Their main thing is to make money, support their family, and send money back home," he said, straightening his glasses. "They feel that if they do not protest or do not become a thorn in somebody's side that they would be left alone. Unfortunately, that's usually not the case." Also, the divisions between immigrant Muslim communities and African American Muslim communities like the ones Shaykh Bashir usually worked with created difficulties in eliciting involvement from immigrant Muslims.[27]

But his final point about Muslim hesitation was the most telling. "The Muslim community is aware [of New Sanctuary] because they saw me on TV, so they're pretty much familiar with it. And sometimes I get calls from the various imams in reference to immigration problems. See, there are organizations that have immigration as their main focus in the Muslim community. But they are not with sanctuary, because sanctuary presents itself basically as a Christian organization." Following up, I asked, "Well, I know they try to be interfaith, but you feel like so far it's mostly been Christian?" He said, "Yeah, singing songs, with lighted candles and what not? That's Christian. That's not Jewish. That's not Muslim. So there's a heavy orientation of that. And so that's not attractive to Muslims, because they feel: why should I be involved with that?"[28] While the practices of singing and lighting candles are more associated with Judaism than his comments indicate, they are much less associated with Muslim traditions, a situation that made New Sanctuary feel less welcoming to potential Muslim participants.

Shaykh Bashir's response suggests that in the opening story, Rabbi Jacob[29] was right to be concerned about a lack of knowledge about (and perhaps, appreciation for) the cultures of religious traditions outside of mainline Protestant and Catholic ones. In another example of religious hegemony, at one of the local New Sanctuary launches, a member of another "newcomer" tradition in the realm of progressive religious activism was silenced so the group could present a more unified front to the press. One early activist, an evangelical pastor who had not participated in much interfaith activism in the past, relayed the following story about his local launch: "When I did my speaking at the press conference, I decided to go for it, and I literally said, 'Where are the evangelicals?' And I was trying to reach out to the evangelicals. I talked about 'quiet times' and I said, 'Our faith isn't in our private, personal quiet times, it's about our life in this world', and I pointed to the family of Bob,[30] his wife and kids, and said, 'How can we allow these parents to be removed from their children?' And I kind of went to a political place that the New Sanctuary Movement didn't want me to go to."

The pastor explained that the other coalition members, many of whom had worked together in interfaith coalitions in the past, wanted to stay on the script they had crafted, which stressed the religious character of New Sanctuary over its political character. According to him, they felt he had strayed from it to speak in the ways he felt would grab the attention of his particular religious community. "I didn't want it to become political either, but I wanted to pierce into the world of evangelicals listening and get them to realize that it [political activism on behalf of immigrants] was something their faith was demanding they should do…So while I'm speaking, Kit[31] [a mainline Protestant pastor] comes over to me at the podium and, smiling in front of everybody, grabs my hand and pulls it down with a way of saying, 'Okay I'm gonna stop you now.' And I didn't want to do anything embarrassing," he said, so he finished what he was saying and stepped away from the microphone.

Reflecting on the experience later, he told me, "I mean afterward I was completely pissed. But now looking back I think it's really funny. But they were not gonna let me go there even though it could have totally helped the whole movement." He believed that greater flexibility in the types of language used to describe New Sanctuary would have allowed him to better reach out to evangelicals by tapping into their own worldviews and assumptions, thereby attracting more evangelical involvement. By his account, his presence had already caused tension at early coalition meetings several times, since he often offered a religious conservative spin on issues that challenged the more progressive stances of most of the other members. For instance, he recommended that in attempting to recruit evangelical churches, the coalition make it clear that they would not be forced to partner with an immigrant who had a criminal conviction, since some evangelicals might have problems with these specific cases while supporting mixed-status families more generally. By his account, these suggestions were largely treated with disdain. Many activists did not want to offer a public religious voice that might be seen as affirming legalistic concerns of the religious right or that focused too much on the rights of the government to dictate religious belief and action. Not long after the launch, this person decided not to remain involved in New Sanctuary, though he said that this was for several reasons and that he remained open to becoming involved again in the future.

The examples of Shaykh Bashir and this evangelical pastor provide a window into the struggles New Sanctuary activists faced in cultivating a more genuinely inclusive religious vision. While they wanted to include Muslims and evangelicals, they did not always have the cultural tools needed to reach out to them, and they often struggled with balancing commitments to dominant progressive religious cultures with openness to newcomers. But they needed Muslims and evangelicals to join the coalition, since they could not fully transform religious communities and American religious culture more broadly without their religious expertise. In response to the lack of success in cultivating religious diversity in its initial months, the New Sanctuary Movement engaged in processes of strategic learning and creativity that enabled them to continue working toward greater religious diversity.

The Process of Strategic Learning

Six months after the official launch, by the time of the national gathering in November 2007, things had changed a little, but not much, as the following story shows: On the second morning of the gathering, activists from all over the country gather for worship in a Latino church in the Pico-Union neighborhood of Los Angeles. At the front of the church gymnasium stand Rev. Salvatierra, Shaykh Bashir, and Rabbi Feinberg. Rev. Salvatierra wears a white robe and a brightly colored stole, Shaykh Bashir wears a small white skullcap and a white and green checked scarf, and Rabbi Feinberg wears a small black yarmulke. In front of them, a folding table is set with a white tablecloth, and several items sit on top, including colorful paper streamers. The service begins in song. The language of the songs is mostly religiously inclusive: the words speak of God and the Lord, for example, with no direct reference to Christ. However, most have been copied directly from a Protestant hymnal. At the top of the song sheet for "The Canticle of the Turning" one can still read the hymnal's subject heading "The Triune God," referring to the Christian doctrine of the Trinity. Similarly, "Make Me a Channel of Your Peace," a lovely song about peace and justice, is clearly attributed to the Prayer of St. Francis, a Catholic saint. The words for "We Are Called" come directly from Micah 6:8, part of Jewish and Christian scriptures. One of its verses is:

> Come! Live in the light!
> Shine with the joy and the love of the Lord!
> We are called to be light for the kingdom,
> To live in the freedom of the city of God!

While associated with the scriptures of particular traditions—the phrase "the kingdom" refers directly to the Christian concept of the Kingdom of God— the room also rings with the more universal dream of religious globalism as people sing the third verse together:

> Sing! Sing a new song!
> Sing of that great day when all will be one!
> God will reign, and we'll walk with each other
> As sisters and brothers united in love!

After the singing concludes, Juan Carlos Ruiz steps forward to give a short reflection. "In New York, people hear me say this over and over. A friend of mine a few weeks back was asked within the context of what is happening in Iraq—violence, brother killing brother, sister killing sister—he was asked, 'What do you mourn?'" Juan Carlos continues, "The thing I mourn the most is the demise of imagination. As a movement we are about awakening that imagination, to embody in symbols and words the hopes of our people."

He tells the story of a woman who was very poor. She had no education, and her house had no electricity. This woman was very worried about her son, who was gravely ill. The doctor lived 20 miles away, so she spent all day traveling to bring him to her home. When he arrived, he said what the son needed to survive was ice, to cool the fever. "Without ice," he said, "the boy will die." The mother left and got a bucket, put it outside and began to pray. Then she started making a peanut butter sandwich. Incredulous, the doctor asked, "What are you doing? Your son is dying, he will die without ice!" The woman answered, "My son likes peanut butter sandwiches. When he wakes up and he is well, he is going to be hungry." She continued, "I talked to my God and told him I needed the ice. And so I am waiting. You go back to my son. I will continue preparing the sandwich." As she sat making the sandwich, the wind of the north and the wind of the south spoke together. The meeting of the two winds created hail and ice, which filled the bucket until it overflowed.

"Our hope, our prayers, and our activities lie in hands that are not our own," Juan Carlos concludes. "We need to take up our buckets. We need to lift our eyes up and speak our words of hope. But what are the words that we will speak?" he asks. Pointing to the colored streamers that sit on the table at the front of the room, he tells everyone to "write down the words of hope that embody our voices, our hopes, our very lives." People pass the streamers around the room, and everyone writes down "a word of hope." Then, people walk up slowly and place their "gifts" on the makeshift altar at the front of the room. Months later, when I visited Liliana's home at the United Church of Christ (UCC) Simi Valley, I saw the streamers again, arranged into a collage and hanging on the wall near her front door.

While the religious leaders of multiple faith traditions are included in this liturgy, and the content refers to *God* rather than *Christ*, in form and content it is almost entirely Christian. Like most Christian worship services, it starts with songs (ones that come largely from Christian hymnals), it moves into a time of speech or sermon making, and it concludes with participants coming together around an altar of Godly gifts. Thus, despite their efforts to be inclusive, the service feels Christian.

On the final day of the gathering, some of these problems related to Christian dominance come to a head. In a session designed to articulate plans for New Sanctuary based on the foregoing discussions at the gathering, Rev.

Juanita,[32] a member of the national coordinating committee, presents an easel of butcher block paper to attendees. On it is an agenda, including the items "Core Vision" and "Structure." Under Core Vision several items are already listed, including being interfaith. However, she poses the question: "Is there really consensus on our core vision?" Under Structure, the group hopes to transition away from the interim national coordinating committee that has been organizing the national New Sanctuary Movement up to this point, replacing it with a more long-term, representative committee that would include the sanctuary families. One activist suggests that the new committee include someone from each local coalition and all of the family members.

Around this time, it begins to emerge that there was a meeting the night before, after the "official" events were over, and that "not everyone was invited." Several people around the room are nodding, seeming frustrated about this. One rabbi who traveled to LA from a coalition in another state, Rabbi Matthew,[33] says "it feels very top down." Rev. Juanita's eyes widen for a moment before she explains, "Well, it was the original coordinating committee who were meeting." Another activist speaks up, saying, "Anyone who wants to help should be invited to meetings like that." Looking defensive, Rev. Juanita responds, "I want to give you some history to discuss why not everyone was invited last night." Suddenly, several hands shoot into the air. Clearly some people have been stewing over this all morning, while those who were in the meeting last night are caught off guard. The tension thickens, as Rev. Juanita and the other members of the coordinating committee look at each other, unsure of what to do next.

Rabbi Matthew says, "We should have been discussing these things during the whole conference." Rev. Juanita responds, "We have been trying to achieve consensus in the past, but it is not always happening. We're trying to figure out how to share power better," she adds. Another activist, red in the face, defends them, shouting, "They have been doing a great job! I can't believe this!" One pastor, a marginal member of New Sanctuary who showed up only for the last day of the gathering, says, "Look, process isn't important. There are urgent strategic decisions to be made." A mainline Protestant from an East Coast coalition disagrees, arguing, "How we work is as important as what we do." Another activist nods, saying, "People are not trusting the building of the movement yet. Representation is an important issue: do people feel represented?"

Rabbi Matthew speaks up again, saying, "Well, I have issues with informal decision-making. I hope the local coalitions will be able to choose their national representatives rather than it being imposed." An LA-area mainline

Protestant pastor says, "Listen, I'm a process person, but we have to figure out how we work together to keep hope alive for the families." Carolyn,[34] a Catholic LA-area activist, asks Liliana for her opinion, and suddenly everyone grows quiet, turning to face her. Liliana speaks in Spanish and Carolyn translates: "The separation of families is the most important thing. How can we help Congress understand what is happening?"

Though the mood of the room has shifted, someone reminds everyone, "We still need to make a decision about structure." Rev. Juanita says, "Well, we could hold a vote, but not everyone is here. But the coordinating committee's legitimacy has been profoundly questioned," she says, indicating that they should not make the decision on behalf of everyone. She suggests that they vote on an idea presented earlier by someone from the crowd: that they have one representative from each city, chosen by that city, and that the sanctuary families can participate as they choose.

However, to maintain some continuity someone also suggests that members of the initial coordinating committee remain on the national steering committee for the time being. Rabbi Matthew shakes his head and looks down at the ground. One activist agrees with the suggestion, saying, "When groups I work with are trying to transition from an old group to a new one, the old people have usually been involved, but sharing with the new." Rev. Juanita names the members of the coordinating committee, who all happen to be mainline Protestant clergy with the exception of Juan Carlos Ruiz and a rabbi who works with CLUE.

After naming the committee members, she gets a little choked up, tears forming in her eyes. "Our goal has always been to be inclusive and effective," she says, her voice shaking, "so it's a little difficult emotionally to get this kind of feedback." Rabbi Matthew says, "I'm sorry, I just don't feel that the leadership has been democratically chosen. And I think historically fuzziness has been our problem."

Another activist jumps in, saying, "Sometimes the focus on 'My own, my own!' from the culture can move into a movement. I'm not a structure person, and I think we should just trust each other. If people come cross-country for a gathering like this, you can trust them." A member of the initial coordinating committee, says, "Form follows function, and whatever structure we choose it needs to facilitate helping the families. You can't just replicate corporate dynamics, business as usual. If we want something new, we must model that."

By now, several of the activists who have worked with the coordinating committee since the beginning are crying. One says, "I just can't leave today without recognizing the work that has been done. We wouldn't be here without the coordinating committee," she says, wiping tears from her cheeks. Emotion pours out of the activists in the room. People are exhausted, frustrated, and hurt. Several hug one of the main coordinators standing in the back of the room, her face red from crying. She says, "All of this had to be discussed, but it isn't easy!" Another member of the initial coordinating committee says, "I want to acknowledge tears of exhaustion for the past year and all of the work that has been done." Laughing a little, she says, "Hey, we have been trying to give birth to something here. But sometimes our children kick us in the chin, saying 'We can do it ourselves!' And we're a bunch of radicals who don't trust authority, so that makes it hard." One of the weepy activists agrees, saying, "Part of it is exhaustion. But I haven't stopped crying since Liliana spoke earlier, sharing her story with us. I just feel so blessed and honored to be joining hands with her."

These issues of inadequate representation were not solely about the need for greater religious diversity. Underneath the surface, much of the contestation was over IWJ and CLUE's organizational control of New Sanctuary, factions within the Chicago coalition, issues related to funding, and the need to increase the power of other regions' coalitions to make it a truly national movement organization. However, the need for other regions to be represented among national leadership, and not just Chicago and Southern California, was partly an issue of religious representation. At the national gathering, Shaykh Bashir was the only Muslim religious leader present, and only a handful of Jewish leaders were there. While Rabbi Matthew may have come off looking like the bad guy with the session ending in tears, his insistence that the coordinating committee better represent the national network's diversity, including its religious diversity, merely called the New Sanctuary Movement to be true to what it claimed was part of its core vision.

Even though the bulk of the participants in the 2007 national gathering were crossover activists and experienced interfaith activists, they still lacked a deep understanding of the cultures, interests, and institutional positions of the few religious minorities in their midst. While interactions like those at the 2007 gathering were difficult, they provided important learning opportunities for activists coming from dominant religious traditions. Grounded in commitment to continue working toward both political and religious change, which required the participation and leadership of a larger number of religious minorities, the crossover actors in both this story and the opening vignette sought to learn from these conflicts. Similarly, in his closing prayer at the beginning of this chapter, Rev. Ford thanked Rabbi Jacob for educating him about Judaism, reporting that his eyes had been opened. Then he prayed a more inclusive prayer than he might have prior to that moment of learning. Like Rev. Ford, many early activists sought to build a greater understanding of and openness to the cultures and representational needs of religious minorities through these sometimes tense interactions, allowing them to better include and recruit more members of these groups. Having engaged in these learning processes, activists used this knowledge in creative ways, constructing innovative, more genuinely inclusive religious rituals for New Sanctuary Movement gatherings.

Using Learning to Creatively Build Greater Inclusion

The foregoing stories from the earliest days of the New Sanctuary Movement show how activists struggled to recruit religious minorities in working toward their inclusive religious vision, but they often faltered because the majority of leaders and participants were themselves mainline Protestants and Catholics, whose religious cultures dominated. Two years later, at the 2009 national gathering, New Sanctuary had taken some important steps toward making its religious culture more genuinely *religious global*. Regarding the sources of innovation, sociologist James Jasper writes, "difference... may be crucial to creativity... Here is the key to innovation and social change: the biographical variation in feelings and visions on the part of individuals... the more there are from which to choose, the more likely we are to find some that do have wide appeal."[35] Despite the small number of religious minorities in New Sanctuary, there were at least a few among the core group of crossover actors, providing New Sanctuary activists with a greater variety of "feelings and visions" on which to draw in building more inclusive movement rituals, bolstering the potential for creativity.

Having learned more about the needs, interests, and cultures of religious minorities through their prior interactions within the New Sanctuary Movement, the core group of crossover activists used this limited knowledge to create a *more* inclusive (though still relatively Christian) religious culture, even in the continued absence of widespread religious diversity. They used three creative strategies for this, represented in the following stories by three different liturgies: (1) traditional (in this case, Christian) content combined with innovative form ("The Welcome Table"); (2) traditional (in this case, Christian) form combined with innovative content ("Desert Prayers"); and (3) traditional content and form from a minority religious tradition ("Kaddish Yatom/The Mourners' Kaddish").

The Welcome Table

The 70 people at the 2009 national gathering of the New Sanctuary Movement stand around round tables in a large room in Riverside Church as Mark,[36] an organizer, walks toward a table in the center of the room. Unlike the other tables in the room, which are mostly bare, this table is dressed with a flowing white tablecloth, champagne flutes, tall silver candlesticks, and china. It is set for four or five people, though there are no chairs around it. As he nears the table, he speaks into the microphone and says, "Someone describe this table for me." A couple of people hesitantly speak up, one saying "elegant" and another saying, "for a few." "Exactly!" he responds. "We have to deconstruct to transform," he continues, referring to the need to challenge the systems that keep immigrants down in order to move toward their full inclusion in society, both legally and religiously. He asks for some help as he walks up to the table and begins "deconstructing" the table by removing the champagne flutes and other table dressings. Two or three people come and help him—a young Latino man, a white woman in a wheelchair. They remove the fancier items and, as Mark explains excitedly, they "make it the People's Table, the Creator's Table!"

Holding up several different loaves of bread in his hands—a dark wheat, a braided challah, and a round, white loaf—he says this table will have no dishes, but it will have bread and room for all. He invites everyone to come and grab on to a piece of the white tablecloth. As people move toward the center of the room, it is clear that there is no way that 70 people will be able to get to the table and grab hold of the tablecloth. However, as the first few people grab on to it and step backward a bit so that others can move in, the tablecloth begins expanding, growing and growing into a gigantic circle of cloth reminiscent of the kinds of parachutes children played with in recess when I was young. Everyone fits around this tablecloth—there is indeed, surprisingly, room for all. Mark begins singing an old African American spiritual, gesturing for everyone else to join in:

> I'm gonna sit at the welcome table
> I'm gonna sit at the welcome table one of these days
> Hallelujah!
> I'm gonna sit at the welcome table
> Gonna sit at the welcome table one of these days

The lyrics of the song are somewhat repetitive and it has a simple melody, so soon everyone in the room is smiling and singing loudly. When the song winds down, Mark says into the microphone, "Here we have three different types of bread, representing three of our major religious traditions. Please pass the bread around and share a piece as we all share this table together." Passing around the loaves, people tear off small bites and chew contentedly as they make their way back to their seats (Figure 7.2).

Desert Prayers

On the final day of the 2009 national New Sanctuary gathering, participants gather in a small, chapel-like room in Riverside Church. Metal folding chairs are set up in an intimate circle surrounding a bare table. As people arrive and choose one of the seats, a member of Riverside plays the piano—a soft, beautiful tune called "You Have Come Down to the Lakeshore." A Latina woman sitting nearby spontaneously begins singing aloud in Spanish to the music, making it all the more beautiful and haunting.

Five people begin bringing items to the table, sent to the gathering by Flor Crisostomo, a woman living in sanctuary in the same church—Adalberto United Methodist Church (UMC)—where Elvira Arellano was in sanctuary prior to her deportation. As the group of 40 or so people watches, the group of

FIGURE 7.2 New Sanctuary activists gather around "The Welcome Table." (Photo by Tom N. Martinez.)

five leaders, including Liliana's husband, unfold a green tablecloth and smooth it on the table. On top of the table, they place a candle, a pitcher of water, an empty bowl, and a T-shirt printed with the words "One Family Under God," with the faces of Liliana and the other LA-area sanctuary families underneath.

When they are finished, a Latino activist rises and reads a prayer in Spanish, "Oración por los Migrantes." According to the worship sheet, it is read every morning during the Migrant Trail: Walk for Life, an annual 75-mile walk from Sásabe, Sonora, to Tucson, Arizona, "in solidarity with our migrant sisters and brothers who have walked this trail and lost their lives." The New Sanctuary coalition in Chicago also uses the prayer—it is prayed each Friday on buses carrying immigrants to be deported from Broadview Detention Center in Illinois.

Stacy,[37] a white activist in her 30s from Chicago, leads the service, saying, "Let's all remember Joe, who has a check-in this morning. We need to lift him up in our thoughts and prayers." She continues, saying, "We are called to move from being strangers to neighbors," asking that these prayers help to create that transformation. Another white woman in her 30s—Karen[38] from Portland— joins her, and everyone stands as the two women begin the first words of a call-and-response: "River of Life, who is known by many names; Over-turner and illuminator of hearts…" As they intone the words, "River of Life," they raise the pitcher of water, pouring it into the empty bowl on the table. It splashes loudly but soothingly in the quiet room. Following their words, everyone reads the response: "We gather with gratitude for the earth and all who journey in it. We give thanks for the interconnectedness of all creation." They continue:

ONE: Source of Justice, who is known by many names,
ALL: Let us not swerve from the path of righteousness
ONE: That leads to just and equitable relationships.
Open our eyes that we may see the immigrant and undocumented
ALL: Give us the will to become your living sanctuary
And claim our place in the movement to transform creation
That our voice, our heart, our spirit
Will join the voice, heart and spirit of all
Who demand to live with respect, justice, and peace.[39]

After the final line, the two women say together, "May it be so. Amen." Karen sits down, and Stacy begins reading a prayer in Spanish written by Flor, the sanctuary immigrant in Chicago with whom her coalition partners. As she reads the prayer, her voice breaks and she pauses, tears rolling down her cheeks. As people in the room watch, several of them begin to tear up as well. She wipes her eyes and continues reading again, more slowly this time. She finishes reading and, her face wet and flushed, sits in a nearby chair. A woman nearby passes her some tissue, and she mouths "thank you" as she wipes her face.

After a soloist sings a song, Karen stands again and shares her reflections on a delegation she led on the Mexican border earlier this year. "Since Operation Gatekeeper in 1994, 5,000 migrants have died in the desert," she says.[40] She tells the story of a woman she met in the desert, a migrant who told her, "We are all migrants from the moment we are born. The migrant's journey is our journey." While she is speaking, the lighted candle starts to smoke, black smoke pouring through the room. Several people look around, wondering what they should do. A few people start to laugh quietly, and finally someone moves over to the table and grabs the candle, taking it outside of the circle to put out the smoke. As she waves the smoke away from her face Karen jokes, "The spirit is filling the room," and everyone laughs.

After this moment of lightness, the mood grows solemn again. A prayer asks those present to acknowledge that "We are all part of your holy family" and to commit to "welcome the stranger in our midst not only because we were once strangers but because we are kin." After a pause, Stacy calls for "a time of remembrance and calling in the spirits of those who have died in the desert." Pablo,[41] a Latino activist from Oregon, reads the names of the 162 migrants who have been found dead in the Sonoran desert since April 2008. After each name, the group says together, "Presente!"—an act of remembrance common in Latin America, signifying the continued presence of those who have died. During the "calling of the names," the activists walk forward one by one, touching the water in the bowl on the table "that connects us all" before once again joining "the circle of unity."

It takes almost 15 minutes for all of the names to be read aloud, a powerful reminder of how many lives have been lost. Once the last name has been spoken, Stacy stands, pausing before she speaks. She says, "We're going to sing a final song together. Music is something that sustains us," she tells the group, asking them to join hands while they sing. Grabbing the hands of the people standing next to them, the group sings "We Shall Overcome" together, following in the footsteps of many activists before them.

Kaddish Yatom/The Mourner's Kaddish

On the second morning of the 2009 gathering, activists enter the large room at Riverside once again, some rubbing the sleep out of their eyes at this early hour. Mark, the leader of yesterday's Welcome Table liturgy, introduces a woman wearing all black and Birkenstock sandals, with very short gray hair and glasses. "This is Rabbi Rachel from Philadelphia,"[42] he says. "She is going to lead this morning's service, which is structured around services in the Jewish tradition." After an opening refrain, "Let my prayer rise before you as incense, the lifting of my hands as the morning sacrifice," based on Psalm 141, the 40 people present all sit in a big circle. Rabbi Rachel says, "It's a miracle that we are here, in body and in spirit. Stretch, feel how good it is to be in your body." People reach their arms into the air, yawns escaping their mouths as they twist their bodies. "Now close your eyes, and think about what you're especially grateful for," she says. As people shut their eyes, she begins to chant a blessing:

> Blessed are you, One God
> Life of all the world
> Who gives all of us so many things
> Blessed are you, One God
> Life of all the world
> For giving me…

As she finishes this last line, people call out the names of people and things for which they are grateful: family, open hearts, being part of the circle, meaningful work, community, this beautiful day. After each person speaks, she quietly chants "Amen." When no one else speaks up, she finishes, chanting, "We give thanks for all of these things and more. Together we all say, 'Amen.'" Everyone repeats, "Amen" as a chant.

Next, the group moves on to a more challenging task, at least for a room filled mostly with non-Jews. Together, everyone sings a line of Hebrew: "Elohay neshamah shenatata bi tehorah hi," which translated means, "My God, the soul you gave to me is pure." Rabbi Rachel begins the song first, chanting softly in a minor key. When people start to pick up the tune, they begin singing along. After repeating the song together for a couple of minutes, Rabbi Rachel switches to singing the same tune, but instead of words merely chanting "ya, dei, dei." Around the room, several people sing with their eyes closed, rocking back and forth slightly, losing themselves in the chanting.

After a couple of readings, the group comes to the next section of the program: a single line written in the Hebrew alphabet. Below, the English translation reads, "Listen Israel: THE ETERNAL is our God, THE ETERNAL ONE alone!" Rabbi Rachel tells the group, "This is one of the most important lines in the Jewish service. It is a call to listen, to hear the oneness of the universe, and of each other. When one hurts, all hurt. We realize it through love." She instructs everyone, "Take out the word Israel, and put in anyone you would like to have listen." People call out the names of people they wish would listen: Sherrif Joe Arpaio, Congress, denominational leaders, President Obama, Minutemen, their neighbors, ICE. She ends by chanting in Hebrew, then in English, "THE ETERNAL is our God, The entire world is one."

A woman starts playing the piano, a very soft, slow, peaceful jazz song. Its tune is quiet yet powerful and full of emotion. Several people sit with their head resting in their hands, thinking and reflecting. Mark puts his arm around Carolyn,[43] an activist who has worked closely with Liliana, and she begins to cry. Liliana has been in sanctuary now for over two years, and Carolyn grieves for the woman who is now a close friend. After the song, someone reads a poem that begins: "And then all that has divided us will merge/And then compassion will be wedded to power" and ends with "And then all will live in harmony with each other and the Earth/And then everywhere will be called Eden once again."[44]

Even after this poem of eschatological hope, there is a quiet, somber mood in the room. Rabbi Rachel moves on to the Kaddish Yatom, or The Mourners' Kaddish. She says, "Mourners say the Kaddish together to remember God's goodness, even in death and loss." She continues quietly, "The Jewish service ends with memory. After we say the kaddish, remember and speak the name of one who has died." She begins chanting in Hebrew: "Yitgadal veyitka-dash shemey raba…" People struggle to respond in Hebrew: "Yehey shemey raba mevarah le'alam ulalmey almaya." Rabbi Rachel continues to chant the kaddish until its close. When she finishes, silence fills the room, the silence as powerful as any of the words that have been spoken or sung. After a few moments, she looks up, smiling and with new energy and enthusiasm. She asks everyone to stand and to sing a final song together. The tune is simple, upbeat, and hopeful, and people join in, singing loudly and strongly. Rabbi Rachel claps with the beat, and soon everyone is joyfully clapping their hands together as they sing.

Compared with the 2007 gathering described earlier, by 2009 the New Sanctuary Movement had made genuine efforts to better live out their goal of becoming religious global, though they still had a long way to go. Each of these three liturgies moved beyond simply having leaders of multiple faiths present or using the language of God instead of more tradition-specific language (like references to Christ). The Welcome Table liturgy had content that was recognizably Christian—for instance, the song "The Welcome Table" comes from Christian tradition—while some aspects of the form were quite innovative, like the use of an expanding table. The Desert Prayers liturgy combined a more traditional Christian form—with songs, candles, the pouring of water (in Christian tradition, used as a reminder of baptism), and call-and-response prayers—with innovative content, such as connecting the water to migrants who have died in the desert rather than to baptism and the reading of migrants' names aloud. Finally, the Mourners' Kaddish was led by a rabbi, included prayers and a structure that were common in Jewish services, and included prayers in Hebrew. In content and form this liturgy was primarily Jewish. Yet by helping move Christians beyond their own religion's cultural dominance it felt more like an introduction to a shared religious liturgy than an imposition of a domineering content and form (Figure 7.3).

By this point in time, a core group of crossover activists had learned from past interactions with religious minorities, using their limited knowledge and creativity to develop a more religious global culture within New Sanctuary.[45] While these liturgies remained predominantly Christian, they also demonstrated efforts to reach out to and include religious minorities, efforts that allowed the New Sanctuary Movement to maintain its commitment to the goal of cultivating a globally inclusive religious vision. It provided a certain legitimacy, both internally and externally, that maintained the possibility of recruiting a larger number of religious minorities.

FIGURE 7.3. A New Sanctuary activist blows a shofar, used in Jewish tradition as a call to repentance and justice, at a street action marking the end of the 2009 national gathering. (Photo by Tom N. Martinez.)

This suggests that initial difficulties with recruiting single-institutional actors, like those revealed in Chapter 6, do not have to spell an end to multi-target social movements. When crossover actors remain committed to multiple targets, engagement in processes of learning and creativity may provide enough knowledge to allow the movement or movement organization to maintain its multiple commitments until it can recruit a larger number of single-institutional actors with the expertise and legitimacy they need. However, this situation cannot be sustained forever. The core group of crossover actors that give birth to a movement will likely eventually burn out.[46] By that time, there must be other activists to replace them, ones with deep investment in and knowledge about the institutions the movement or movement organization seeks to change.

Conclusion

Beyond mainline Protestants, liberal Catholics, and Reform Jews, there was little involvement from members of other religious traditions during the first two years of the New Sanctuary Movement. At the 2009 national gathering, one rabbi even pointed out that "no Muslims are at this gathering": even Shaykh Bashir was not present, as he had begun devoting his time to other activities that he felt were bigger priorities for him and his community. There had long been little to no evangelical involvement at the national level. The goal of building a religiously diverse coalition in the New Sanctuary Movement proved too challenging, at least during that period, making New Sanctuary's vision more focused on bringing into being the Christian "kingdom of God" than a more religiously inclusive eschatological realm.

But the commitment to religious change was kept alive, at least temporarily, by the interfaith commitments of a core group of crossover activists and their willingness to engage in processes of learning and creativity in reaching out to religious minorities and building an internally inclusive religious culture. For a truly religious global culture, whether within New Sanctuary or within the broader religious culture, activists needed to develop shared liturgies that not only had inclusive, innovative content and innovative forms but that also incorporated the embodied rituals and styles of multiple religious traditions. But to do this, they needed a larger number of members from these traditions to join, sharing their expertise on minority religious cultures and institutions, something New Sanctuary never fully achieved during its early years.

CONCLUSION

The scent of spicy food wafts through the air of the gymnasium at Riverside Church. Lunchtime has arrived on the first day of the 2009 national gathering, and a smorgasbord of beef with broccoli, garlic shrimp, noodles, and dumplings from Joe's restaurant tempt the activists, who pile food onto their plates before sitting back down at their tables. Before heading to the growing food line, I chat with two activists about the state of the New Sanctuary Movement two years after its launch, one from Chicago and one from Washington, D.C. Stacy,[1] the Chicago activist, admits, "Another immigrant rights activist in Chicago once told me that sanctuary is a bridge to nowhere." In Chicago, sanctuary has mostly taken a traditional form, with both Elvira and her sanctuary successor, Flor, living in the offices of Adalberto United Methodist Church.[2] Mark,[3] the D.C. activist, replies, "Well, we don't *want* to keep doing sanctuary, to incarcerate families."[4] Stacy elbows Mark: "But that's not the only definition of sanctuary," she exclaims, teasing him since he has often made that argument in the past. He chuckles, but says, "Yeah. But you know, that's not what was put out there at the beginning of the movement. It was the old kind of sanctuary." Stacy nods and says, "We need to keep putting it out there that we are communities of sanctuary and refuge, not buildings for people to live in."

After heading to the food table, I settle in beside two women, a national organizer and a New York activist. They are discussing the potential strength of "everyone doing different things in different places," of responding to local needs. They talk about the need to expand available options for how people can get involved and for who counts as a "sanctuary group." The national organizer says her local coalition stopped using the sanctuary pledge over a year ago. "If they're doing the work, they're sanctuary," she says. Gina,[5] the New York activist, has been working on Joe's case by meeting with staff at his congresswoman's office. She looks tired and heavy-laden when she talks about the work, saying she feels divided between being here at the gathering and needing to be off working on his case. "I mean, I need to get a better idea about what the *purpose* is of the national movement," she says.

After the national organizer leaves the table, she airs more of her frustration: "I'm sorry, but more and more I have clear opinions about things and that just leads to more conflict." I say that her comments earlier in the day about the need for concrete networking and plans for action seemed like good ideas. "But see—I don't understand why the national gatherings are so abstract and reflective," she says. "It feels too much like patting ourselves on the back." By now, Jean has come over to the table, and she asks him what he thinks the national organization should be doing. "We need funding and staff," he says with certainty, between bites of beef with broccoli. "And we really need a sense of urgency," he says. Gina nods in agreement. He mentions all of the small, storefront churches in the outer boroughs of the city, saying, "We need them. That's where the immigrants are." "And the Catholics," adds Juan Carlos, sitting down with his plate of food and joining in the conversation.

Gina mentions a meeting they have tomorrow about working with the U.S. Department of Homeland Security, but Juan Carlos and Jean both shake their heads, as if to say they don't think this will do much good. Gina continues, "How we could make this movement really stand out from the immigrant rights movement is to connect it to wider prison justice issues." "Talk about bringing brown and black together!" Juan Carlos responds. Jean adds, "Yeah, but we really need someone to take charge nationally. Leaders and followers. They're both important roles, but we need someone to lead." I point to him, and everyone at the table smiles. Jean says, "Yeah, but it's a lot of risk and sacrifice. Juan Carlos has wanted me to be the leader, but I don't have the power." Juan Carlos says, "Yeah, but now people in Congress know you. They will listen to you." Gina smiles, shakes her head, and mumbles, "Troublemaker..." The tired faces around the table break into laughter.

As the New Sanctuary Movement entered its third year in late 2009, its membership still lacked the religious and ethnic diversity it hoped for and needed, though as the last chapter showed, committed activists continued working hard to increase a sense of inclusion and openness in New Sanctuary that might help them recruit other participants. At the same time, as this story suggests, sanctuary as identity, strategy, tactic, and even moniker was becoming increasingly contested. The national New Sanctuary Movement was dwindling, with activists becoming more deeply involved with local causes, many of which had little to do with sanctuary—including in places like Los Angeles that were central to organizing New Sanctuary in its early days. In what follows, I explain these transitions, including what these changes reveal about multi-target social movements and their likely trajectories.

Shifting Contexts

By fall 2009, religious and political contexts in the United States had changed significantly compared to late 2006 and early 2007, when the New Sanctuary Movement began taking shape and articulating its goals and strategies. In many ways, the religious landscape had become less contested, for three primary reasons: (1) the 2008 election of Barack Obama as president of the United States; (2) the declining emphasis in the United States on the so-called War on Terror, including the wars in Iraq and Afghanistan; and (3) the lack of emergence of a national religious movement against immigrant rights. On the other hand, many recent immigration reforms had created a more hostile, threatening political climate for immigrants and their partners.

The Religious Context

From 2000 to 2008, the presidency of George W. Bush became a symbol of the power and authority of the religious right. Very public about his evangelical faith as the source of his conservative politics, President Bush was adored by the religious right as much as he was disliked by many religious people who were not conservative, people who claimed he distorted the core values of religion through his administration's war making, use of torture, and implementation of economic policies they believed favored the wealthy.[6]

During the 2008 presidential election cycle, Barack Obama emerged as a candidate that was both public about his Christian faith and theologically and politically progressive, a clear alternative to the type of public religiosity embodied by both Bush and his supporters. And while Obama's association with Rev. Jeremiah Wright and black liberation theology was controversial among many Americans, his refusal to entirely disown Wright and his theology was a victory for religious Americans who saw their own religious visions reflected in these more progressive religious traditions. Obama's election as president in 2008 was a triumph not only for Democrats but also for religious people hoping to challenge the dominance of the religious vision popularized by the religious right.

At the same time, by 2009 eight years had passed since the 9/11 attacks and the official start of the War on Terror and the related wars in Iraq and

Afghanistan. These wars created a revival of religious nationalism, with the United States once again depicted as divinely blessed compared to other nations,[7] who were often compared with satanic forces in national political and religious language, embodied in the use of terms like "Axis of Evil" to refer to North Korea, Iran, and Iraq. Similarly, support among many religious groups for the wars (despite the harm they would cause to people in other nations), the proliferation of calls to "pray for our troops," and the frequent use of the phrase "God bless America" made some religious leaders increasingly uncomfortable and even angry, leading people like the New Sanctuary activists to push for a more religious global perspective and practice.[8] But by 2009, these wars and the religious support behind them had moved to the background of the American consciousness, both because of a degree of stabilization in the conflicts and because of the economic recession that captured much of the public imagination at the time.

Finally, an important achievement of the New Sanctuary Movement by 2009 was that they may have played at least a small role, as one of many religious immigrant rights organizations in the United States, in making the public religious voice on immigration a progressive religious voice, one that sought broader inclusion of immigrants rather than tighter controls on immigration.[9] Though it did not receive overwhelming attention from the media, New Sanctuary was covered in several national news outlets, many local newspaper and television stories, and religious media outlets.[10] While at least one major national anti-immigration organization attempted to popularize a religious anti-immigrant perspective,[11] it was not taken up by any activist group associated with the religious right. In media stories, while "the other side"—supporters for tighter immigration controls—were often cited, it was typically a secular anti-immigrant group rather than a religious voice that was presented.[12] In the rare case when a religious anti-immigrant view was offered, it was almost always by one person representing a denomination's supposed position on the issue rather than any type of religious movement or movement organization for tighter immigration controls.[13] As of this writing, this remains true, with some religious leaders and groups strongly associated with the religious right, such as Focus on the Family and former Southern Baptist Convention leader Richard Land, taking more *pro-immigration* positions by publicly supporting comprehensive immigration reform.[14] To summarize, by the 2009 gathering no organized public voice had emerged that represented a religious movement on the right offering a position that countered that of the New Sanctuary Movement and other religious immigrant rights organizations, such as the Catholic Justice for Immigrants campaign, No More Deaths, and Humane Borders.[15]

This should not imply that New Sanctuary itself created these changes in the religious context. The first two changes were clearly out of activists' control. But by joining its voice with other religious immigrant rights organizations, the early mobilization of New Sanctuary, its explicitly interfaith identity, and its public development of a pro-immigrant theology may have made it more difficult for people against immigrant rights to successfully mobilize in an explicitly religious way. With both the religious right and religious nationalism holding less sway in the public conversation, the need for religious conversion and transformation no longer existed to the same degree. While most religious communities remained segregated by ethnicity and national origin and the religious right's view of religion remained dominant, the decrease in religious threats to progressive religious people made the religious goals of the New Sanctuary Movement less urgent.

The Political Context

In contrast, as of 2009 the political context was even more urgent than in 2007, both in the case of the sanctuary families themselves and in the national immigration context. By September 2009, Liliana had been living in sanctuary for over two years, as had the other three immigrants living in churches in the Los Angeles area. As Karen and Mark's conversation suggests, activists were increasingly concerned about families being stuck in church buildings, with no end in sight. While the New York coalition had recently scored a victory, with one of its sanctuary family members being granted asylum, most of the New York families' cases were still in limbo or had worsened.

On the national level, the failure of Comprehensive Immigration Reform (CIR) efforts in summer 2007 and the inability of immigrant rights activists to revive these efforts provided activists with little hope for national policy change. For a few early activists and the foundations funding them, sanctuary was meant largely as a short-term effort to achieve CIR, making it unviable as soon as CIR failed. However, as I have shown throughout this book, many activists had more long-term visions when they began organizing the national New Sanctuary Movement, recognizing from the beginning that sanctuary had limited potential for creating short-term political changes like passing CIR. According to this vision, sanctuary might have been "a bridge to nowhere" for short-term political change but not necessarily for other activist goals of long-term political and religious change.

Though the 2008 election of Barack Obama as U.S. president revived some activists' hopes that political change might be possible, many realized that a new president would not be able to make sweeping changes right away. With national reform stymied, state and local officials began considering their own immigration reforms, often much harsher than national policies. And the anti-immigrant practices of local law enforcement officers drew increasing attention, such as dramatically increasing arrest quotas for ICE Fugitive Operations Teams and Sherriff Joe Arpaio's alleged racial profiling of immigrants in Arizona.[16]

The increasing political threats and decreasing religious ones, coupled with a continuing lack of immigrant participants, led New Sanctuary activists to rethink their targets and associated identities, strategies, and tactics. In this environment, sanctuary no longer seemed as appealing. And since the national network's unity and identity was rooted in sanctuary—the source of its uniqueness—the glue holding it together was being called into question as well.

These shifts help explain the informal conversations at the 2009 gathering relayed at the beginning of this chapter. Activists were increasingly questioning both the utility of sanctuary, with its religious symbolism and fit to religious goals, as well as the purpose of working together nationally as opposed to focusing on their own local contexts and the families in their midst. By the time of the 2009 gathering, most of the activists involved in the Los Angeles New Sanctuary coalition had largely moved on to other strategies and tactics, even as the coalition's sanctuary families were still living in local churches. And while the New York coalition retained the moniker of New Sanctuary in its work, its tactical focus had already begun moving in different directions, changes that continued to a large degree in the coming years.

Activists Respond: Changes in the New Sanctuary Coalition of NYC

My primary time in the field lasted from 2007 to 2009. However, several important changes occurred in the years following 2009, necessitating some updates on New Sanctuary. Coalition emails, informal conversations with activists, news coverage, website updates, and field notes from the New York coalition's 2010 and 2011 annual retreats provided me with a rough sketch of some of the changes occurring in New Sanctuary after 2009, especially in the New York coalition.

First, while some New Sanctuary activists hoped that the Obama administration would turn to CIR after overcoming the obstacle of passing health-care legislation, by fall 2010 it was clear that this was not going to happen during his first term. Though Obama received praise from some immigration activists for his 2012 statement in support of DREAMers, there were few opportunities for wide-reaching policy change at the national level.[17] However, directly following President Obama's reelection in November 2012, New Sanctuary activists anticipated that CIR would be on the table again in 2013 (which, as of this writing, still looks like a good possibility), which may shift New Sanctuary's focus again toward the national.

While little changed in the years directly following 2009 on the national front, the political context at the state level shifted drastically. In 2010, the state legislature of Arizona passed a controversial law seeking to eradicate undocumented immigration.[18] The Support Our Law Enforcement and Safe Neighborhoods Act (SB 1070), passed in April 2010, instructed local police not only to cooperate with federal immigration agents but also to engage in their own attempts to reveal the status of people living in the state without papers. A particularly controversial aspect of the legislation empowered local police to stop any cars whose drivers "look illegal"—critics argued that this is merely a legalization of racial profiling.

In the wake of the passage of the Arizona law, several other states began campaigns to approve similar legislation, including Indiana, Georgia, and Florida. By 2011, a law widely regarded as even harsher than Arizona SB 1070 passed in Alabama—the Hammon-Beason Alabama Taxpayer and Citizen Protection Act (HB 56).[19] The law enshrined such strict measures that, in response to the bill, a group of Alabama clergy sued the state, claiming that "the Law will prohibit members of these mainstream congregations from being able to freely practice their faith to minister to all of God's children without regard to immigration status."[20] Similar to Cardinal Mahony's argument about the Sensebrenner Bill, they contended that ministering to people in need was central to their religious practice and that having to ask for people's papers before doing so would amount to an infringement of their religious liberties.

At the same time, the national "Secure Communities" program gained prominence through its continued implementation on the state and local levels.[21] Designed to provide incentives to local law enforcement for cooperating with ICE, it arguably conflicted with existing "sanctuary city" ordinances in some places.[22] For instance, New York City's Executive Order 41 made it illegal for local police to ask people for proof of their immigration status, arguing that cooperation between federal and local officials actually makes communities less secure. This is because undocumented immigrants will be less likely to report crimes if they fear that police will discover their immigration status, a situation that can increase rather than decrease local problems with crime. But as a state-level program, Secure Communities has the potential to override local orders like New York City's Executive Order 41, creating further danger for undocumented immigrants seeking to avoid deportation. In summer 2011, New York's governor Andrew Cuomo opted out of the Secure Communities program, considered by some to be a major victory for groups like the New Sanctuary Movement, despite it being unclear exactly what opting out of the program would mean. But in other parts of the country and in New York, major threats to undocumented immigrants remained.

While immigration policies were becoming increasingly threatening, the New York coalition also faced two more concrete threats. First, sanctuary immigrant Jean was suddenly and unexpectedly detained by ICE around the start of 2010, leaving his wife and children devastated and alone. This gave birth to the Bring Jean Home campaign,[23] which gained national media attention and provided New Sanctuary activists with an increased sense of political urgency—ironically, just what Jean said they needed in the 2009 story that opened this chapter (Figure 8.1).[24] New York activists shifted their focus almost entirely to partnering with other local immigrant rights groups to advocate for Jean's release, committing civil disobedience in front of the Varick Street Detention Center that had become a regular site for coalition vigils.[25]

FIGURE 8.1 New Sanctuary activists join Jean's wife and son in demanding his release from detention in early 2010. (Photo by Mizue Aizeki.)

Jean was detained for weeks, transported to a prison in Pennsylvania, and almost deported to Haiti, as his family and supporters desperately sought information on his status and whereabouts. Just before his scheduled deportation, a major disaster struck Haiti: a catastrophic earthquake that killed more than 200,000 people.[26] While the earthquake was a tragedy for his birthplace, it was paradoxically a reprieve for Jean himself. Since he could not be deported to a country in the midst of devastation, Jean was returned to his family in New York—but without any guarantee that the same thing would not happen again in the future.[27] Second, having run out of legal appeals, Patty, the NYC sanctuary immigrant married to a U.S. citizen named Jarrett, received a final deportation order, choosing to voluntarily leave the United States for Guatemala a few days later so she could take their infant child along with her.

Thus, between the time of the September 2009 national gathering and the New Sanctuary Coalition of NYC's annual retreat in September 2010, political threats had only increased, especially on the state and local levels. Facing little opportunity nationally and rising threats locally, by fall 2011 the New Sanctuary Movement shifted from a national network of movement organizations with both political and religious targets to a very loose network of local coalitions with primarily political targets. Related to these changes, the identity, strategy, and tactics of these coalitions moved away from sanctuary and toward family unity and immigrant advocacy more broadly.[28]

As part of this shift, in March 2010 the New York coalition hired a new local organizer—an undocumented immigrant. They started a new program called the Jericho Walk that combined religious and political imagery in a weekly march outside of the ICE headquarters at Federal Plaza, but the walk was geared toward political, not religious, change.[29] At the same time, the coalition's leadership was increasingly moving from a steering committee model that included leaders from a variety of congregations to an advisory committee model that included a small number of elected leaders and staff. As a result, some of the religious leaders and congregations that had played a central role in the coalition's past began playing more marginal roles, backgrounding the coalition's religious aims.[30]

When I attended the 2010 New Sanctuary Coalition of NYC retreat, there was noticeably less discussion of sanctuary and of religion, as this vignette demonstrates: As I arrive at Judson Church around 7 p.m., I discover a table with piles of retreat agendas and information packets on the New Sanctuary Coalition of NYC, which still identifies itself as part of the national New Sanctuary Movement. On the front of the packet is the new logo from last year, with two hands joined around a heart. But this year, rather than "Radical Welcome," the theme of the meeting is "Year of Change." Downstairs, people are meeting in one of the larger meeting rooms at Judson, one where most of the steering committee meetings took place during my study.

Metal folding chairs are set up in rows facing the front of the room, where Jean stands and gives an update on his family. The room is full, with around 40 people present—not bad for a weeknight. While there are definitely clergy collars around the room, at least half of the people appear to be laypeople. I later learn that around 10 are immigrants, suggesting that more immigrants are involved now than there were formerly. On the other hand, there is little religiously diversity. While Rabbi Michael Feinberg is here, I recognize no other Jewish or Muslim attendees.

The new coalition organizer stands after Jean finishes his update. Tall and broad-shouldered, with a long black ponytail touched with hints of gray, he immigrated to the United States from Trinidad. He tells the people in the room, "We need you there [at our immigration check-ins] because ICE is nicer. They would be nastier if you weren't there." He talks about his own case for a moment, lifting up his ankle to show everyone the ankle bracelet he has to wear as part of ISAP, and people around the room gasp and shake their heads. After he speaks, organizer Angad Bhalla comes to the front. He wears a navy blue T-shirt and cargo pants, his black hair pulled back in a long ponytail. He sets up a TV in the front of the room for the screening of the new documentary film he just finished making. He says the goal of the documentary is to help not only the sanctuary families but also all mixed-status families because they recognize that this is a problem affecting many people. He mentions the ICE out of Rikers campaign as one way they are trying to address that, calling it one of "our main campaigns," and the documentary film focuses on the stories of immigrants at Rikers.

After the film, a white man raises his hand and reminds everyone that the DREAM Act is up for a vote and that it could help one of the immigrants in the video, who is a student at a local college. "We need a sense of optimism," he says. Picking up on his lead, another activist says that "Rikers has made some changes" in response to their ongoing campaign to force ICE agents to identify themselves to inmates at the local jail. Now, ICE agents must wear uniforms, whereas before they could just wear plainclothes and trick immigrants into thinking they were lawyers. Also, now immigrants must sign a consent form before correctional officers will take them to see ICE. A young, white male around 30 from a secular immigrant rights organization in New York comes to the front next, saying they have worked with the New

Sanctuary Movement on the ICE out of Rikers campaign and want to invite coalition members to join them in an upcoming march to put pressure on local law enforcement to stop collaborating with ICE.

At this point, Rev. Schaper comes to the front of the room. Tonight's guest of honor, Rev. John Fife, the founder of the 1980s Sanctuary Movement introduced in Chapter 2, has arrived. He comes to the front of the room, wearing a very similar outfit to the one he wore at last year's national gathering: a button-down shirt, jeans, and a large belt buckle. He says Rev. Schaper told him to "say something religious and something from the Southwest." But he talks about human rights law more than he talks explicitly about religion, and he mentions sanctuary only rarely in his speech.

From Multiple to Single Targets

By the 2010 retreat, the New Sanctuary Coalition of NYC had indeed begun a "year of change." While mentions of religion and sanctuary were still present, they were much less central than they once were. But by the following year's retreat in 2011, the coalition had become even more political, no longer focusing on recruiting congregations as part of its main strategy.[31] Other than the coalition's name and history, there was no discussion of sanctuary as identity, strategy, or tactic on its website.[32] The 2011 retreat focused almost entirely on political campaigns such as the ICE out of Rikers campaign, with a ceremony honoring the New York University lawyers who had helped achieve victories in that area. Fewer clergy were present at the retreat than in years past, and only one of the sanctuary families was present. However, more immigrants were present than in past years, and the coalition had begun accompanying several undocumented immigrants who were not part of mixed-status families, expanding the types of immigrants with whom they were working. Likewise, fewer than five members of the original coalition steering committee and organizers were present, signifying a shift away from the core group of crossover activists and their commitment to multiple targets of change.

While its practices had not completely changed—the coalition still focused on volunteers accompanying immigrants to their check-ins, for example—these were no longer intimate, long-term partnerships between select immigrant families and congregations. They were no longer framed in terms of sanctuary and were less often discussed in religious terms. At the 2011 retreat, one long-term coalition member, who had seen the coalition through many changes, explained to me: "The model has been shifting. Before, families were tied to a congregation. Now, we are still focused on family. But for change, we need a lot more faces. That's what grassroots movements have to do—change to grow. Some people aren't happy about that. It's hard to let go of the old models."

These shifts in the New Sanctuary Coalition of NYC do not merely represent a change in strategies and tactics, which research shows are difficult to weather in and of themselves.[33] Rather, New Sanctuary appears to be undergoing a process of change not only in strategies and tactics but also targets, associated goals, and even identity. It is transitioning from a multi-target social movement with political and religious targets into a single-target social movement focused solely on changing the state, though using religious framing and including religious participants.

These changes are not unique to the New Sanctuary Coalition of NYC, though the shifts taking place have varied in different coalitions. In Los Angeles, while a few immigrant–congregation partnerships remain, the coalition has long since moved away from a focus on the identity, tactic, and even moniker of sanctuary. Part of this change paralleled a major victory in Liliana's case in 2010: she was granted deferred action that allowed her to move back home with her husband and children, at least temporarily.[34] However, this occurred after the Los Angeles coalition began moving away from a focus on sanctuary, not before. Similarly, one of the first coalitions in the New Sanctuary Movement—the Kansas City coalition, where one of the group's national paid organizers was located for a time—no longer uses the language or model of sanctuary, calling itself the Immigrant Justice Advocacy Movement.[35] However, the New York coalition is not the only local coalition maintaining the moniker of sanctuary, if not the practice of it. For example, as of this writing, local coalitions in Philadelphia and Boston still call themselves sanctuary coalitions, even as their strategies and tactics have shifted away from the use of sanctuary partnerships, whether physical or otherwise.[36]

These updates on the New Sanctuary Movement provide two additional insights about multi-target social movements. First, multi-target movements may change into something more closely resembling a single-target movement over time. This may be a particularly likely trajectory for this type of movement or movement organization, as the delicate balance discussed in Chapters 5, 6, and 7 is difficult to achieve and sustain.[37] Second, multiple targets may be especially likely in the initial stages of a social movement or movement organization, when activists are still attempting to define its focus and when they may be at their most energetic and optimistic regarding their ability to achieve change. In fact, it may be the case that all multi-target movements eventually morph into single-target movements over time, especially if their distinct goals require strategies and tactics that conflict in practice.

Toward a Theory of Multi-target Social Movements

In the foregoing pages of this book, I introduced the concept of the multi-target social movement, defining it and distinguishing it from other types of social movements and movement organizations. The insights emerging from the New Sanctuary Movement provide a rough foundation for a research agenda on multi-target social movements, producing hypotheses about how and why they differ from other movements and movement organizations that can offer a fuller understanding of movement diversity and complexity.

First, multi-target social movements appear more likely to emerge in times and places in which a group of crossover actors perceives new opportunities or threats in multiple institutional contexts simultaneously, prompting them to build a movement or movement organization seeking to respond to all of these shifts at once. I hypothesize that multi-target social movements will emerge *less frequently* than other types of social movements though not necessarily *infrequently*, since many institutions are overlapping and nested and therefore change in relation to each other.[38] This pattern will vary according to the types of institutions being targeted. For instance, because of religion's focus on transcendence and divine purpose, shifts in the religious context may be interpreted as divine calls to action, potentially making it easier to mobilize multi-target social movements that include religion as a target compared to other kinds of multi-target social movements.

Second, decision-making about strategies and tactics will also differ in multi-target social movements, since activists targeting multiple institutional arenas for change will be more inclined to seek crossover strategies that will be appropriate fits for changing multiple targets at once. I hypothesize that the process of strategy selection in multi-target social movements will be longer and more contested than in other movements or movement organizations, since fewer crossover strategies exist. However, I also hypothesize that a genuinely fitting crossover strategy can produce a greater degree of change in each institutional arena being targeted by a multi-target social movement than would have been created in a single-target movement. Because actors in single-target movements must select strategies and tactics from their own cultural tool kits, ones that will resonate with their institutional contexts, these strategies also run the danger of merely replicating existing institutional models rather than challenging them, particularly if the activists involved are part of the institutions they seek to change.[39] In contrast, because they contain multiple symbols and ideas, crossover strategies have the potential to resonate in multiple institutional arenas while also bringing innovative symbols and ideas to each of those arenas, creating the potential for crossover strategies to both resonate with and simultaneously challenge the rules of the game in each institutional arena being targeted.

Third, even more than other movements and movement organizations, multi-target social movements must devise careful, intentional tactics for attracting new members, since a delicate balance of crossover actors and single-institutional actors is necessary for maintaining focus on multiple targets. The adoption of crossover strategies can throw a wrench into these efforts, since single-institutional actors may find crossover strategies less resonant and less fitting for their needs. However, a core, committed group of crossover actors engaging in processes of learning and creativity can respond to these challenges, maintaining a sense of openness and responsiveness that may ultimately attract more single-institutional actors. Related to this, I hypothesize that multi-target social movements will be more likely than other movements and movement organizations to develop innovative ways of framing causes and engaging with outsiders (whether effective or not), since creativity is essential to attracting involvement from such a diverse group of actors.

Finally, the case of the New Sanctuary Movement suggests that over time multi-target social movements are likely to turn into something more like a single-target movement, given the challenges of transitioning from an initial group of crossover actors to a balanced group of single-institutional actors. Nascent social movement organizations may be especially likely to have multiple targets, though as they grow and change they may be forced to choose between their targets, either consciously or otherwise.

Most of these insights emerged from the case of the New Sanctuary Movement inductively and are hypotheses to be tested using other cases rather than conclusive statements about the way multi-target social movements work. Future research should explore these issues through the examination of present-day movements and movement organizations as well as through applying this theoretical lens to the analysis of older movements and movement organizations. This approach could even reveal new insights about the most commonly studied social movements.

Take, for example, the Civil Rights Movement. While most accounts of the Civil Rights Movement recognize the centrality of religious actors and religious discourse to the movement's mobilization and eventual success, they also almost exclusively emphasize the movement's state targets.[40] Of course, expanding African American legal and political rights was an urgent and completely sufficient goal. But the perspective I have advanced in this book raises the question: was the state in fact the movement's only target? If not, how might that change interpretations of the movement's emergence, decision-making, internal and external conflicts, and eventual successes?

A cursory examination of the statements and actions of movement leaders suggests that some could have been targeting religion as well as the state for change. In his seminal work *The Origins of the Civil Rights Movement*, sociologist Aldon Morris briefly discusses the Southern Christian Leadership Conference's goal of "refocusing black religion" through "revivals" that emphasized revolutionary religious themes in black Christianity over the more common theological focus on comfort in the next life.[41] Martin Luther King Jr.'s famous 1963 "Letter From Birmingham Jail" was addressed directly to clergy and, to a great extent, challenged his fellow clergy's views on religion and morality rather than solely making arguments for political change.[42]

King saw religious transformation in both black and white churches as necessary for political change, but that does not mean he and other leaders did not also seek religious change as an important end in and of itself, an aim that may have guided their strategic decisions and actions. In his doctoral dissertation in theology, King engaged in a battle over religious ideas, opposing his own ideas about God's relationship to humanity with those of popular theologians of the day, suggesting an early investment in challenging dominant religious authority.[43] In his book *The Beloved Community*, religion scholar Charles Marsh argues that many civil rights leaders were invested in religious and spiritual transformation as well as political change and that scholars and activists have ignored this history.[44] A multi-target social movements approach might systematically examine whether some Civil Rights activists did, in fact, have multiple targets for change, a question that would require researchers to look for evidence of other targets and to ask how having additional targets might change dominant interpretations of the movement.

For example, sociologist Doug McAdam discusses how changes in the southern black church between 1931 and 1954—an increase in the average size of black congregations and a shift away from otherworldly theological orientations—made it possible for civil rights organizing to occur. However, he does not interpret these changes as representing shifts in the religious context or religious opportunities but as changes in organizational capacity to provide resources for political organizing.[45] If instead we thought about these changes as responses to or causes of shifts in the power and authority of certain religious ideas and institutions, what kinds of new data would that require us to gather, and what kinds of insights might we gain about how movements emerge and the dilemmas they face?

Regarding religious context, sociologist Robert Wuthnow has argued that the decades following the end of World War II (the years leading up to the Civil Rights Movement) were ones of upheaval for America's religious institutions.[46] Just as the war disrupted traditional practices in many arenas of American society, religious institutions faced shortages in trained clergy, a lack of building materials for church renovations, and declines in contributions from members during the war. Many saw the war as a "rite of passage from adolescence to maturity" for American Christianity,[47] adopting an openness to change regarding the postwar future of the church. Wuthnow writes, "Clergy were admonished to regain the apostolic vision of what the church could become, to quit tradition, to be imaginative, and to support the great causes that needed their attention."[48]

While Wuthnow mobilizes these data to highlight how they led to a decline in denominationalism, movement scholars might analyze the ways this new religious flexibility created openings in the religious institutional context that would allow for the emergence of a movement of black churches challenging not only political marginalization and societal segregation but also the segregation of religious institutions and the traditional theological understandings of God and of humanity that upheld this segregation. Perhaps the movement would not have emerged without these shifts in the religious context and related hopes of changing the dominant religious vision. If the Civil Rights Movement did target religion to a greater extent than has been recognized in past analyses, this might change our understandings not only of the factors leading to its emergence but also of its decisions about strategies and tactics, the types of coalitions it formed, its trajectory, and its consequences. An approach that recognizes the possibility that movements have multiple targets for change shifts our focus, asking us to look for different kinds of data and different kinds of explanations for seemingly familiar events.

Religious Change and Multi-target Social Movements

The case of the New Sanctuary Movement also provides several insights that challenge trends in the study of religion and activism more specifically.[49] First, it challenges an exclusive focus on religion as an independent variable exerting influence on social movement activism. While religion often shapes social movements in important ways, certain social movement organizations also seek to shape religion by challenging existing religious power and authority structures. In such cases, the focus regarding the relationship between religion and activism shifts from how and why religion shapes social movements to whether, how, and why social movements shape religion as a *dependent variable*. As such, the study of religion and social movements can contribute more substantially to conversations about religious contestation and religious change.

Melissa Wilde's book *Vatican II* is an important example of what studies of religion and social movements can contribute if they focus not only on how religion shapes movements but also on how movements shape religion.[50] Her examination of social movement organizations at the Second Vatican Council demonstrates how and why activists were able to create significant changes in the oldest and most powerful religious institution in the world. Still, these movement organizations were intrainstitutional rather than multi-target, leaving room for further elucidation of how having multiple targets—only one of which is religious—might change the ways movement activism matters for religious change. How do multi-target movements' efforts at religious change differ from those of movements whose sole focus is on religious transformation? Further, how do movement attempts to create religious change differ from other types of religious change?

A focus on movement attempts to create religious change might improve theories of religious change by expanding the conversation about religious change beyond debates over secularization and theories of religious markets. Instead, a multi-target social movements approach focuses attention on the ways that religious people and their allies contest existing religious authority, making religious change less about *quantities* (i.e., growth or decline in members of certain religious traditions) and more about *qualities* (i.e., changes in the form, content, and characteristics of various religious traditions). Sometimes, social movement organizations form with the goal of challenging existing religious authority, hoping to change the qualities of religion that dominate in a particular public or institutional setting. While no movement is free of obstacles, multi-target movements may paradoxically fare better than single-target movements in changing religion due to their expanded cultural tool kits and the ways these repertoires can aid them in changing religious institutions rather than merely replicating them or being absorbed by them, as Tricia Bruce predicts for intrainstitutional social movements.[51]

In addition to highlighting the importance of religion as a dependent variable, this book matters for research on religion and activism in a second way. In recent years, research and theorizing on religion's relationship to movement activism has fallen victim to an overall trend of focusing on culture as a resource for activism while neglecting its role as constraint,[52] with virtually all research on the topic focusing on religion as a "resource" for mobilization.[53] A few studies have pointed out how religion can constrain movement activism,[54] but most have focused on religion's enabling role. David Smilde and Matthew May criticize their fellow sociologists of religion for tending to stress religion's beneficial characteristics for society in general.[55]

This trend has led to a neglect of the ways religion can limit activism, not only in the way Karl Marx recognized (by discouraging people from challenging injustice to begin with) but also by exerting influences that limit the ability of movement organizations to grow, diversify, and thrive.[56] How and why does religion sometimes enable, but sometimes constrain, social movement activism? In particular, how might this happen in multi-target social movements compared to state-centered groups or intrainstitutional social movements geared toward changing religious institutions?

The case of the New Sanctuary Movement suggests that, compared with single-target movements, in multi-target movements religious mechanisms are not either resources *or* constraints; they do not merely operate as a resource under some circumstances but a constraint under others. Rather, a particular religious mechanism can simultaneously operate as both resource and constraint. In New Sanctuary, religious identities and strategies served as a resource for its religious goals while also constraining its attempts to change public policy. In contrast, in single-target movements, religious identities and strategies will be more likely to either help or hinder the group's ability to change its target. In these ways and others, a theory of multi-target social movements can expand not only social movement studies but also ideas about religious change and religion's influence on public life.

The New Sanctuary Movement, Immigration Politics, and Religion in Public Life

The New Sanctuary Movement confirms that native-born religious activists are interested in immigrant rights. Many are deeply concerned about what they see as an increasingly harsh political and cultural environment for immigrants in the United States. They feel called by their religious beliefs to create more accepting, compassionate policies and communities. In some ways, they are using religion as a resource to create this kind of change. Along with other accounts of religious activists working for immigrant rights,[57] the case of the New Sanctuary Movement demonstrates that immigrant rights activism can draw strength from American religious traditions and institutions.

But New Sanctuary activists and others who see immigration as a religious issue remain a minority. And while religion has the potential to be a powerful force for immigrant rights activism, in some ways religion constrained New Sanctuary's political goals because of its at times competing goals of religious change. Religion's effects on immigrant rights activism therefore appear to depend on the specifics of the concrete context rather than religion always clearly being a benefit or a limitation for changing immigration policy. This complicates the picture provided in other accounts of religious immigrant rights activism, which have primarily highlighted the ways religion provides resources for immigrant rights activists.[58]

While the case of New Sanctuary demonstrates the complexities involved in multi-target movements that target both the state and religion, this should not be taken by activists and religious leaders to mean that religious targets should never be combined with political ones. Having multiple targets does complicate things like strategic decision-making and processes of activist recruitment, potentially resulting in more serious dilemmas than those faced by other movements and movement organizations. But as I have argued, in the right circumstances a crossover strategy might actually be more effective than strategies that target only one institutional arena. And multi-target movements may be especially likely to build new relationships between previously unconnected groups of activists or to produce innovations in strategy, tactics, and cultural forms.

This potential for bridge building and innovation may be especially important as the United States becomes increasingly global. The New Sanctuary Movement shows that one way immigration is changing religious activism in the United States is by pushing religious people to reach across divides that have often separated them, such as differences in religious, ethnic, and national background. The growing numbers and relative power of immigrants in the U.S. religious landscape encourages activists to build new kinds of interethnic and interfaith coalitions, both for political and religious reasons. In this context, distinctions between religious progressives and religious conservatives may become even less clear, as more evangelical Protestants join coalitions that include Muslims, liberal Protestants, and Jews.

New Sanctuary shows that the line dividing religion from politics remains contested in the United States, perhaps even more so in the context of the new immigration and the accompanying diversification in understandings of the appropriate relationship between religion and the state. The New Sanctuary Movement demonstrates that when religious people participate in public life explicitly as religious people, their actions often have relevance beyond the specific political issue at hand. Whether intentionally or not, when religious people engage in activism, their actions are also public representations of what it means to be religious. These representations then shape religious people's self-understandings, those of their religious communities, and broader societal understandings of what it means to be a religious citizen. Should battles over what it means to be religious take place in the public sphere? Should religious citizens make their religious identities and religious reasons explicit in their activism, or should they merely allow their religious beliefs to influence their participation in otherwise secular political endeavors? And what are the implications of major shifts in religious understanding, such as a move from civil religion to religious globalism or from more conservative to more progressive forms of religious authority, for the democratic public sphere?

While some political theorists have argued that religious reasons are best left to the private sphere,[59] contending that only rational, secular reasons can be understood by all members of society and therefore only they should form a basis for democratic deliberation, less attention has been paid to the latent functions of the use of explicitly religious reasons and identities in public. When religious people use religious reasons in the public sphere, they are not only trying to win people over to their particular political position—at times, they are also attempting to define and argue over what it means to be religious in the first place. Perhaps all members of society, secular people included, should have an interest in who wins the battle over what it means to be religious. While in the short run New Sanctuary's insistence on an inclusive, global religious vision constrained its goals of justice for immigrants, in the long run they hoped it would lead to a dominant American religious culture that values justice and compassion for "the other," regardless of the specific political issue at hand. Tying religion to immigration—seeking to make it a religious, moral issue—could change not only the religious but also the political context in a nation in which only 7% of people with a position on immigration say that religion is the most important influence on their views.[60]

Perhaps the important questions are not the ones focusing on whether religion is good or bad for the public sphere but those asking when, how, and why religion is good or bad for *particular aspects* of our shared public discourse and lives. The New Sanctuary Movement suggests that progressive religion in contemporary America may be good for cultivating a more global political perspective, for helping citizens reach across new lines of religious, cultural, and ethnic difference, and for pushing states to imagine new ways of relating to citizens of other states. Even if a rise in religious globalism were to move the United States away from a civil religion that sanctifies and upholds its democratic public sphere, it could support democratic deliberation in new and different ways, ones that might turn out to be both better and necessary for an increasingly global age.[61]

Allowing, even encouraging, discussions using religious reasons in the public sphere through efforts like the New Sanctuary Movement may actually benefit democratic society by enabling all citizens to more fully participate in the construction of the religious and political futures of the nation. In an ideal model of rationality, collective deliberation regarding the definition of religion would lead to a more compassionate, just conception of the religious life and the religious citizen, one that would be as amenable to democracy as possible. While New Sanctuary's multiple targets produced little change for millions of undocumented immigrants in the short run (though, after a period of several years, they did help Liliana), in the long run a more compassionate and inclusive religious public might be more open to people like Liliana from the beginning. The case of the New Sanctuary Movement suggests that many religious people are willing to have these religious debates in public—maybe Americans, religious and secular, should take them up on it.

One Family Under God

When I finished my research in 2009, Liliana was still living in sanctuary in the United Church of Christ (UCC) Simi Valley, more than two years after leaving her home and family to move into a church. She had become a regular fixture at the church, having been there longer than some of its members who joined through more traditional methods. Congregation members had been transformed by her presence, their religious vision shifting from an emphasis on helping their fellow citizens to helping all people as they would their own brothers and sisters, no matter their country of origin, the language they spoke, or their immigration status.

Yet while Liliana, UCC Simi Valley, and their partners had created a new kind of relationship, one that signified one human family, Liliana was still forced to live under a separate roof from her husband and her children. She was waiting for the day when her immigration status might change, when her family would be united again. In the meantime, she had become a face for the New Sanctuary Movement and for families like hers across the United States. During her first years in sanctuary, invited groups would come to the church house and visit her, asking her questions about her case and listening as she shared intimate details of her life with them, coaxing them into more fully changing their hearts and minds. She also started writing poetry, including a piece called "Justice: A General Definition" that the New Sanctuary Movement used multiple times in public events and newsletters. An excerpt reads:

> The definitions of justice and crime are so equivocal, so fragile. When I saw the tears in my children's eyes because I was leaving, when my husband couldn't release my hand to let me go, I felt the earth slip out from under my feet and I fell all the way down, I felt completely alone... alone with Pablito, who was barely a month old...
>
> Ah no, no. It doesn't matter if I last just one or thousands more days. This holy sanctuary is less of a sacrifice when I think (and I'm convinced) that our efforts will be rewarded with the infinite peace and humanity that the whole world deserves.[62]

Participation in the New Sanctuary Movement was a sacrifice for Liliana. In sanctuary, she lived apart from her family for multiple years, though she was closer to them than she would have been if she had been deported to Mexico. But her public participation ensured that she could not leave the church without facing the immediate risk of being detained and deported, and after two long years the strategy of sanctuary had not helped her individual legal case or her chance for legalization through a change in immigration policy.

But while Liliana changed other New Sanctuary activists, they changed Liliana as well, lifting her up as a leader with the power to transform her oppressors. As an activist said in Chapter 5, she became "both victim and prophet at the same time." Her story, her friendship, and her dream of "peace and humanity for the whole world" were sources of religious conversion for her UCC Simi Valley partners and others who worked with and visited her, who like the Fox News reporter in Chapter 2 were changed by the enduring hospitality of someone who had been treated so inhospitably. Their overlapping experiences of change and conversion, moving slowly toward both religious and political change, suggest that perhaps neither is fully achievable without the other.

When I visited Liliana at the church house in June 2008, she greeted me at the door, hugging me with one arm as she held Pablito in the other. She gave me a tour of the house, including her own private sanctuary: an unfinished section of the house that she had turned into a space for prayer. Colorful images of the Virgin of Guadalupe dangled above a small makeshift altar. A Jewish prayer shawl was draped over a kneeler, and a tiny doll painted to look like the infant Jesus sat on the altar's wooden surface. "Gifts from people in the movement," she explained in Spanish. Back in the kitchen, my stomach growled. She insisted on making me a sandwich, pulling bread and cheese from a refrigerator covered with colorful drawings by her children. We laughed and talked together, and for a moment she was just a smart, friendly woman around my age, like a friend or sister. But as I left, thanking her for her hospitality and hugging her goodbye, I saw a sign posted just left of the door, instructing church members on what to do if immigration agents came knocking. The world is not one family yet.

STORYTELLING AND TERMINOLOGY

Notes on Storytelling

When I first encountered the New Sanctuary Movement in August 2007, the story of Liliana and her sanctuary partners was just emerging. Few people outside of small circles in the Los Angeles area knew her story. But by the time I traveled to Los Angeles in November for the 2007 national gathering of the New Sanctuary Movement, Liliana's story had become a paradigmatic example of stories in the group's narrative life. I heard the stories of her migration from Mexico, her visit from Immigration and Customs Enforcement (ICE) agents, her family, and her experience with sanctuary more times than I can count. At national and local gatherings, in media accounts and press releases, from Liliana herself and from other activists, in public and in private: Liliana's story and the stories of immigrant families like hers were central to New Sanctuary and to its strategy of transformation through sanctuary.

In a similar way, activists repeatedly invoked stories of congregations like the United Church of Christ (UCC) Simi Valley. As a mostly white, native-born faith community that was transformed by forming a close relationship with an undocumented immigrant, the "conversion narrative" of UCC Simi Valley provided a success story for the New Sanctuary Movement, an example of a group of people whose religious and political visions shifted through the practice of sanctuary. Though a few leaders of UCC Simi Valley started with a commitment to immigrants and religious globalism, acting as the driving force for the congregation's involvement in New Sanctuary, today far more of the church members embrace undocumented immigrants as central to their religious community than before. While these stories were told more in private than in public, they too were central to New Sanctuary's narratives, practice, and identity.

Because of the centrality of stories in the New Sanctuary Movement, both immigrants' stories and the stories of transformation in religious communities, I intentionally foreground stories in this book. While I hope they make for more interesting reading, as an ethnographer, I also seek to give the reader a sense of what it feels like to be involved. To be a part of the New Sanctuary Movement was to be immersed in these stories: to hear them told and retold and for the stories to become part of you. The New Sanctuary Movement went beyond stories to building relationships, a point I highlight in Chapter 3. But it began with stories.

As I tell it in the book's opening, Liliana's story is a New Sanctuary Movement narrative, a story retold by activists in their regular movement activities. I was not present to personally witness all parts of the story—instead, I offer the story as an archetype of New Sanctuary Movement narratives, mobilized to touch the hearts of listeners. Throughout the book, I include stories of this type alongside stories from my field notes and direct quotes from my interviews, such that secondhand history intermingles with firsthand observations. Since the purpose of the storytelling is to immerse readers in the lives of New Sanctuary and its participants, I offer little in-text commentary on the source of each of the stories. Instead, to avoid disruption in the narrative, I describe sources for each story in the notes.

Finally, the story of the New Sanctuary Movement this book tells is a limited one: it focuses solely on its first two years. The claims I make about its practices and the insights I gather from them are most relevant to its earliest period, from 2007 to 2009. This also means that almost all of the action presented in this book occurred several years before its publication. Since as of this writing the New Sanctuary Movement still exists, changing as all activist networks do, the image depicted in these pages necessarily differs in important ways from New Sanctuary as current activists and allies know and experience it. As a result, most of my description and analysis of the New Sanctuary Movement uses the past tense. Nonetheless, many of the ethnographic narratives in this book are told using the present tense to further the cause of active storytelling and as a reminder that, for now, the New Sanctuary Movement's work continues, even if its current incarnation differs from the early form that is the focus of this book.

Notes on Terminology

In writing about controversial topics like religion and immigration, words take on a special kind of power, as social movement theories of framing remind us.[1] The use of certain terms rather than others privileges particular understandings of the world and therefore has political ramifications as well as scholarly ones. Because of this, I thought very carefully about my use of terms in this book, doing my best to offer a fair depiction and analysis but also to stick as closely to my empirical case as possible.

Religion or Christianity?

Like Liliana and UCC Simi Valley, most of the sanctuary immigrants and faith communities involved in the New Sanctuary Movement were Christian, particularly mainline Protestant or Catholic. Still, I use the term *religious* in describing New Sanctuary and its aims rather than *Christian*. While there are obviously important differences between religious traditions, I use the umbrella terms religion and religious for two reasons, one empirical and one theoretical.

The New Sanctuary Movement itself spoke of faith communities or congregations when referring to local churches, synagogues, and mosques and of people of faith when referencing the American religious public. They intentionally avoided the terms churches or Christians, seeking to be more inclusive in their language and their aims. Thus, while most participants were Christians and their focus was primarily on changing churches and the public image of Christianity, my use of the term religious reflects their emphasis on religious solidarities that extended beyond traditional divisions. If one takes New Sanctuary's discourse and language seriously, its goal was not merely to change churches and Christianity but also to transform a diverse group of religious communities and public conceptions of faithfulness beyond definitions of Christianity. More particularly, while most religious conservatives in America are Christian, activists more often talked about the religious right rather than the Christian right, a term that recognizes the religious diversity in conservative organizations despite the fact that they are predominantly Christian. I therefore follow them in using this more inclusive language.

My empirical case—the New Sanctuary Movement—therefore dictates my use of the term religion rather than Christian. Beyond this, using the broader term better enables me to engage with sociological theories of religion, which tend to analyze traditions together under the umbrella term religion rather than developing separate theories of distinct traditions. With few exceptions, scholars of religion and activism have typically talked of the influence of religious resources on activism rather than analyzing whether Christianity might shape activism differently from Judaism or Islam. Because the topics of these studies are almost always Christian groups, this creates problems, since the patterns may very well hold only for Christian groups and not for other religious traditions. However, it is likely that all religious communities have some commonalities that are relevant for activism, such as social networks and financial resources. Similarly, using the term religious rather than focusing in on one particular tradition allows me to theorize a broader phenomenon while recognizing the limits that my theories of religious change might have for religions other than Christianity and for religious communities outside of the United States.

Undocumented or Illegal?

Many mainstream media outlets, politicians, and conservative political groups use terms like illegal immigrants, illegals, and criminal aliens to describe immigrants who are in the United States without proper authorization. These terms sensationalize immigrants by constructing them as threats, a practice corresponding to the goals of groups seeking increased restrictions on immigration.[2] Terms like illegal immigrant also misrepresent the diversity of immigrants without papers, many of whom—like Jean—have become deportable despite having legal residency. Many other concerns have also been raised about the use of these terms, in particular the ways in which they have been intentionally used in the past as slurs to further marginalize the most vulnerable ethnic groups of the day.[3]

As a result, immigration scholars tend to avoid using these terms, instead preferring the terms unauthorized immigrants and undocumented immigrants, which better capture the diversity of immigrants living in the United States without permission.[4] As immigrant rights activists, New Sanctuary activists rarely used the term "illegals," invoking it only to condemn it. They argued that the discourses around immigrants in the mainstream media were inaccurate, insulting, and dehumanizing. Given the lack of consensus around terminology and concerns about the ways terms like "illegal" further dehumanize and marginalize immigrants, in this book I use the terminology that New Sanctuary activists used, identifying them as undocumented immigrants.

RESEARCH METHODOLOGY

Around the time that I started looking for a topic for my dissertation at New York University, I heard about the New Sanctuary Movement through a local friend. A mutual friend had recently started volunteering for the New Sanctuary Coalition of New York City. As a scholar of religious social movements, I was familiar with the 1980s Sanctuary Movement and was intrigued by the idea of a new incarnation of that movement. I asked the volunteer if I could join her at a coalition meeting.

A few days later, in August 2007, I went to a church in New York for my first New Sanctuary Movement meeting. When we arrived, only 15 people were present. Though I was surprised, I also recognized that this was a real benefit for my research. The organization was in the initial stages of mobilization and formation, so I would be able to study it largely as it happened, privy to its growing pains and struggles as well as its triumphs. This is unusual for social movement studies, which often rely on historical accounts and retrospection for their data. I realized it could therefore reveal important new insights about nascent movements and movement organizations.

Another unexpected boon was that the activist who ran that first meeting turned out to be another acquaintance. I now had two contacts in the group who supported me, and they were instrumental in helping me gain access to the organization's meetings and events. I decided to focus on the New York coalition, supplementing that focus with research on the national network's activities. It was only later, when I realized that a larger, more diverse sample would help answer more of my emerging questions, that I decided to also include the Los Angeles coalition in my study.

Through my two acquaintances, I obtained initial access to the New Sanctuary Coalition of New York City. Once I began attending meetings, group leaders gave me the green light to continue conducting research on the New Sanctuary Movement. They insisted they were trying to be more public with their activities compared with the 1980s Sanctuary Movement. While I struggled to remain in the loop regarding some more private group activities, there were also times when I was convinced I had obtained a measure of insider status.

This happened much more quickly in New York than in Los Angeles, where I had fewer contacts and had to begin interviewing almost immediately after entering the field. Even in LA, though, more than one of my interview respondents told me about a secret event that was approaching, something only insiders knew about. In this case, one of the immigrants living in physical sanctuary was being moved from the church where he had been living for the past three months to a new church in another part of the city, after which the coalition planned to hold a service welcoming him to the new church. Since there were real dangers involved in revealing this information, the sharing of this secret represented a high level of trust, something I appreciated and guarded carefully.

Methodological Approach

This study of the New Sanctuary Movement uses an ethnographic case study approach. The case study approach has both strengths and weaknesses: it allows for depth while sacrificing breadth.[1] Ethnography as a method has both strengths and weaknesses as well. The strength of ethnography lies in its ability to collect detailed data on practice, to capture subtleties in discourse and tensions in action, and to document complex social processes over time, making it a useful tool for developing theoretical innovation.[2] The participant observation in this study took place anywhere that New Sanctuary activities took place,[3] allowing for (1) "thick description" of processes *as they happened*, which provided the nuance necessary for theory building; and (2) a check on the interviewing data and the extent to which accounts respondents gave in the interviews were reflected in group practice.

The ethnographic data presented in this study were collected at New Sanctuary meetings, vigils, protests, religious services, congregation town halls, immigration check-ins, national gatherings, workshops, and a variety of other events in the New York City and Los Angeles areas. Acting as a participant observer at group activities over the span of approximately a year and a half allowed me to keep track of recruitment and membership, to develop rapport with members that was helpful in the interviews, and—most importantly—to observe changes over time as the new organization struggled to grow and to balance its targets, goals, strategies, and identities.

Most of the ethnographic observations took place in the New York City coalition. The Los Angeles observations lasted for approximately 2 months (May–June 2008), while the New York observations lasted around 16 months (August 2007–April 2008 and July 2008–January 2009). While an imbalance exists in the amount of time I spent with each, my time in LA provided enough data to provide a broader sense of the New Sanctuary Movement's diversity. I also observed two three-day national gatherings, one in November 2007 in Los Angeles and the other in September 2009 in New York. During all of my fieldwork, I entered detailed notes into a journal and later expanded them using a computer.

After close to a year of ethnographic research, once I had developed rapport with the activists, I began conducting in-depth interviews. I interviewed 70 people total in both New York and Los Angeles. I conducted interviews with New Sanctuary participants (48) and potential participants (22): people who did not join despite the group's attempts to recruit them. Because all respondents were asked questions about themselves as individuals and about their congregations (for my purposes they served as representatives of their congregations), in effect I conducted interviews with 70 religious individuals and 40 congregations (20 who joined and 20 who did not). I selected congregations and individuals using purposive sampling from organizational contact lists, interviewing between one and three individuals from each congregation. Interviews lasted between 30 minutes and two hours, though the average length was one hour. All but two were recorded using a digital recorder. The interviews were semi-structured yet open-ended enough to allow the respondents to tell their stories in their own ways.[4] Also, to avoid leading questions about the role of religion in various group processes, I asked questions about religion only once the respondent had already mentioned it. Thus, activists' commitments to religious goals could be even stronger than they appear in this study.

Lastly, New Sanctuary Movement documents, press coverage, and other related media gave background and context for the national network and the two local coalitions. They provided important information about how New Sanctuary framed itself (both to insiders and outsiders), how its framing changed over time, what its main strategies and tactics were, and how those strategies changed over time. I analyzed documents and media including New Sanctuary brochures, flyers, websites, and newsletters; newspaper and magazine articles about the group; video footage of televised interviews; video footage of select public events; organizational videos; and group training materials.[5] All of the ethnographic, interviewing, and document data were analyzed using Atlas.ti. They were coded both deductively and inductively, with some of the coding categories taken from theory and others emerging from the data.

Ethics and the Position of Researcher/Activist

As a native-born, white American with the privileges that accompany those statuses, I had not dealt with the U.S. immigration system prior to beginning this research. However, in previous research and community work, I had encountered and befriended immigrants whose stories inspired me to learn more about immigration in the United States. Initially, one of the reasons I found the New Sanctuary Movement compelling was that it offered a way for me to explore my own personal views about the complex issues surrounding undocumented immigration. In other words, I did not enter the field as a committed immigration activist but as a curious and concerned citizen. Over time, the stories I heard, the friendships I formed with sanctuary immigrants, and the complexities I learned about made it clear to me that overall I was on the side of the New Sanctuary Movement, both in its political and religious goals.

Despite identifying in some ways with the group and its cause, I did not "go native." Still, going from a place of relative ignorance and ambivalence to a more educated and actively concerned position is a similar journey to how some New Sanctuary participants experienced the process of change. Having had this experience myself, I could better understand the experiences some of my study participants were having. Of course, sharing the experiences of the people you are observing is what participant observation is all about, and that is one of its greatest strengths as a research method. While I shared the experiences of Anglo and other activists who were new to the realm of immigrant rights activism, as a native-born American I necessarily shared fewer of the experiences of immigrants themselves. Because of this, I paid special attention to immigrants' experiences with New Sanctuary, talking regularly with the immigrants involved and interviewing immigrants who chose not to join.

I have tried to represent the New Sanctuary Movement and its critics, whether native-born or immigrant, in ways they would recognize as valid. I have not sidestepped the struggles and, at times, failures of New Sanctuary, which may make some of its participants unhappy. I have also focused more on its more latent, contested target and goals—those related to religious authority and identity—than on its goals of changing immigration policy, which may surprise some activists or leave them frustrated that it does not capture their impression of the New Sanctuary Movement's main emphasis. The role of the participant observer is to capture nuances and a variety of perspectives, particularly surprising ones that others, including some activists themselves, might miss. I hope that by pointing out what I see as some of the underlying problems with the New Sanctuary Movement, its leaders can better see what does and does not work well in achieving its goals.

Though it is never possible (and perhaps inadvisable) to be a completely objective researcher, it is especially difficult when studying vulnerable populations. This seems appropriate—such situations call for care and compassion, not inhuman objectivity. One of New Sanctuary's leaders warned me at the start of my interview with her that "it's a violation to do this kind of research and not follow it with some kind of action." While I'm not sure I agree, given that the added costs of participating in this study were relatively low compared with the costs immigrants and activists were already experiencing as part of such a public group, I recognize the vulnerable situation the families were in, am grateful for their willingness to share their stories, and have done my best to represent their struggles adequately. There were many times when the hardships of the families involved brought me to tears or filled me with anger. Some of that emotion no doubt made its way into this study, but I see this as a strength rather than a weakness of this type of research.

There were two main ethical concerns in this project. First, I wanted to make sure that my research in no way put the sanctuary families into a more difficult position than they were already in. Second, I needed to protect the identities of the activists to the best of my ability. Though the New Sanctuary Movement is not doing anything strictly illegal, it is challenging the state and the law in provocative ways. Familiar with past infiltration of social movements (including the 1980s Sanctuary Movement) by the Federal Bureau of Investigation (FBI), I was especially careful to keep information protected and confidential.

Still, both the families themselves and the faith communities and individual activists involved had very public stories by virtue of the coverage of the New Sanctuary Movement in the media. As a result, it made little sense to me, ethically or empirically, to use pseudonyms when telling the history of the group or when discussing nonsensitive topics. On the contrary, part of the purpose of this book is to document the New Sanctuary Movement, its leaders, and their sacrifices. One of the only ways I can repay those who participated in my research is by highlighting the often courageous things they did by using their actual names, with their permission, in the telling of the story.

However, as the first book-length account of the New Sanctuary Movement, this is both a book of history that seeks to document activists' efforts and a book on a still-existing activist network with vulnerabilities. My desire to publicize the courageous work of activists is balanced by the need to protect their identities. When discussing rank-and-file activists, I use pseudonyms. For instance, in the introductory chapter, "Pastor Michaels" is a pseudonym. However, I often use the same pseudonyms repeatedly to provide continuity in character and action throughout the text.

In contrast, when I describe leaders, including the sanctuary families, I typically use their actual names. Again, in the opening story, Liliana's actual name is Liliana, though I refrain from using her last name since New Sanctuary has kept it private. In fact, all of the LA sanctuary families adopted the last name Santuario, the Spanish word for sanctuary. Because of extensive media coverage, leaders' identities are already well-known in public: a simple Google search would reveal their identities. Liliana herself has been the subject of countless media stories, and her photograph is all over the Internet. Similarly, I use the actual names of congregations and organizations that were leaders in the early New Sanctuary Movement—such as UCC Simi Valley—whose names were regularly associated with New Sanctuary online and in the media. This allows me to better contextualize and document their work. However, for congregations and individuals whose participation is less publicly documented, I use pseudonyms. Whenever I stray from these general rules, I note the difference.

NOTES

INTRODUCTION

1. For instance, one of the church's main focuses had been lesbian, gay, bisexual, and transgender (LGBT) rights. Though LGBT activism can be transnational, this church's focus was on LGBT rights in denominational and national political contexts.

2. For example, see Michael D. Shear, "Demographic Shift Brings New Worry for Republicans," *New York Times*, November 7, 2012, Retrieved November 20, 2012 (http://www.nytimes.com/2012/11/08/us/politics/obamas-victory-presents-gop-with-demographic-test.html?pagewanted=all&_r=0); Donna St. George and Dennis Brady, "Growing Share of Hispanic Voters Helped Push Obama to Victory," *Washington Post*, November 7, 2012, Retrieved November 20, 2012 (http://www.washingtonpost.com/politics/decision2012/growing-share-of-hispanic-voters-helped-push-obama-to-victory/2012/11/07/b4087d0a-28ff-11e2-b4e0-346287b7e56c_story.html); and Molly Henneberg, "Republicans Losing Ground Among Hispanic Voters," FoxNews.com, November 9, 2012, Retrieved November 20, 2012 (http://www.foxnews.com/politics/2012/11/09/republicans-losing-ground-among-hispanic-voters/).

3 Cadge 2004; Eck 2002; Kurien 2007; McCarthy 2007; Wuthnow 2005.

4. Jenkins 2002; Levitt 2007; Matovina 2012; Pew 2007, 2012.

5. See Eck 2002.

6. See Hondagneu-Sotelo 2007, 2008.

7. Pew Research Center Report, "Few Say Religion Shapes Immigration, Environment Views," Washington, DC, 2010.

8. For example, see Castañeda-Liles 2005; Davis, Martinez, and Warner 2010; De La Torre 2003; Espinosa, Elizondo, and Miranda 2005; Gonzalez and Rosario 2009; Haddad 2009; Hondagneu-Sotelo 2007, 2008; Rey and Stepick 2010; Wilson 2008.

9. See Edles 2013. In this book, I focus on many religious groups and activists that identified variously as progressive, liberal, liberationist, radical, or leftist in their theologies and politics. (A few identified as conservative, but they were a small minority.) I do not use the terms interchangeably, since they clearly have different genealogies and meanings. Instead, I refer to the groups with what I (and many of them) see as the most inclusive and least politically laden of these terms: *progressive*. However, when referring specifically to "liberal Protestants," I use the term liberal rather than progressive since it is the term most often used in the social scientific literature to describe this religious tradition, whether aptly or not.

10 For details, see Tom Kisken, "Five Years Later, Oxnard Woman Continues Fight Against Deportation Threat," *Ventura County Star*, July 9, 2012, Retrieved November 20, 2012 (http://m.vcstar.com/news/2012/jul/09/five-years-later-oxnard-woman-continues-fight/).

11. Ibid.

12. The opening story about Liliana is a retelling of her story as it is repeatedly told by members of the movement, both in public events and in private interview settings. While I was present for some of these events, I was not present for them all. The story should be read not as firsthand observation but as movement narrative. I confirmed many of the details of the story through my own fieldwork and through firsthand journalistic accounts of Liliana and the United Church of Christ (UCC) Simi Valley.

13. See "An Assessment of United States Immigration and Customs Enforcement's Fugitive Operations Teams," Department of Homeland Security, Office of Inspector General, March 2007.

14. For more on the history of sanctuary, see Cunningham 1995. For more on Elvira Arellano, see Kathy L. Gilbert, "Church Rallies around Woman Battling to Stay in U.S.," *United Methodist News Service*, August 17, 2006, Retrieved October 16, 2012 (http://www.umc.org/site/c.gjJTJbMUIuE/ b.2020711/k.DCD3/ Church_rallies_around_woman_battling_to_stay_in_US.htm)

15. Coutin 1993; Crittenden 1988; Cunningham 1995; Lorentzen 1991; Nepstad 2004a; Smith 1996b.

16. See Smith 1996. Also, see McAdam 1988 for a discussion of how participation in social movements can change the biographies of those involved, training future generations of activists.

17. Yukich 2012.

18. The New Sanctuary Movement emphasized that many sanctuary immigrants were part of larger families, but they still focused much of their public attention on the undocumented family member in particular. Since I hope to represent the movement's actions and narratives as closely as possible, I also privilege the stories of individual undocumented immigrants over those of their families (for example, by focusing primarily on Liliana rather than on the rest of her family).

19. Barkan 1979; Ganz 2000, 2009; King and Cornwall 2005; McAdam 1983; McCammon 2003; Minkoff 1999; Taylor and Van Dyke 2004; Yukich 2012.

20. See Yukich 2012.
21. See Yukich 2011.
22. For example, see Harris 1999; Hart 2001; Hondagneu-Sotelo 2008; Lichterman 2005; Morris 1984; Smith 1991, 1996a, 1996b; Swarts 2008; Williams 1995, 1996; Wood 1999, 2002.
23. See Bartley 2007; DeSoucey 2010; King and Pearce 2010; Isaac 2009. See also Jasper's calls to focus on culture (Jasper 1997) and on strategic dilemmas (Jasper 2006) as central to understanding protest, including the recognition that the state is not always the target of protest.
24. See Castañeda-Liles 2005; Davis, Martinez, and Warner 2010; De La Torre 2003; Espinosa, Elizondo, and Miranda 2005; Gonzalez and Rosario 2009; Haddad 2009; Hondagneu-Sotelo 2007, 2008; Rey and Stepick 2010; Wilson 2008.
25. Levitt 2007.
26. See Hart 2001; Lichterman 2005, 2008, 2012; Stout 2010; Swarts 2008; Warren 2001; Wood 1999, 2002.
27. See Beyerlein 2010; Davis, Martinez, and Warner 2010; Hondagneu-Sotelo 2007, 2008.
28. By my definition, the Los Angeles New Sanctuary Coalition included activists both in Los Angeles and in nearby Ventura County, where UCC Simi Valley is located, despite the fact that activists usually spoke of them as separate coalitions. I do this not only because of Ventura County's proximity to Los Angeles but also because (1) the Ventura County coalition was very small, with Liliana as the only sanctuary family; (2) it was supported largely by CLUE networks; and (3) it interacted with the LA coalition a great deal. Also, Liliana started out in sanctuary in an LA church and only later moved to Ventura County, so placing both coalitions under one "Los Angeles area" umbrella better represents the way the group worked in practice.
29. See Caminero-Santangelo 2009; Freeland 2010; Irazabal and Dyrness 2010 for brief accounts of specific New Sanctuary Movement coalitions, including coalitions in locales other than New York and Los Angeles.
30. See Appendix B for a more detailed account of my methodology.
31. Polletta 2004.
32. McAdam 1982; McAdam, Tarrow, and Tilly 2001; McCarthy and Zald 1977; Polletta 2008.
33. See Beyerlein 2010; Hondagneu-Sotelo 2007, 2008; Pallares and Flores-González 2010; Voss and Bloemraad 2011.
34. The association between organized religion and conservatism is so dominant in the United States that Hout and Fischer 2002 suggested that some liberals who believe in God, pray, or even attend religious services often eschew religious identification to avoid being labeled as conservative.
35. The notion of "one human family" is similar to the idea of the *beloved community* that other observers have associated with progressive religious activists (see Marsh 2005; Williams 2002). However, New Sanctuary activists rarely talked about the beloved community. Instead, their family-focused discourse mirrored their

emphasis on immigrant families and highlighted the *intimate* and *transnational* nature of human connectedness in today's world. In contrast, the term community does not connote the same level of intimacy as the term family, and though the beloved community was originally conceived as global in scope it has often been associated specifically with seeking to transcend racial divides in the United States rather than with crossing national borders.

36. See Armstrong and Bernstein 2008.
37. See King and Pearce 2010; Van Dyke, Soule, and Taylor 2004.
38. See Aronowitz 1992; Calhoun 1993; Habermas 1981; Klandermans and Tarrow 1986; Laraña, Johnston, and Gusfield 1994; Melucci 1980; Offe 1985; Pichardo 1997; Touraine 1981.
39. Armstrong and Bernstein 2008.
40. See Billings 1990; Morris 1984; Nepstad 2004a, 2008; Smith 1991, 1996a, 1996b; Williams 1995, 1996; Wood 1999, 2002.
41. See Hannigan 1991 for a discussion of this. Davis and Robinson's 2012 book *Claiming Society for God* is a rare but excellent example of a study that challenges this theoretical distinction between religious movements and social movements. Michael Young's 2006 work suggests that religion accounts for the rise of the very form of collective action that we think of as the contemporary social movement.
42. Bruce 2011; Katzenstein 1998; Wilde 2007.
43. See Bruce 2011. For example, Melissa Wilde's 2007 book *Vatican II* asks how the types of social movement organizations that Catholic bishops developed at the Second Vatican Council helped determine their degree of success in achieving the religious changes they sought, changes that drastically transformed the largest religious institution in the world and that challenge sociological theories of religious change.
44. See Bender et al. 2012.
45. See Hefner 2009; Mahmood 2005; Metcalf 2004; Peacock 1978; Zaman 2007. Davis and Robinson 2012 make a similar argument about several movements—Muslim, Christian, and Jewish—in four different nations.
46. Davis and Robinson 2012.
47. Pseudonym.

CHAPTER 1

1. The opening vignette is based on the author's field notes.
2. While Rev. Fife is joking here, some New Sanctuary activists in fact did not like the term *new*, for a variety of reasons. At various times and in various places, some activists dropped the term new and just called themselves *sanctuary*, though they were still affiliated with the national New Sanctuary network and had adopted similar practices.
3. See Chapter 3 of this book, as well as Cunningham 1995, for a history of the practice of sanctuary.

4. For example, see: McAdam 1982; McAdam, McCarthy, and Zald 1996; McCarthy and Zald 1977; Tarrow 1994. Political process theorists refer to these three variables using a variety of terms. For instance, one of the more well-known explications of the theory uses the terms political opportunities, mobilizing structures, and cultural framings (McAdam, McCarthy, and Zald 1996). I use the terms political context, organizational resources, and revolutionary consciousness here because I see them as the basic ideas underlying the many different terminologies (see Goodwin and Jasper 1999 for more on the different terms used by political process theorists).

   In making political context, organizational resources, and revolutionary consciousness central to the study of social movement emergence, proponents of political process perspectives emphasize the intentionality and rationality of collective action. However, their models assume the state is the target for change. Changing political opportunities depend on shifting relationships with the state, organizational resources are defined as those best suited for challenging the state, and the concept of revolutionary consciousness roots injustice and its eradication in the power and authority of the state. As social movement scholars are beginning to appreciate, the dominance of these perspectives limits recognition of nonstate movement targets and the related ability to explain the emergence of a diverse array of social movements and movement organizations.

5. See Matthew 7:12, NRSV.

6. Michael Falcone, "100,000 Parents of Citizens Were Deported Over 10 Years," *New York Times*, February 13, 2009, Retrieved November 30, 2012 (http://www.nytimes.com/2009/02/14/us/14immig.html?_r=0).

7. Cunningham 1995.

8. Perla and Coutin 2012.

9. Cunningham 1995; Lippert and Rehaag 2012.

10. See Yukich 2012.

11. Smith 1996b.

12. Both CLUE-LA and CLUE-Ventura County played a role in the New Sanctuary Movement in the Los Angeles area. While they typically distinguished between the LA and Ventura County New Sanctuary coalitions, their geographic proximity and organizational ties meant that there was some overlap in the institutions and activists involved. As mentioned earlier, for the sake of simplicity I describe them all as part of the LA coalition in this book. However, Liliana's sanctuary cluster was technically part of the Ventura County coalition.

13. When I describe New Sanctuary Movement activists as either mainline Protestant or evangelical Protestant, I am using the denomination-based classification scheme established by Steensland et al. 2000. While there is debate about whether it is best to classify people according to denominational affiliation or theological beliefs, since I did not have the opportunity to investigate each activist's theological beliefs, I opted to classify them according to denominational affiliation. For instance, members of churches belonging to the Episcopal Church or the American Baptist

Churches in the U.S.A. are mainline Protestants, while members of churches belonging to the Southern Baptist Convention or members of nondenominational Christian churches are evangelical Protestants, with this distinction reflecting broad differences in history, theology, and practice. However, if a member of a mainline congregation self-identified as evangelical, I classify them as evangelical here. This was the case for a few Latino members of mainline congregations.

14. Yolanda and her daughter are the focus of a documentary called "Sanctuary's Daughter," Retrieved November 30, 2012 (http://www.sanctuarysdaughter.com/).

15. I use pseudonyms for them both, as they have chosen to keep their identities more private in the media and on the web.

16. This is a pseudonym as she has chosen to keep her identity private for most movement purposes.

17. Tichenor 2002.

18. Pew Research Center, "America's Immigration Quandary," Washington, DC, 2006, Retrieved November 30, 2012 (http://people-press.org/report/274/americas-immigration-quandary).

19. 2007 American Community Survey. Data from Elizabeth Grieco, "Race and Hispanic Origin of the Foreign-Born Population in the United States: 2007," American Community Survey Reports, 2010.

20. Foreign-born refers to people living in the United States who were not U.S. citizens at birth. Data Source: 2007 American Community Survey; Census 2000; Campbell Gibson and Emily Lennon, "Historical Census Statistics on the Foreign-Born Population of the United States: 1850 to 1990," U.S. Census Bureau Working Paper 29, U.S. Government Printing Office, Washington, DC, 1999.

21. Marrow 2011; Massey 2008.

22. For instance, see Lee and Bean 2010.

23. Data Source: US Census Bureau, Decennial Censuses 1960 to 2000 and 2007 American Community Survey. Data from Elizabeth Grieco, "Race and Hispanic Origin of the Foreign-Born Population in the United States: 2007," American Community Survey Reports, 2010.

24. See Brodkin 2012; Lee and Bean 2004, 2007, 2010.

25. Chavez 2008.

26. As discussed in Appendix A, in this book I use the term undocumented immigrants when describing this group, since this is the term typically used by New Sanctuary activists.

27. See Michael Hoefer, Nancy Rytina, and Bryan C. Baker, "Estimates of the Unauthorized Immigrant Population Residing in the United States: January 2007," U.S. Department of Homeland Security, 2008.

28. More recent research suggests that the number of undocumented immigrants in the United States has declined since 2008, in part because of the economic recession. See Passel and Cohn 2010.

29. Passel and Cohn 2009.

30. Ibid.

31. See Guskin and Wilson 2007. For instance, in 2010 comedian Stephen Colbert testified before the U.S. Congress about the undesirability of farm labor, using satire to draw attention to the hardships facing immigrant farmworkers.

32. Passel and Cohn 2009.

33. See Scott Keeter, "Where the Public Stands on Immigration Reform," Pew Research Center, 2009, Retrieved November 30, 2012 (http://pewresearch.org/pubs/1421/where-the-public-stands-on-immigration-reform).

34. See Gregory A. Smith, "Attitudes Toward Immigration: In the Pulpit and the Pew," Pew Research Center, 2006, Retrieved November 30, 2012 (http://pewresearch.org/pubs/20/attitudes-toward-immigration-in-the-pulpit-and-the-pew).

35. These stereotypes are just that: stereotypes, not realities. See Chaves 2008; Guskin and Wilson 2007; Smith 2006.

36. Two particularly well-known examples are the Chinese Exclusion Act (1882) and the National Origins Act (1924). See Tichenor 2002; Jasso and Rosenzweig 2011.

37. Brotherton and Kretsedemas 2008.

38. Kurzban 2008: 64.

39. Brotherton and Kretsedemas 2008.

40. Sheik 2008.

41. More specifically, there was a 27% increase between 1996 and 1997 and a 23% growth between 2001 and 2002. See the U.S. Department of Justice Immigration and Naturalization Service, *Budget Requests to Congress, 1985–2002* and *Budget of the United States Government, Appendix 1985–2003*; Migration Policy Institute, "Immigration Enforcement Spending Since IRCA," Independent Task Force on Immigration and America's Future, Migration Policy Institute, Washington, DC, 2005.

42. U.S. Department of Homeland Security, *Budget-in-Brief, Fiscal Year 2007*.

43. U.S. Department of Homeland Security, *2007 Yearbook of Immigration Statistics*.

44. Kerwin and Lin 2009.

45. Data Source: U.S. Department of Homeland Security, *2007 Yearbook of Immigration Statistics*.

46. Michael Falcone, "100,000 Parents of Citizens Were Deported Over 10 Years." *New York Times*, February 13, 2009.

47. Human Rights Watch, "Forced Apart (By the Numbers): Non-Citizens Deported Mostly for Nonviolent Offenses," Human Rights Watch, New York, 2009.

48. H.R. 4437, THOMAS, Library of Congress.

49. "A Day Without an Immigrant," Indymedia, February 17, 2006, Retrieved November 2, 2012 (http://indymedia.us/en/topic/immigrantrights/archive8.shtml).

50. See Bloemraad, Voss, and Lee 2011, especially Table 1.1 on p. 8.

51. Ibid. Also see "Over 500,000 Protest Anti-Immigrant Law in Downtown Los Angeles," Indymedia, March 25, 2006, Retrieved November 2, 2012 (http://la.indymedia.org/archives/archive_by_id.php?id=1073&category_id=3).

52. Cordero-Guzmán, Martin, Quiroz-Becerra, and Theodore 2008; Martinez 2008; Pantoja, Menjívar, and Magannaga 2008; Voss and Bloemraad 2011.

53. "US Immigrants Stage Boycott Day," BBC News, May 2, 2006, Retrieved February 4, 2010 (http://news.bbc.co.uk/2/hi/americas/4961734.stm).

54. "Senate Passes Immigration Bill," CNN.com, May 26, 2006, Retrieved June 3, 2009 (http://www.cnn.com/2006/POLITICS/05/25/immigration/index.html).

55. Pew Hispanic Center, "2007 National Survey of Latinos: As Illegal Immigration Issue Heats Up, Hispanics Feel a Chill," Washington, DC, 2007.

56. Deborah White, "Catholic Cardinal Mahony Slams House Bill HR 4437: Tells Bush That Priests Will Not Verify Legal Status." About.com Guide, 2006, Retrieved February 4, 2010 (http://usliberals.about.com/od/immigration/a/RMahony.htm).

57. Ibid.

58. At the time, Bishop Carcaño was serving as bishop of the Phoenix Episcopal Area.

59. McAdam 1982.

60. Ganz 2000, 2009; Milkman 2011; Shaw 2008, 2011; Voss and Bloemraad 2011.

61. Ganz 2000, 2009.

62. Shaw 2008.

63. Ibid.

64. Milkman 2006, 2011.

65. Shaw 2008.

66. Milkman 2011; Shaw 2011.

67. Das Gupta 2006; Shaw 2008.

68. Bloemraad and Voss 2011; Félix, González, and Ramírez 2008.

69. Bloemraad and Voss 2011.

70. Félix, González, and Ramírez 2008.

71. Heredia 2011; Milkman 2011; Shaw 2011; Voss and Bloemraad 2011.

72. See Nepstad 2004b, 2008 on how religious identity shapes decisions about movement involvement, such as tactical choice.

73. For example, see Alba, Raboteau and DeWind 2009; Cadge 2004; Cadge and Ecklund 2007; De La Torre 2003; Ebaugh and Chafetz 2000, 2002; Ecklund 2006; Espinosa, Elizondo and Miranda 2005; Guest 2003; Haddad, Smith and Esposito 2003; Kurien 2007; Kwon, Kim and Warner 2001; Leonard, Stepick, Vasquez and Holdaway 2005; Levitt 2007; McAlister 2001; Min and Kim 2002; Mooney 2009; Prothero 2006; Stepick, Rey and Mahler 2009; Tweed 1997; Vasquez and Marquardt 2003; Warner and Wittner 1998.

74. Kurien 2007.

75. Castañeda-Liles 2005; Davis, Martinez and Warner 2010; De La Torre 2003; Espinosa, Elizondo, and Miranda 2005; Gonzalez and Rosario 2009; Haddad 2009; Hondagneu-Sotelo 2007, 2008; Jeung 2007; Mooney 2007; Rey and Stepick 2010; Wilson 2008.

76. See Jeung 2007; Mooney 2007. Of course, joining groups based on ethnicity or other shared identities and focusing activist efforts on that group's own interests is not a pattern unique to immigrants or to immigrant congregations.

77. Davis, Martinez, and Warner 2010.
78. Davis, Martinez, and Warner 2010; Heredia 2011.
79. Heredia 2011.
80. "National Evangelical Hispanic Alliance Formed," *Christian Examiner Online*, 2006, Retrieved October 16, 2012 (http://www.christianexaminer.com/Articles/Articles%20Mar06/Art_Mar06_18.html).
81. Beyerlein 2010; Hagan 2007; Hondagneu-Sotelo, Gaudinez, and Lara 2007.
82. Hondagneu-Sotelo 2008; Leonard 2007.
83. Hagan 2007; Hondagneu-Sotelo, Gaudinez, and Lara 2007.
84. Heredia 2011; Mooney 2007.
85. McCarthy and Zald 1977.
86. McAdam 1982.
87. See Hondagneu-Sotelo 2008 for more on CLUE's role in immigrant rights activism.
88. The activists' local observations in 2005 and 2006 were reflected in national-level survey data showing that more than half of all Hispanic adults (regardless of status) were worried that they, a family member, or a close friend could be deported. Additionally, two-thirds of U.S. Hispanics said the failure of Congress to enact immigration reform had made life more difficult for all Latinos. See Pew Hispanic Center, "2007 National Survey of Latinos: As Illegal Immigration Issue Heats Up, Hispanics Feel a Chill," Pew Hispanic Center: Washington, D.C.
89. See Smith 1996b.
90. While the head of an interfaith organization sat on the initial steering committee of the New Sanctuary Coalition of NYC, the organization itself played a more limited role in the coalition's work.
91. Kateel and Shahani 2008: 259.
92. I do not use the traditional honorific for priest (Father) when referring to Ruiz because while he had been ordained as a priest and still identified as one in some ways, in other ways he no longer identified as a priest. He did not use the honorific himself and did not serve in a parish, and I never heard anyone refer to him in this way.

CHAPTER 2

1. The opening story about Rev. Schaper is based on the written text of one of her sermons, field notes on her sermon-making style, and in-depth interviews with Schaper.
2. See Stout 2010.
3. A prolific writer, she has authored more than 30 books, though her writings on immigration are uncollected.
4. Excerpt from the pamphlet by Rev. Schaper.
5. Sociologist Rhys Williams refers to this as "tribal" civil religion. See Williams Forthcoming, 2013.
6. Religious globalism is my term, not theirs. I use this term rather than transnationalism, which Rev. Schaper uses in her writing, because my conceptualization of the

phenomenon is based on the work of Peggy Levitt 2007, who uses the term religious globalism.

7. Pseudonym.

8. The opening story about Rev. Salvatierra is based on video footage of the San Juan event, field notes, and in-depth interviews with Salvatierra.

9. Personal communication from Rev. Salvatierra, October 30, 2012.

10. Stout 2010.

11. From field notes, September 2009.

12. Hondagneu-Sotelo 2008.

13. Alexia Salvatierra, "Sanctuary Breaks an Unjust Law," God's Politics, July 2007, Retrieved November 23, 2012 (http://blog.beliefnet.com/godspolitics/2007/07/alexia-salvatierra-sanctuary-b.html).

14. Pseudonym.

15. Pseudonym.

16. This story is based on field notes.

17. Wellman 2008. See also Edles 2013.

18. See Imam Ali Siddiqui, "Immigration on the Minmber," Humane Immigration Rights, Indymedia, 2006, Retrieved November 30, 2012 (http://indymedia.us/en/2006/10/20391.shtml).

19. Wilcox 2006.

20. See Bellah 1967.

21. See Bellah 1967; Demerath and Williams 1985; Williams Forthcoming, 2013. See also Robert N. Bellah, "Is a Global Civil Religion Possible?" The Immanent Frame, December 24, 2007, Retrieved November 27, 2012 (http://blogs.ssrc.org/tif/2007/12/24/is-a-global-civil-religion-possible/).

22. See the 2012 Rasmussen poll results: "Only 43% Now Believe America Is the Last Best Hope of Mankind," Rasmussen Reports, July 2, 2012, Retrieved November 27, 2012 (http://www.rasmussenreports.com/public_content/lifestyle/general_lifestyle/june_2012/only_43_now_believe_america_is_the_last_best_hope_of_mankind); and McDaniel, Nooruddin, and Shortle 2011.

23. Levitt 2007.

24. Marsh 2005; Warren 2010; Williams 2002.

25. In other examples, Rev. Schaper appeared on Fox News's show The O'Reilly Factor with controversial host Bill O'Reilly to talk about the New Sanctuary Movement. She also appeared alongside her congregation's sanctuary partner—Jean and his family—on the network's show Geraldo at Large with Geraldo Rivera.

26. Anderson 1983.

27. Heredia 2011.

28. Hondagneu-Sotelo, Gaudinez, and Lara 2007.

29. McAdam 1982; McCarthy and Zald 1977; McAdam, Tarrow, and Tilly 2001.

30. Armstrong and Bernstein 2008.

31. See Armstrong 2002; Armstrong and Bernstein 2008; Jasper 2006; Snow 2004.

32. Armstrong 2002; Armstrong and Bernstein 2008; Bruce 2011; King and Pearce 2010; Van Dyke, Soule, and Taylor 2004; Wilde 2007.

33. See Armstrong 2002; King and Pearce 2010; Van Dyke, Soule, and Taylor 2004.

34. Armstrong and Bernstein 2008.

35. Armstrong and Bernstein 2008; Bruce 2011; Snow 2004.

36. Weber [1904] 2002.

37. Armstrong 2002.

38. See Marsh 2005.

39. See Casanova 1994.

40. For a discussion of similar themes, see Demerath and Williams 1985; Lichterman 2012.

41. See Wellman 2008.

42. Bruce 2011; Katzenstein 1998; Wilde 2007.

43. Bruce 2011: 150.

44. Nepstad 2004b, 2008.

45. Stout 2010.

46. Lichterman 2005, 2008; Swarts 2008; Wood 1999, 2002.

47. See Lichterman 2012.

48. Wilde 2004, 2007.

49. Williams 2004.

50. Bruce's 2011 discussion of religious opportunities is an important exception.

51. The pamphlet was published by Interfaith Worker Justice, one of the organizations that helped start the New Sanctuary Movement and that continued supporting it by providing staff, limited financial assistance, and members during New Sanctuary's early years.

52. Interfaith Worker Justice, "For You Were Once a Stranger: Immigration in the U.S. Through the Lens of Faith," 2007, p. 24.

53. Wuthnow 2009.

54. Ibid., 27.

55. Ibid., 162.

56. Ibid., 162.

57. Roof 1978; Warner 2005.

58. Ammerman 2005.

59. Wuthnow 2009: 164.

60. De La Torre 2003; Mooney 2009.

61. Goldberg 2006; Wilcox 2006.

62. Smith 2003.

63. Smith 2003; Warner 2005; Wuthnow 1988.

64. See Wuthnow 1988.

65. For example, see Farrell 2011 and Smith and Johnson 2010 for different views on whether young evangelicals are becoming more liberal theologically and politically. For instance, Smith and Johnson 2010 show that less than 25% of members of

evangelical denominations, whether young or old, identify as Democrats, and fewer than 20% identify as liberal. Also, see Guth et al. 2003; Smith et al. 1998.

66. Chaves 1994; Wuthnow and Evans 2002.

67. Hout, Greeley, and Wilde 2001.

68. See Diamond 1998; Wilcox 2006. Also see Frederick Clarkson, "The Battle for the Mainline Churches," Public Eye Magazine, Spring 2006, Retrieved October 12, 2012 (http://www.publiceye.org/magazine/v20n1/clarkson_battle.html).

69. See Luker 1985; Munson 2009.

70. Guth et al. 2003.

71. Hout and Fischer 2002.

72. For instance, while survey data show that evangelical Protestants are more likely to say that religion is "very important" in their lives than mainline Protestants are, the majority of mainliners nonetheless claim that religion is "very important" to them, and almost 90% assert that it is either very important or somewhat important in their lives. See Pew Forum on Religion and Public Life, "U.S. Religious Landscape Survey," Washington, DC, 2008.

73. See Edles 2013; Wuthnow and Evans 2002. This salience of religious identity was likely especially strong for progressive religious leaders, as "culture wars" are more likely to occur among elites. Often, laypeople are less concerned with battles over religious authority (Danielsen 2013; Uecker and Lucke 2011).

74. The national characteristic of both the religious threats and of the political threats of the immigration context made the New Sanctuary Movement more likely to combine these targets. This is in opposition to FBCO efforts, which are often more local or regional and therefore have fewer reasons to engage in or combat national religious or political battles. This may, in part, explain why the religious context affected New Sanctuary activists differently than some of the local religious activists Lichterman 2012 has studied, who did not highlight issues of religious identity. The more specific ways that changes in religious context do or do not impact different groups of religious activists is something that should be further explored in future research.

75. Interfaith Worker Justice, "For You Were Once a Stranger," p. 37.

76. Ibid., 32.

77. This is in line with Pierre Bourdieu's 1991 conception of the *religious field* as a site of struggle between various religious groups and their leaders over the power and authority to determine what constitutes religion. It also shares certain ideas in common with Fligstein and McAdam's 2012 notion of strategic action fields.

78. See McAdam, Tarrow, and Tilly 2001. I say "often" because, in many studies using the political process approach, the political context is not well defined (see Goodwin and Jasper 1999 for more on this).

79. Warner 2002.

80. The closing story about Rev. Schaper is based on field notes and in-depth interviews.

CHAPTER 3

1. Pseudonym. Because Joe has taken a more active, public role than his wife, and his name is typically used in movement correspondence while hers is not, I follow the same pattern here.

2. It is worth noting that these practices have, at times, led to the detention and deportation of U.S. citizens, when officials assumed they were undocumented and they did not have ID with them to counter these accusations. For example, see Sandra Hernandez, "Immigration: Another U.S. Citizen Deported," *Los Angeles Times*, January 5, 2012, Retrieved November 21, 2012 (http://opinion.latimes.com/opinionla/2012/01/immigration-us-citizen-deported.html).

3. Passel 2005; Passel and Cohn 2009.

4. Meyer and Staggenborg 1996; McCammon et al. 2008; Pietersen 2002.

5. See Downey 1986 and Epstein 1991 for a discussion of the distinction between rational, instrumental decisions about strategy versus decisions that are not rooted in cost–benefit analysis, such as the desire to express one's beliefs.

6. Ammerman 2005; Chaves 2004; Warner 2005.

7. See The Lutheran Church of the Good Shepherd's website, Retrieved October 4, 2011 (http://www.goodshepherdbayridge.org).

8. However, research suggests that the missionary tradition at times leads to more revolutionary forms of consciousness. Examples of this can be seen in the 1980s Sanctuary Movement and other U.S.-Central American Solidarity Movements, where missionary relationships (particularly in Catholic religious orders) inspired activist mobilization. See Smith 1996b, Nepstad 2004a.

9. "Congregation Trend Report: Good Shepherd Lutheran Church," ELCA Research and Evaluation, 2012, Retrieved March 30, 2013 (http://archive.elca.org/ScriptLib/RE/Trendnet/cdsTrendNet.asp?Id=C4C1C4CECAB9CCCBA7C6E09096B7C8F177E2C2DEEDB383C2B3A5CCA497A5B0BBC4B3A9BF9EE09C8D).

10. Emerson and Woo 2006.

11. Source: U.S. Census Bureau, 2007–2011 American Community Survey 5-Year Estimates. Statistics for Bay Ridge, Brooklyn are based on the zip code 11209 and compared with statistics for New York City, New York as a whole.

12. Kasinitz, Mollenkopf, and Waters 2006.

13. Emerson and Woo 2006.

14. Ammerman 2005; Chaves 2004; Warner 2005; Wuthnow 2009.

15. Meyer and Staggenborg 1996; McCammon et al. 2008; Pietersen 2002.

16. Social movement scholars disagree about how best to define strategies and tactics, with some using the terms interchangeably and others arguing for the need for clear distinctions (see Ganz 2000; King and Cornwall 2005; McCammon 2003; Minkoff 1999). These distinctions are important for theorizing movement activities and outcomes. Still, they can obscure the possibility that a single symbol can serve as identity, strategy, and tactic at once, which is the role sanctuary played in the New Sanctuary Movement. At times, sanctuary as it had

historically been practiced was used as a tactic in the New Sanctuary Movement, but it was not the movement's primary tactic. Instead, sanctuary operated as a general strategy, including both nonconfrontational and more disruptive tactics (see Yukich 2012).

17. According to the instrumental–expressive binary, which despite criticism still underlies much research on strategic choice, the only explanation for the choice of sanctuary given its lack of fit to the political context is that New Sanctuary activists chose to forego a rational approach to choosing strategies, instead concerning themselves with a feel-good expression of their existing values (see Polletta 2004 for a discussion and criticism of this binary). But this explanation does not fit the actual process of strategic choice engaged in by the activists who formed New Sanctuary. Instead, as the example of the Good Shepherd member shows, these activists sought to recruit at least some people who were not already committed to immigrant rights—such as lay members of churches like Good Shepherd—who would not have felt a push to express commitments they did not yet share.

18. Lippert and Rehaag 2012.

19. Numbers 35:9–15, NRSV.

20. Cunningham 1995.

21. Ibid.

22. Cunningham 1995; Lippert and Rehaag 2012.

23. There are several excellent accounts of the 1980s Sanctuary Movement. Crittendon 1988 offers a good overall introduction to the movement. For social scientific analyses of the movement, see Coutin 1993; Cunningham 1995; Lorentzen 1991; Nepstad 2004a; and Smith 1996b.

24. They were trained at the School of the Americas, a U.S. military school in Ft. Benning, Georgia, and received funding from the Ronald Reagan administration. For more on this, see Nepstad 2004a and Smith 1996b.

25. Smith 1996b: 66.

26. Ibid., 67.

27. Ibid.

28. Yukich 2012.

29. Swidler 1986, 2001.

30. Pseudonym.

31. Pallares and Flores-González 2010; Voss and Bloemraad 2011.

32. Jasper 2006.

33. Ibid., 141.

34. Linda S. Rhodes, "Church Continues to Offer Sanctuary for Mother, Son," *United Methodist News Service*, 2006, Retrieved October 23, 2012 (http://www.umc.org/site/c.gjJTJbMUIuE/b.2028577/ k.D9D7/Church_continues_to_offer_sanctuary_for_mother_son.htm).

35. Hondagneu-Sotelo 2008.

36. There was disagreement among my interview participants regarding precisely what groups and foundations provided initial funding for New Sanctuary, so I do not

name them here. It was a controversial topic in part because early leaders disagreed about where funding should come from given its potential to shape the focus and growth of New Sanctuary.

37. My interviews with early, prelaunch organizers suggest there was a good deal of controversy in the months leading up to the launch around issues like whether to focus on sanctuary at all and whether to focus on sanctuary for all victims of raids or on sanctuary only for a subset of mixed-status families. Those who disagreed with the choice of sanctuary for mixed-status families as the strategic focus of the growing network either chose not to become very involved in the national network (e.g., Adalberto United Methodist Church) or were somewhat marginalized in the network at least in its initial years (e.g., the Portland coalition did not participate in the national New Sanctuary Movement launch). These disagreements were rooted in differences in local political context, in different levels of investment in religious goals, and in differences of opinion about the advisability of accepting funding tied to particular kinds of strategies and tactics.

38. "An Invitation to Join the New Sanctuary Movement," *Faith Works: Newsletter of Interfaith Worker Justice,* May 2007, p. 5–8.

39. Polletta et al. 2011.

40. Kroll-Smith 1980; Philibert and Hoge 1982; Yamane 2000.

41. In the past, most religion scholars have used the term *conversion* to refer to the adoption of a new religious institutional affiliation or identity, such as conversion from Buddhism to Islam or from an indigenous religion to Christianity (see Lofland and Stark 1965; Stark and Bainbridge 1980; Stark and Finke 2000). The logic undergirding the concept of conversion is that changing from one tradition to another shifts one's beliefs, practices, and culture so profoundly that other major changes will accompany these religious alterations. However, it is possible for such profound religious changes to occur in individuals or congregations even without any shifts in denomination or religious tradition, such that the term conversion need not be reserved for religious switching.

42. James 1902.

43. Williams 1964.

44. See Ellison and Powers 1994; Hayes and Dowds 2006.

45. Warren 2010.

46. Ellison and Powers 1994.

47. Lippert 2005.

48. Buber [1923] 1958.

49. Yukich 2010.

50. Armstrong and Bernstein 2008; McAdam, Tarrow, and Tilly 2001; Swidler 1986, 2001.

51. Armstrong and Bernstein 2008.

52. See Yukich 2012.

CHAPTER 4

1. Language taken from a flyer for the vigil.
2. According to Passel and Cohn 2009, in 2008 there were 10.4 million undocumented adults in the United States. Of those, only 3.8 million were members of mixed-status families.
3. Warner 2002.
4. Williams 2002.
5. Passel and Cohn 2009; Suárez-Orozco, Todorova, and Louie 2005.
6. See Yukich 2012.
7. Perla and Coutin 2012.
8. Cunningham 1995.
9. Coontz 1992; Gillis 1997.
10. Pallares 2010; Pallares and Flores-González 2011.
11. For instance, see Das Gupta 2012; Pallares and Flores-González 2011; Yukich 2013.
12. As I show in the book's conclusion, over time the New York coalition moved toward this model of sanctuary, increasing the numbers of immigrants involved in the movement.
13. See Rehaag 2009 on merit-based screening practices in Canadian sanctuary.
14. Pallares and Flores-González 2011; Williams 2002.
15. Shaw 2011; Wellman 2008.
16. Pallares and Flores-González 2011.
17. Ibid., 166.
18. For more, see Kateel and Shahani 2008.
19. Martinez 2011; Pallares and Flores-González 2011.
20. See Yukich 2013.
21. Pallares and Flores-González 2011: 166.
22. Coontz 1992; Gillis 1997.
23. Fetner 2008.
24. Diamond 1998; Fetner 2008; Hunter 1991; Wilcox 2006.
25. Fetner 2008; Wilcox 2006.
26. Ribuffo 1989.
27. Ibid.
28. Fetner 2008; Gillis 1997; Hunter 1992; Wilcox 2006; Williams 2002.
29. Hout, Greeley, and Wilde 2001; Hunter 1992; Wuthnow 1988; Wellman 2008.
30. Wuthnow and Evans 2002.
31. Edles 2013; Gaddy 2005; Hout and Fischer 2002; Schmalzbauer 2005; Slessarev-Jamir 2011; Wellman 2008.
32. Fetner 2008; Hout and Fischer 2002; Luker 1985; Putnam and Campbell 2010; Wilcox 2006.
33. Gaddy 2005; Wilcox 2006.
34. Wilcox 2006.
35. See Luker 1985 for a discussion of the importance of ideas about womanhood and motherhood in shaping positions on abortion, for instance.

36. Wilcox 2006.
37. G. Jeffrey Macdonald, "Liberal Journals Wither Despite Rising Christian Left," *Washington Post*, December 2, 2006, Retrieved March 30, 2013 (http://www.washingtonpost.com/wp-dyn/content/article/2006/12/01/AR2006120101211.html).
38. See Danielsen 2013; Edles 2013; Farrell 2011; Slessarev-Jamir 2011. See, for example, Jim Wallis, "What Do Values Voters Value Most?" Sojomail, September 20, 2006, Sojourners, Washington, DC, Retrieved November 30, 2012 (http://sojo.net/sojomail/2006/09/20).
39. Yoshikawa 2011.
40. Pseudonym.
41. Pseudonym.
42. Pseudonym.
43. Levitt 1998, 2007.
44. See Imam Ali Siddiqui, "Immigration on the Minmber," Indymedia, 2006, Retrieved November 30, 2012 (http://indymedia.us/en/2006/10/20391.shtml).
45. See the New Sanctuary Movement's original website, 2007, Retrieved June 1, 2011 (http://www.newsanctuarymovement.org).
46. Matthew 25:35, NRSV.
47. Referencing Leviticus 19:33–34.
48. Pseudonym.
49. See the New Sanctuary Movement's second website, 2009, Retrieved June 1, 2011 (http://www.sanctuarymovement.org).
50. See Snow et al. 1986.
51. Wellman 2008.
52. Wellman 2008: 273–274.
53. Danielsen 2013; Edles 2013; Farrell 2011; McDaniel, Nooruddin, and Shortle 2011.
54. Wellman 2008: 255.
55. Danielsen 2013; Diamond 1998; Farrell 2011; Putnam and Campbell 2010; Smith and Johnson 2010; Uecker and Locke 2011.
56. Wellman 2008.
57. Ibid., 273.
58. See Dan Zanes' website, Retrieved June 1, 2011 (http://www.danzanes.com/albums/the-welcome-table).
59. Anderson 1983.
60. See Williams 2007.

CHAPTER 5

1. Pseudonym.
2. Pseudonym.
3. Pseudonym.
4. Pseudonym.
5. Ganz 2000, 2009; Brown-Saracino and Ghaziani 2009; Lichterman 1995; Polletta 2002.

6. Armstrong and Bernstein 2008; Friedland and Alford 1991.

7. Ganz 2000, 2009.

8. See Armstrong and Bernstein 2008. Also, see Fligstein and McAdam's 2012 discussion of the embeddedness of strategic action fields, or the idea that among institutional arenas "there can be a form of embedding whereby actors that make up smaller collectivities are located within larger strategic action fields that contain larger collectivities" (p. 59).

9. Evans 2010: 8.

10. Swidler 1986, 2001.

11. Wuthnow 2011: 15.

12. Yamane 2000.

13. Evans 2010; Swidler 2001; Vaisey 2009; Wuthnow 2011; Zubrzycki 2006.

14. While approximately two-thirds of my respondents were active New Sanctuary participants, about one-third were people who New Sanctuary tried to recruit but who chose not to participate in its activities. See Appendix B for details on my interviewing methods.

15. See Swidler 2001.

16. Wellman 2008. Also, see Putnam and Campbell 2010 for a discussion of evangelical Christian views on salvation. Their survey data suggest that evangelical views on salvation are much more diverse (and more inclusive) than has often been assumed, to the chagrin of some evangelical Protestant leaders. For instance, 83% of evangelical Protestants believe that good people who are not evangelicals can go to heaven. Further, 54% believe that people of non-Christian faiths can go to heaven. Belief that members of other religions are "saved" appears related to whether one has a family member or close friend of a different faith, which Putnam and Campbell refer to as the "Aunt Susan" phenomenon. If you are Christian and your good and beloved Aunt Susan is Muslim, it might be harder for you to believe that all non-Christians deserve to be and will be eternally damned.

17. See Beyerlein and Chaves 2003.

18. Smith et al. 1998.

19. Associated Press, "New York Lawmakers Reject Gay Marriage Bill," NBC News, 2009, Retrieved November 30, 2012 (http://www.msnbc.msn.com/id/34242872/ns/us_news-life/t/new-york-lawmakers-reject-gay-marriage-bill/#.ULvHyXHR2pI).

20. Crawford and Olson 2001; Guth et al. 1997; Smith 1998.

21. Pseudonym.

22. See Lichterman 2012.

23. The "clergy" category includes seminarians on an ordination track.

24. This parallels Uecker and Lucke 2011, who found substantial engagement in culture wars by Protestant clergy from a variety of backgrounds. They argue that the much-debated *culture wars thesis* (see Hunter 1991) was originally rooted in debates among religious elites and should therefore be tested using data on clergy rather

than on the attitudes of the American public, who typically have less power over and less investment in struggles over religious authority.

25. Armstrong and Bernstein 2008; Thornton and Ocasio 1999.
26. Thornton and Ocasio 1999: 804.
27. Becker 1999.
28. Ganz 2000, 2009.
29. See the New Sanctuary Movement's original website, 2007, Retrieved January 10, 2012 (http://www.newsanctuarymovement.org/invitation.htm).
30. For instance, expanding the faith-based campaigns of Democrats might have the potential to both challenge the view that the Democratic Party is primarily for secular Americans (political discourse) and challenge the view that religious people are mostly conservative (religious discourse).
31. See the New Sanctuary Coalition of NYC's website, Retrieved January 10, 2012 (http://newsanctuarynyc.wordpress.com/).
32. City of New York Department of Correction, "DOC Statistics," Retrieved November 30, 2012 (http://www.nyc.gov/html/doc/html/stats/doc_stats.shtml).
33. See Lippert and Rehaag 2012; Tramonte 2009.
34. City of New York Department of Correction Directive, April 7, 2005, Retrieved November 30, 2012 (http://www.nyc.gov/html/doc/downloads/pdf/6000RA.pdf).
35. From author's field notes from a meeting between the New York coalition and representatives from New York University's Immigrant Rights Clinic, November 5, 2007.
36. Pseudonyms.
37. See Tramonte 2009.
38. At first, the campaign was known as the Immigration out of Rikers Campaign.
39. Retrieved January 10, 2012 (http://newsanctuarynyc.wordpress.com).
40. Ganz 2000, 2009.
41. Jasper 2006: 90.
42. Armstrong and Bernstein 2008.
43. Smith 1996b; Summers-Effler 2010.

CHAPTER 6

1. Chavez 2008.
2. Pseudonym.
3. For an example of liberation theology, see Gutierrez 1973; for a history of the Latin American liberation theology movement, see Smith 1991.
4. Epstein 1991.
5. In 2008, the Mexican American Cultural Center became Mexican American Catholic College.

6. Though I distinguish between themes of charity and justice here, charity work is not necessarily distinct from justice or counterrevolutionary, as is sometimes assumed. At times, charity work can become the root of social justice-oriented revolutionary action. See Boudewijnse, Droogers, and Kamsteeg 1998 for more on this.

7. Slessarev-Jamir 2011.

8. Ibid.

9. Lippert and Rehaag 2012.

10. Perla and Coutin 2012.

11. Lippert 2005.

12. See Lippert and Rehaag 2012. Also, Perla and Coutin 2009 highlight the involvement of Central American activists in the 1980s Sanctuary Movement. However, they also demonstrate the ways their involvement was largely deemphasized and hidden for strategic reasons. This is one of the factors that kept the Sanctuary Movement's legacy from spreading in Central America the way it did in the United States.

13. Pseudonym.

14. Slessarev-Jamir 2011.

15. Pseudonym.

16. See Smith 1996a.

17. Lippert and Rehaag 2012.

18. Voss and Bloemraad 2011.

19. While these two quotes suggest that immigrants who understand sanctuary as charitable aid are opposed to others receiving that aid, there are many immigrants who engage in mutual aid and support in a variety of forms, including offering private forms of sanctuary for immigrants in their own congregations.

20. See Lippert and Rehaag 2012; Tramonte 2009.

21. Jake Tapper with Ron Claiborne, "Romney: Giuliani's NYC 'Sanctuary' for Illegal Immigrants," ABC News, 2007, Retrieved November 30, 2012 (http://abcnews.go.com/Politics/story?id=3459498&page=1#.ULvLlHHR2pI).

22. Swidler 1986, 2001; McAdam, Tarrow, and Tilly 2001.

23. Edwards 2008a, Edwards 2008b; Pitt 2010.

24. Andersen 2003; Bonilla-Silva 2001; Gallagher 2003; Lewis 2004; Lipsitz 1998.

25. Eliasoph and Lichterman 2003.

26. Lichterman 2005.

27. Becker 1999.

28. Becker 1999; Espinosa, Elizondo, and Miranda 2005; Wilson 2008.

29. See Lichterman 1995. For a different view, see Polletta (2002, 2004), who has shown that participatory democracy as an organizational form has been used by social movement organizations with diverse membership backgrounds, not only by white, middle-class people.

30. Leondar-Wright 2005.

31. See the New Sanctuary Movement's original website, 2007, Retrieved May 26, 2011 (http://www.newsanctuarymovement.org).

32. Leondar-Wright 2005; Lichterman 1995
33. Stout 2010; Wood 2002.
34. Pseudonym.
35. Pseudonym.
36. Pseudonym.
37. See Smith 1996b.
38. Yukich 2012.
39. Foucault 1975.
40. Wiltfang and McAdam 1991.
41. Pew Hispanic Center, "2007 National Survey of Latinos: As Illegal Immigration Issue Heats Up, Hispanics Feel a Chill," Pew Hispanic Center Report 84, Washington, DC, 2007.
42. Brotherton and Kretsedemas 2008.
43. See Voss and Bloemraad 2011.
44. Brotherton and Krestsedemas 2008; Hondagneu-Sotelo 2008.
45. See Hart 2001; Lichterman 2005; Smith 1996a, 1996b; Stout 2010; Wood 2002.
46. Morris 1984; Smith 1996a.
47. Lichterman 2005, 2008; Stout 2010; Wood 1999, 2002.
48. Pseudonym.
49. Since my Spanish was not fluent, I received translation assistance from the church's pastor.
50. In 2007, ICE Fugitive Operations Teams arrested 30,407 immigrants compared with 15,462 in 2006. See Margot Mendelson, Shayna Strom, and Michael Wishnie, "Collateral Damage: An Examination of ICE's Fugitive Operations Program," Migration Policy Institute, Washington, DC, 2009.
51. While several New Sanctuary coalitions held Know Your Rights events, including the New York coalition, activities like this never became as central as sanctuary in most coalitions.
52. Levitt 2007.
53. Pallares and Flores-González 2011.
54. Pseudonym.
55. Pseudonym.

CHAPTER 7

1. Pseudonym.
2. Pseudonym.
3. Pseudonym.
4. In the coalitions I studied, there was no participation from other non-Western religious traditions, such as Hinduism or Buddhism.
5. Eck 2002.
6. Ganz 2009.

7. Wuthnow 2005.

8. See U.S. Religious Landscape Study, Pew Forum on Religion & Public Life, 2008, Retrieved November 30, 2012 (http://religions.pewforum.org/affiliations) for a full breakdown of American's religious affiliations.

9. Unaffiliated status should not be equated with irreligiosity. Rather, studies have shown that even people who do not affiliate with any religious tradition often report beliefs and behaviors traditionally associated with religiosity, such as belief in God or prayer. Only some members of this group are professed atheists or agnostics, while a large number might fall into the category of "spiritual but not religious," perhaps for reasons related to political identity (see Hout and Fischer 2002).

10. Herberg 1955.

11. Smith 2003; Wuthnow 2006.

12. Warner 2005; Wuthnow 2006.

13. Hout, Greeley, and Wilde 2001; Smith 2003; Wuthnow 2006.

14. Wuthnow 2006: 133.

15. See, for example, Cadge 2004; Kurien 2007.

16. Levitt 2007; Matovina 2012.

17. Wuthnow 2006.

18. Hondagneu-Sotelo 2007, 2008.

19. Ecklund 2006.

20. Beyerlein 2010; Hondagneu-Sotelo 2007, 2008.

21. Hondagneu-Sotelo 2008:21.

22. Weiner 2010.

23. Jasper 1997: 11.

24. Hondagneu-Sotelo 2008; Leonard 2007.

25. See, for example, Ahmed 2011; Hondagneu-Sotelo 2008.

26. Edwards and McCarthy 2004; McAdam 1988.

27. See Leonard 2007 for more on the tensions between immigrant and indigenous Muslim communities in the United States.

28. Though I would argue that singing and lighting candles is in fact an important part of many Jewish traditions, Shaykh Bashir's point that these are practices associated with some traditions (such as Christianity and Judaism) but not with others (such as Islam) still stands.

29. Pseudonym.

30. Pseudonym.

31. Pseudonym.

32. Pseudonym.

33. Pseudonym.

34. Pseudonym.

35. Jasper 1997: 341.

36. Pseudonym.

37. Pseudonym.

38. Pseudonym.

39. The worship sheet for the Desert Prayers liturgy indicated that the Call to Worship, Prayer of Invocation, and Prayer of Commitment used in the service were adapted from "From Stranger to Neighbor: Worship Toward Sane, Humane Immigration Policies," written by Rev. Loren McGrail and Rev. Michael Mulberry, United Church of Christ.

40. For more on the role of Operation Gatekeeper in migrant deaths at the border, see Nevins 2010.

41. Pseudonym.

42. Pseudonym.

43. Pseudonym.

44. Attributed to Judy Chicago.

45. While it might seem contradictory that crossover activists with experience with interfaith activism would need to learn how to engage with religious minorities, much of their prior interfaith activism was focused on shared goals that did not include religious globalism, meaning that the emphasis of New Sanctuary demanded deeper levels of engagement than those they were often used to.

46. Smith 1996b; Summers-Effler 2010.

CONCLUSION

1. Pseudonym.

2. See Slessarev-Jamir 2011.

3. Pseudonym.

4. While some activists compared the situations of the sanctuary families in physical sanctuary (who were unable to leave their sanctuaries without the risk of deportation) to a form of imprisonment or incarceration, others were uncomfortable with this analogy, feeling it was an inapt comparison given the terrible conditions often associated with actual incarceration.

5. Pseudonym.

6. Wellman 2008; Wilcox 2006.

7. Goldberg 2006.

8. Wellman 2008.

9. Beyerlein 2010; Heredia 2011; Hondagneu-Sotelo 2008.

10. See, for example, Gretchen Ruethling, "Chicago Woman's Stand Stirs Immigration Debate," *New York Times,* August 19, 2006, Retrieved November 30, 2012 (http://www.nytimes.com/2006/08/19/us/19immigrant.html?scp=1&sq=elvira%20arellano&st=cse); David Van Biema, "A Church Haven for Illegal Aliens," *TIME Magazine,* July 19, 2007, Retrieved November 30, 2012 (http://www.time.com/time/magazine/article/0,9171,1645169,00.html); and "Feature: Immigrant Sanctuary Movement," *Religion & Ethics NewsWeekly,* June 15, 2007, Retrieved November 30, 2012 (http://www.pbs.org/wnet/religionandethics/week1042/

feature.html). Most of the national coverage during the 2007–2009 period occurred early in the group's mobilization, but coverage in smaller news outlets was more frequent.

11. James R. Edwards Jr., "A Biblical Perspective on Immigration Policy," Center for Immigration Studies, 2009.

12. "Feature: Immigrant Sanctuary Movement," *Religion & Ethics NewsWeekly*, June 15, 2007, Retrieved November 30, 2012 (http://www.pbs.org/wnet/religionandethics/week1042/feature.html).

13. Ibid. For instance, Richard Land, a Southern Baptist representative, was quoted in this PBS story from 2006, before the New Sanctuary Movement even began.

14. See, for example, Paloma Esquivel, "Focus on the Family Joins Evangelical Call for Immigration Reform," *Los Angeles Times*, June 12, 2012, Retrieved November 21, 2012 (http://latimesblogs.latimes.com/lanow/2012/06/conservative-ministry-immigration-reform.html); and Richard Land, "God and Immigration Reform," *USA Today*, August 15, 2010, Retrieved November 21, 2012 (http://www.usatoday.com/news/opinion/forum/2010-08-16-column16_ST_N.htm).

15. Beyerlein 2010; Hagan 2007; Heredia 2011; Hondagneu-Sotelo 2008.

16. See Margot Mendelson, Shayna Strom, and Michael Wishnie, "Collateral Damage: An Examination of ICE's Fugitive Operations Program," Migration Policy Institute, 2009; William Finnegan, "Profiles: Sherriff Joe," *New Yorker,* 2009.

17. As of this writing, the Child Citizen Protection Act (CCPA), the only proposed policy to have received the New York coalition's official support, had still not passed. Some activists continued to emphasize its importance, while others feared that passing "piecemeal" legislation—the act would give immigration judges more freedom in deciding the cases of specific immigrants—would discourage supportive legislators from pushing for more comprehensive reform. Similarly, while they generally supported the 2010 push for the passage of the DREAM Act, national legislation that would enable undocumented immigrant students to seek legal status, New Sanctuary activists were less involved in this drive because of their emphasis on mixed-status immigrant families. In the end, the DREAM Act failed to pass at that time, and despite President Barack Obama's support for DREAMers, as of this writing there is still no legislation protecting them.

18. See Randal C. Archibold, "Arizona Enacts Stringent Law on Immigration," *New York Times*, April 23, 2010, Retrieved November 30, 2012 (http://www.nytimes.com/2010/04/24/us/politics/24immig.html).

19. See Richard Fausset, "Alabama Enacts Anti-Illegal-Immigration Law Described as Nation's Strictest," *Los Angeles Times*, June 10, 2011, Retrieved November 30, 2012 (http://articles.latimes.com/2011/jun/10/nation/la-na-alabama-immigration-20110610).

20. *Parsley et al. v. Bentley,* Civil Action File 2011:2, Retrieved November 30, 2012 (http://www.nytimes.com/2011/08/14/us/14immig.html?scp=1&sq=alabama%20immigration%20law%20clergy&st=cse).

21. See U.S. Immigration and Customs Enforcement website, "Secure Communities," Retrieved November 30, 2012 (http://www.ice.gov/secure_communities/).

22. See Tramonte 2009.

23. See the New Sanctuary Coalition of NYC's website, Retrieved March 30, 2013 (http://newsanctuarynyc.wordpress.com/about-jean/).

24. See Kirk Semple, "Demonstrators Press for Haitian Advocate's Release," *New York Times*, January 14, 2010, Retrieved November 30, 2012 (http://www.nytimes.com/2010/01/15/nyregion/15deport.html?scp=2&sq=jean%20montrevil&st=cse).

25. A few months later, the detention center closed, though it was likely due more to the high costs associated with jailing immigrants there than to opposition to the detention center. See Nina Bernstein, "Immigrants in Detention to Be Sent Out of State," *New York Times*, January 14, 2010, Retrieved November 21, 2012 (http://www.nytimes.com/2010/01/15/nyregion/15ice.html).

26. See Oxfam International's website, "Haiti Earthquake 2010," Retrieved November 25, 2012 (http://www.oxfam.org/en/haitiquake).

27. While Haitian immigrants facing deportation were granted Temporary Protected Status in the earthquake's aftermath, protecting them temporarily from deportation, this protected status did not apply to immigrants like Jean with past criminal convictions. See Jorge Rivas, "Temporary Protected Status for Haitians Begins Today, but Doesn't Apply to Everyone," *ColorLines*, January 21, 2010, Retrieved November 25, 2012 (http://colorlines.com/archives/2010/01/temporary_protected_status_for_haitias_begins_today_but_doesnt_apply_to_everyone.html).

28. For instance, in the New York coalition's main brochure, the two programs highlighted were immigrant check-in accompaniment and immigrant legal clinics: no mention of partnerships between mixed-status families and congregations as a major activity.

29. See the New Sanctuary Coalition of NYC's website, Retrieved November 21, 2012 (http://www.newsanctuarynyc.org/jericho.html).

30. Oral communications to author from two coalition activists, November 2012.

31. Author's field notes.

32. See the New Sanctuary Coalition of NYC's website, Retrieved January 19, 2012 (http://newsanctuarynyc.wordpress.com/).

33. Ganz 2009; Hannan and Freeman 1984; McAdam 1983; McCammon 2003; McCammon et al. 2008; Minkoff 1999.

34. According to LA area activists, deferred action status protects Liliana from deportation temporarily, but it must be renewed each year. So far, it has been renewed in both 2011 and 2012, and her partners and lawyers hope it will be renewed in future years as well. Also, see Tom Kisken, "Five Years Later Oxnard Woman Continues Fight Against Deportation Threat," *Ventura County Star*, July 9, 2012, Retrieved November 21, 2012 (http://m.vcstar.com/news/2012/jul/09/five-years-later-oxnard-woman-continues-fight/).

35. See the Immigrant Justice Advocacy Movement's website, Retrieved November 30, 2012 (http://www.ijamkc.org/).

36. See the New Sanctuary Movement of Philadelphia's website, Retrieved November 30, 2012 (http://www.sanctuaryphiladelphia.org/); and the Boston New Sanctuary Movement's website, Retrieved November 30, 2012 (http://www.bostonnewsanctuary.org/).

37. See Nepstad 2008 for a discussion of theories about what shapes movement trajectories. Most theories focus on structural factors, such as expanding or contracting political opportunities. New Sanctuary also highlights how changes in structural factors (e.g., the religious and political contexts) may shape movement trajectories—in this case, by encouraging activists to shift from an emphasis on multiple targets to a focus on a single target.

38. Armstrong and Bernstein 2008.

39. See Bruce 2011; Jasper 1997.

40. See Andrews 2004; Harris 1999; McAdam 1982; Morris 1984.

41. Morris 1984: 97–98.

42. See King 2000.

43. See the Martin Luther King Jr. Research and Education Institute, Retrieved November 23, 2012, (http://mlk-kpp01.stanford.edu/index.php/encyclopedia/encyclopedia/enc_dissertation_of_martin_luther_king_jr_1955/).

44. See Marsh 2005.

45. See McAdam 1982, esp. pp. 90–92.

46. Wuthnow 1988.

47. Ibid., 37.

48. Ibid., 38.

49. Smilde and May 2010; Yukich 2011.

50. Wilde 2007.

51. Bruce 2011: 154.

52. Brown-Saracino and Ghaziani 2009.

53. Morris 1984; Smith 1991, 1996a, 1996b; Williams 1995, 1996; Wood 1999, 2002.

54. Mirola 2003; Wilde 2004.

55. Smilde and May 2010.

56. See Marx [1844] 1978.

57. Beyerlein 2010; Davis, Martinez, and Warner 2010; Heredia 2011; Hondagneu-Sotelo 2007, 2008; Hondagneu-Sotelo, Gaudinez, and Lara 2007; Menjivar 2007; Slessarev-Jamir 2011.

58. See Beyerlein 2010; Davis, Martinez, and Warner 2010; Hondagneu-Sotelo 2007, 2008; Slessarev-Jamir 2011; Voss and Bloemraad 2011.

59. While Habermas 1985 and Rawls 1997 offered two of the most important examples of this position, both later changed their positions slightly, especially Habermas. In fact, in a later essay, he argues that it may be unfair to ask religious participants in the public sphere to translate their religious reasons into secular ones and that to completely eradicate religious language from the public might

weaken the democratic public sphere (Habermas 2006). For more on the changing philosophical debates around these issues, see Mendieta and VanAntwerpen 2011.

60. Pew Research Center, "Few Say Religion Shapes Immigration, Environment Views," Pew Research Center, Washington, DC, 2010.

61. Mendieta and VanAntwerpen 2011.

62. See Liliana Santuario, "Justice: A General Definition," *National Newsletter of the New Sanctuary Movement*, January 2008, p. 12.

APPENDIX A

1. See Snow et al. 1986.

2. See Brotherton and Kretsedemas 2008; Chavez 2008.

3. See Charles Garcia, "Why 'Illegal Immigrant' Is a Slur," 2012, Retrieved November 23, 2012 (http://www.cnn.com/2012/07/05/opinion/garcia-illegal-immigrants/index.html).

4. Chavez 2008; Passell and Cohn 2008, 2009.

APPENDIX B

1. Case studies play an important role in social scientific research (Ragin and Becker 1992). Single case studies, no matter how detailed, are limited in the extent to which they are generalizable. In other words, they trade breadth for depth. But because they delve deeply into the specifics of a particular case, uncovering information that allows the linking of observations in innovative and contextually grounded ways, case studies are an indispensable tool for theory building and theory testing.

2. Babbie 2005; Emerson, Fretz, and Shaw 1995.

3. Hannerz 2003.

4. Weiss 1994.

5. As is typical of websites, as of this writing, some of the websites I analyze and cite in this book are no longer operational either because they have not been maintained or because their content was replaced at some point with more recent content.

REFERENCES

2007. *New Revised Standard Version Standard Bible*. New York: HarperCollins.

Ahmed, Leila. 2011. *A Quiet Revolution: The Veil's Resurgence, from the Middle East to America*. New Haven, CT: Yale University Press.

Alba, Richard, Albert J. Raboteau, and Josh DeWind, eds. 2009. *Immigration and Religion in America: Comparative and Historical Perspectives*. New York: New York University Press.

Ammerman, Nancy T. 2005. *Pillars of Faith: American Congregations and Their Partners*. Berkeley: University of California Press.

Andersen, M.L. 2003. "Whitewashing Race: A Critical Perspective on Whiteness." Pp. 21–34 in *White Out: The Continuing Significance of Racism*, edited by A.W. Doane and E. Bonilla-Silva. New York: Routledge.

Anderson, Benedict. 1983. *Imagined Communities: Reflections on the Origins and Spread of Nationalism*. Verso.

Andrews, Kenneth T. 2004. *Freedom Is a Constant Struggle: The Mississippi Civil Rights Movement and Its Legacy*. Chicago: University of Chicago Press.

Armstrong, Elizabeth A. 2002. *Forging Gay Identities: Organizing Sexuality in San Francisco, 1950–1994*. Chicago: University of Chicago Press.

Armstrong, Elizabeth A. and Mary Bernstein. 2008. "Culture, Power, and Institutions: A Multi-Institutional Politics Approach to Social Movements." *Sociological Theory* 26:74–99.

Aronowitz, Stanley. 1992. *The Politics of Identity*. New York: Routledge.

Babbie, Earl. 2005. *The Basics of Social Research*. Belmont, CA: Thomson Wadsworth.

Barkan, Steven E. 1979. "Strategic, Tactical and Organizational Dilemmas of the Protest Movement against Nuclear Power." *Social Problems* 27:19–37.

Bartley, Tim. 2007. "Institutional Emergence in an Era of Globalization: The Rise of Transnational Private Regulation of Labor and Environmental Conditions." *American Journal of Sociology* 113:297–351.

Becker, Penny Edgell. 1999. *Congregations in Conflict: Cultural Models of Local Religious Life*. New York: Cambridge University Press.

Bellah, Robert N. 1967. "Civil Religion in America." *Daedalus* 96:1–21.

Bender, Courtney, Wendy Cadge, Peggy Levitt, and David Smilde, eds. 2012. *Religion on the Edge: De-centering and Re-centering the Sociology of Religion*. New York: Oxford University Press.

Beyerlein, Kraig. 2010. "Understanding the Dynamics of Congregation-Based Mobilization Efforts: The Case of Humanitarian Aid Efforts for Migrants Along the Sonora-Arizona Border." Paper presented at the annual meeting of the Society for the Scientific Study of Religion, Baltimore, MD.

Beyerlein, Kraig and Mark Chaves. 2003. "The Political Activities of Religious Congregations in the United States." *Journal for the Scientific Study of Religion* 42:229–46.

Billings, Dwight B. 1990. "Religion as Opposition: A Gramscian Analysis." *American Journal of Sociology* 96:1–31.

Bloemraad, Irene, Kim Voss, and Taeku Lee. 2011. "The Protests of 2006: What Were They, How Do We Understand Them, Where Do We Go?" Pp. 3–43 in *Rallying for Immigrant Rights*, ed K. Voss and I. Bloemraad. Berkeley: University of California Press.

Bonilla-Silva, Eduardo. 2001. *White Supremacy and Racism in the Post-Civil Rights Era*. Boulder, CO: Lynne Rienner.

Boudewijnse, Barbara, André Droogers, and Frans Kamsteeg. 1998. *More Than Opium: An Anthropological Approach to Latin American and Caribbean Pentecostal Praxis*. Lanham, MD: Scarecrow Press.

Bourdieu, Pierre. 1991. "Genesis and Structure of the Religious Field." *Comparative Social Research* 13:1–44.

Brodkin, Karen. 2012. "How Jews Became White Folks." Pp. 45–57 in *White Privilege: Essential Readings on the Other Side of Racism*, edited by P.S. Rothenberg. New York: Worth.

Brotherton, David and Philip Kretsedemas, eds. 2008. *Keeping Out the Other: A Critical Introduction to Immigration Enforcement Today*. New York: Columbia University Press.

Brown-Saracino, Japonica and Amin Ghaziani. 2009. "The Constraints of Culture: Evidence from the Chicago Dyke March." *Cultural Sociology* 3:51–75.

Bruce, Tricia C. 2011. *Faithful Revolution: How Voice of the Faithful Is Changing the Church*. New York: Oxford University Press.

Buber, Martin. [1923] 1958. *I and Thou*. Trans. Ronald Gregor Smith. New York: Charles Scribner's Sons.

Cadge, Wendy. 2004. *Heartwood: The First Generation of Theravada Buddhism in America*. Chicago: University of Chicago Press.

Cadge, Wendy and Elaine Howard Ecklund. 2007. "Immigration and Religion." *Annual Review of Sociology* 33:359–379.

Calhoun, Craig. 1993. "What's New About New Social Movements? The Early 19th Century Reconsidered." *Social Science History* 17:385–427.

Caminero-Santangelo, Marta. 2009. "Responding to the Human Costs of US Immigration Policy: No More Deaths and the New Sanctuary Movement." *Latino Studies* 7:112–122.

Casanova, José. 1994. *Public Religions in the Modern World*. Chicago: University of Chicago Press.

Castañeda-Liles, Socorro. 2005. "Spiritual Affirmation and Empowerment: The Mexican American Cultural Center." Pp. 111–125 in *Latino Religions and Civic Activism in the United States*, edited by G. Espinosa, V. Elizondo, and J. Miranda. New York: Oxford University Press.

Chaves, Mark. 1994. "Secularization as Declining Religious Authority." *Social Forces* 72:749–774.

———. 2004. *Congregations in America*. Cambridge, MA: Harvard University Press.

Chavez, Leo. 2008. *The Latino Threat: Constructing Immigrants, Citizens, and the Nation*. Palo Alto, CA: Stanford University Press.

Coontz, Stephanie. 1992. *The Way We Never Were: American Families and the Nostalgia Trap*. New York: Basic Books.

Coutin, Susan Bibler. 1993. *The Culture of Protest: Religious Activism and the U.S. Sanctuary Movement*. Boulder, CO: Westview Press.

Cordero-Guzmán, Hector, Nina Martin, Victoria Quiroz-Becerra, and Nik Theodore. 2008. "Voting With Their Feet: Nonprofit Organizations and Immigrant Mobilization." *American Behavioral Scientist* 52:598.

Crawford, Sue E.S. and Laura R. Olson, eds. 2001. *Christian Clergy in American Politics*. Baltimore, MD: Johns Hopkins University Press.

Crittenden, Ann. 1988. *Sanctuary: A Story of American Conscience and the Law in Collision*. New York: Grove Press.

Cunningham, Hilary. 1995. *God and Caesar at the Rio Grande: Sanctuary and the Politics of Religion*. Minneapolis: University of Minnesota Press.

Danielsen, Sabrina. 2013. "Fracturing Over Creation Care? Shifting Environmental Beliefs Among Evangelicals, 1984–2010." *Journal for the Scientific Study of Religion* 52:198–215.

Das Gupta, Monisha. 2006. *Unruly Immigrants: Rights, Activism, and Transnational South Asian Politics in the United States*. Durham, NC: Duke University Press.

———. 2012. "Don't Deport Our Daddies: Gendering State Deportation Practices and Anti-Deportation Organizing." Paper presented at the annual meeting of the American Studies Association, San Antonio, TX.

Davis, Nancy J. and Robert V. Robinson. 2012. *Claiming Society for God: Religious Movements & Social Welfare*. Bloomington: Indiana University Press.

Davis, Stephen P., Juan R. Martinez, and R. Stephen Warner. 2010. "The Role of the Catholic Church in the Chicago Immigrant Mobilization." Pp. 76–96 in ¡*Marcha! Latino Chicago and the Immigrant Rights Movement*, edited by A. Pallares and N. Flores-González. Urbana: University of Illinois Press.

De La Torre, Miguel A. 2003. *La Lucha for Cuba: Religion and Politics on the Streets of Miami*. Berkeley: University of California Press.

Demerath III, N.J. and Rhys H. Williams. 1985. "Civil Religion in an Uncivil Society." *ANNALS of the American Academy of Political and Social Science* 480:154–166.

DeSoucey, Michaela. 2010. "Gastronationalism: Food Traditions and Authenticity Politics in the European Union." *American Sociological Review* 75:432–455.

Diamond, Sara. 1998. *Not By Politics Alone: The Enduring Influence of the Christian Right*. New York: Guilford Press.

Downey, Gary L. 1986. "Ideology and the Clamshell Identity: Organizational Dilemmas in the Anti-Nuclear Power Movement." *Social Problems* 33:357–371.

Ebaugh, Helen Rose and Janet Saltzman Chafetz, eds. 2000. *Religion and the New Immigrants: Continuities and Adaptations in Immigrant Congregations*. Walnut Creek, CA: Altamira Press.

Eck, Diana. 2002. *A New Religious America: How a "Christian Country" Has Become the World's Most Religiously Diverse Nation*. San Francisco: HarperSanFrancisco.

Ecklund, Elaine Howard. 2006. *Korean American Evangelicals: New Models for Civic Life*. New York: Oxford University Press.

Edles, Laura Desfor. 2013. "Contemporary Progressive Christianity and Its Symbolic Ramifications." *Cultural Sociology* 7:3–22.

Edwards, Bob and John D. McCarthy. 2004. "Resources and Social Movement Mobilization." Pp. 116–152 in *The Blackwell Companion to Social Movements*, edited by D. Snow, S. Soule, and H. Kriesi. Malden, MA: Blackwell Publishing.

Edwards, Korie L. 2008a. "Bring Race to the Center: The Importance of Race in Racially Diverse Religious Organizations." *Journal for the Scientific Study of Religion* 47:5–9.

———. 2008b. *The Elusive Dream: The Power of Race in Interracial Churches*. New York: Oxford University Press.

Eliasoph, Nina and Paul Lichterman. 2003. "Culture in Interaction." *American Journal of Sociology* 108:735–794.

Ellison, Christopher G. and Daniel A. Powers. 1994. "The Contact Hypothesis and Racial Attitudes among Black Americans." *Social Science Quarterly* 75:385–400.

Emerson, Michael O. with Rodney M. Woo. 2006. *People of the Dream: Multiracial Congregations in the United States*. Princeton, NJ: Princeton University Press.

Emerson, Robert M., Rachel I. Fretz, and Linda L. Shaw. 1995. *Writing Ethnographic Fieldnotes*. Chicago: University of Chicago Press.

Epstein, Barbara. 1991. *Political Protest and Cultural Revolution: Nonviolent Direct Action in the 1970s and 1980s*. Berkeley: University of California Press.

Espinosa, Gaston, Virgilio Elizondo, and Jesse Miranda, eds. 2005. *Latino Religions and Civic Activism in the United States*. New York: Oxford University Press.

Evans, John H. 2010. *Contested Reproduction: Genetic Technologies, Religion, and Public Debate*. Chicago: University of Chicago Press.

Farrell, Justin. 2011. "The Young and the Restless? The Liberalization of Young Evangelicals." *Journal for the Scientific Study of Religion* 50:517–532.

Félix, Adrian, González, Carmen, and Ricardo Ramírez. 2008. "Political Protest, Ethnic Media, and Latino Naturalization." *American Behavioral Scientist* 52:618–634.

Fetner, Tina. 2008. *How the Religious Right Shaped Lesbian and Gay Activism*. Minneapolis: University of Minnesota Press.

Fligstein, Neil and Doug McAdam. 2012. *A Theory of Fields*. New York: Oxford University Press.

Foucault, Michel. 1975. *Discipline and Punish: The Birth of the Prison*. New York: Random House.

Freeland, Gregory. 2010. "Negotiating Place, Space and Borders: The New Sanctuary Movement." *Latino Studies* 8:485–508.

Friedland, Roger and Robert R. Alford. 1991. "Bringing Society Back In: Symbols, Practices, and Institutional Contradictions." Pp. 232–263 in *The New Institutionalism in Organizational Analysis*, edited by W. W. Powell and P. J. DiMaggio. Chicago: University of Chicago Press.

Gaddy, C. Welton. 2005. "God Talk in the Public Square." Pp. 43–48 in *Quoting God: How Media Shape Ideas About Religion and Culture*, edited by C. Badaracco. Waco, TX: Baylor University Press.

Gallagher, Charles A. 2003. "Color-Blind Privilege: The Social and Political Functions of Erasing the Color Line in Post Race America." *Race, Gender & Class* 10:1–17.

Ganz, Marshall. 2000. "Resources and Resourcefulness: Strategic Capacity in the Unionization of California Agriculture, 1959–1966." *American Journal of Sociology* 105:1003–1062.

———. 2009. *Why David Sometimes Wins: Leadership, Organization, and Strategy in the California Farm Worker Movement*. New York: Oxford University Press.

Gillis, John. 1997. *A World of Their Own Making: Myth, Ritual, and the Quest for Family Values*. New York: Basic Books.

Goldberg, Michelle. 2006. *Kingdom Coming: The Rise of Christian Nationalism*. New York: W.W. Norton.

Gonzalez III, Joaquin Jay and Claudine del Rosario. 2009. "Counterhegemony Finds Place in a Hegemon: Activism through Filipino American Churches." Pp. 285–310 in *Religion at the Corner of Bliss and Nirvana*, edited by L.A. Lorentzen, J.J. Gonzalez, K.M. Chun, and H.D. Do. Durham, NC: Duke University Press.

Goodwin, Jeff and James M. Jasper. 1999. "Caught in a Winding, Snarling Vine: The Structural Bias of Political Process Theory." *Sociological Forum* 14:27–54.

Guest, Kenneth J. 2003. *God in Chinatown: Religion and Survival in New York's Evolving Immigrant Community*. New York: New York University Press.

Guskin, Jane and David L. Wilson. 2007. *The Politics of Immigration: Questions and Answers*. New York: Monthly Review Press.

Guth, James L. 1997. *The Bully Pulpit: The Politics of Protestant Clergy*. Lawrence, KS: University Press of Kansas.

Guth, James L., Linda Beail, Greg Crow, Beverly Gaddy, Steve Montreal, Brent Nelsen, James Penning, and Jeff Walz. 2003. "The Political Activity of Evangelical Clergy in the Election of 2000: A Case Study of Five Denominations." *Journal for the Scientific Study of Religion* 42:501–514.

Gutiérrez, Gustavo. 1973. *A Theology of Liberation: History, Politics, and Salvation*. Maryknoll, NY: Orbis Books.

Habermas, Jürgen. 1981. "New Social Movements." *Telos* 49:33–37.

———. 1985. *The Theory of Communicative Action: Reason and the Rationalization of Society*. Boston: Beacon Press.

———. 2006. "Religion in the Public Sphere." *European Journal of Philosophy* 14:1–25.

Haddad, Yvonne Yazbeck. 2009. "The Shaping of Arab and Muslim Identity in the United States." Pp. 246–276 in *Immigration and Religion in America*, edited by R. Alba, A.J. Raboteau, and J. DeWind. New York: New York University Press.

Haddad, Yvonne Yazbeck, Jane I. Smith, and John L. Esposito, eds. 2003. *Religion and Immigration: Christian, Jewish, and Muslim Experiences in the United States.* Walnut Creek, CA: Altamira Press.

Hagan, Jacqueline Maria. 2007. "The Church vs. the State: Borders, Migrants, and Human Rights." Pp. 93–103 in *Religion and Social Justice for Immigrants*, edited by P. Hondagneu-Sotelo. New Brunswick, NJ: Rutgers University Press.

Hannan, M.T. and J. Freeman. 1984. "Structural Inertia and Organizational Change." *American Sociological Review* 49:149–164.

Hannerz, Ulf. 2003. "Being There…and There…and There! Reflections on Multi-site Ethnography." *Ethnography* 4:201–216.

Hannigan, John A. 1991. "Social Movement Theory and the Sociology of Religion: Toward a New Synthesis." *Sociological Analysis* 52: 311–331.

Harris, Fredrick C. 1999. *Something Within: Religion in African-American Political Activism.* New York: Oxford University Press.

Hart, Stephen. 2001. *Cultural Dilemmas of Progressive Politics: Styles of Engagement among Grassroots Activists.* Chicago: University of Chicago Press.

Hayes, Bernadette C. and Lizanne Dowds. 2006. "Social Contact, Cultural Marginality or Economic Self-Interest? Attitudes Towards Immigrants in Northern Ireland." *Journal of Ethnic and Migration Studies* 32: 455–476.

Hefner, Robert W., ed. 2009. *Making Modern Muslims: The Politics of Islamic Education in Southeast Asia.* Honolulu: University of Hawai'i Press.

Herberg, Will. 1955. *Catholic-Protestant-Jew: An Essay in American Religious Sociology.* Garden City, NY: Doubleday.

Heredia, Luis. 2011. "From Prayer to Protest: The Immigrant Rights Movement and the Catholic Church." Pp. 101–122 in *Rallying for Immigrant Rights*, edited by K. Voss and I. Bloemraad. Berkeley: University of California Press.

Hondagneu-Sotelo, Pierrette, ed. 2007. *Religion and Social Justice for Immigrants.* New Brunswick, NJ: Rutgers University Press.

———. 2008. *God's Heart Has No Borders: How Religious Activists are Working for Immigrant Rights.* Berkeley: University of California Press.

Hondagneu-Sotelo, Pierrette, Genelle Gaudinez, and Hector Lara. 2007. "Religious Reenactment on the Line: A Genealogy of Political Religious Hybridity." Pp. 122–138 in *Religion and Social Justice for Immigrants*, edited by Pierrette Hondagneu-Sotelo. New Brunswick, NJ: Rutgers University Press.

Hout, Michael and Claude S. Fischer. 2002. "Why More Americans Have No Religious Preference: Politics and Generations." *American Sociological Review* 67:165–190.

Hout, Michael, Andrew Greeley, and Melissa J. Wilde. 2001. "The Demographic Imperative in Religious Change in the United States." *American Journal of Sociology* 107:468–500.

Hunt, Larry L. and Janet G. Hunt. 1977. "Black Religion as BOTH Opiate and Inspiration of Civil Rights Militance: Putting Marx's Data to the Test." *Social Forces* 56:1–14.

Hunter, James Davison. 1991. *Culture Wars: The Struggle to Define America*. New York: Basic Books.

Irazabal, Clara and Grace R. Dyrness. 2010. "Promised Land? Immigration, Religiosity, and Space in Southern California." *Space and Culture* 13:356–375.

Isaac, Larry. 2009. "Movements, Aesthetics, and Markets in Literary Change: Making the American Labor Problem Novel." *American Sociological Review* 74:938–965.

James, William. 1902. *The Varieties of Religious Experience*. London: Longmans, Green & Co.

Jasper, James M. 1997. *The Art of Moral Protest: Culture, Biography, and Creativity in Social Movements*. Chicago: University of Chicago Press.

———. 2006. *Getting Your Way: Strategic Dilemmas in the Real World*. Chicago: University of Chicago Press.

Jasso, Guillermina and Mark R. Rosenzweig. 2011. "Characteristics of Immigrants to the United States: 1820–2003." Pp. 328–358 in *A Companion to American Immigration*, edited by R.Ueda. Wiley-Blackwell.

Jenkins, Philip. 2002. *The New Christendom: The Coming of Global Christianity*. New York: Oxford University Press.

Jeung, Russell. 2007. "Faith-Based, Multiethnic Tenant Organizing: The Oak Park Story." Pp. 59–73 in *Religion and Social Justice for Immigrants*, edited by P. Hondagneu-Sotelo. New Brunswick, NJ: Rutgers University Press.

Kasinitz, Philip, John H. Mollenkopf, and Mary C. Waters, eds. 2006. *Becoming New Yorkers: Ethnographies of the New Second Generation*. New York: Russell Sage Foundation.

Kateel, Subash and Aarti Shahani. 2008. "Families for Freedom: Against Deportation and Delegalization." Pp. 258–287 in *Keeping Out the Other: A Critical Introduction to Immigration Enforcement Today*, edited by D. Brotherton and P. Kretsedemas. New York: Columbia University Press.

Katzenstein, Mary Fainsod. 1998. *Faithful and Fearless: Moving Feminist Protest Inside the Church and Military*. Princeton, NJ: Princeton University Press.

Kerwin, Donald and Serena Yi-Ying Lin. 2009. *Immigration Detention: Can ICE Meet Its Legal Imperatives and Case Management Opportunities?* Washington, DC: Migration Policy Institute.

King, Brayden G. and Marie Cornwall. 2005. "Specialists and Generalists: Learning Strategies in the Woman Suffrage Movement, 1866–1918." *Research in Social Movements, Conflicts and Change* 26:3–34.

King, Brayden G. and Nicholas A. Pearce. 2010. "The Contentiousness of Markets: Politics, Social Movements, and Institutional Change in Markets." *Annual Review of Sociology* 36:249–267.

King Jr., Martin Luther. 2000. *Why We Can't Wait*. Signet Classics.

Klandermans, Bert and Sidney Tarrow. 1986. "Mobilization Into Social Movements: Synthesizing American and European Approaches." Pp. 1–38 in *From Structure to Action: Comparing Social Movement Research Across Cultures*, edited by B. Klandermans, H. Kriesi, and S. Tarrow. Greenwich, CT: JAI.

Kroll-Smith, J. Stephen. 1980. "The Testimony as Performance: The Relationship of an Expressive Event to the Belief System of a Holiness Sect." *Journal for the Scientific Study of Religion* 19:16–25.

Kurien, Prema. 2007. *A Place at the Multicultural Table: The Development of an American Hinduism.* New Brunswick, NJ: Rutgers University Press.

Kurzban, Ira J. 2008. "Democracy and Immigration." Pp. 63–78 in *Keeping Out the Other: A Critical Introduction to Immigration Enforcement Today,* edited by D. Brotherton and P. Kretsedemas. New York: Columbia University Press.

Kwon, Ho-Youn, Kwang Chung Kim, and R. Stephen Warner, eds. 2001. *Korean Americans and Their Religions: Pilgrims and Missionaries from a Different Shore.* New York: New York University Press.

Laraña, Enrique, Hank Johnston and Joseph R. Gusfield, eds. 1994. *New Social Movements: From Ideology to Identity.* Philadelphia: Temple University Press.

Lee, Jennifer and Frank D. Bean. 2004. "America's Changing Color Lines: Immigration, Race/Ethnicity, and Multiracial Identification." *Annual Review of Sociology* 30:221–242.

———. 2007. "Reinventing the Color Line: Immigration and America's New Racial/ Ethnic Divide." *Social Forces* 86:561–586.

———. 2010. *The Diversity Paradox: Immigration and the Color Line in Twenty-First Century America.* New York: Russell Sage.

Leondar-Wright, Betsy. 2005. *Class Matters: Cross-Class Alliance Building for Middle-Class Activists.* Gabriola Island, BC: New Society Publishers.

Leonard, Karen. 2007. "Finding Places in the Nation: Immigrant and Indigenous Muslims in America." Pp. 50–58 in *Religion and Social Justice for Immigrants,* edited by P. Hondagneu-Sotelo. New Brunswick, NJ: Rutgers University Press.

Leonard, Karen I., Alex Stepick, Manuel A. Vasquez, and Jennifer Holdaway, eds. 2005. *Immigrant Faiths: Transforming Religious Life in America.* Walnut Creek, CA: Altamira Press.

Levitt, Peggy. 1998. "Local-Level Global Religion: The Case of U.S.-Dominican Migration." *Journal for the Scientific Study of Religion* 37:74–89.

———. 2007. *God Needs No Passport: Immigrants and the Changing American Religious Landscape.* New York: New Press.

Lewis, Amanda E. 2004. "'What Group?' Studying Whites and Whiteness in the Era of 'Color Blindness.'" *Sociological Theory* 22:623–646.

Lichterman, Paul. 1995. "Piecing Together Multicultural Community: Cultural Differences in Community Building Among Grass-Roots Environmentalists." *Social Problems* 42:513–534.

———. 2005. *Elusive Togetherness: Church Groups Trying to Bridge America's Divisions.* Princeton, NJ: Princeton University Press.

———. 2008. "Religion and the Construction of Civic Identity." *American Sociological Review* 73:83–104.

———. 2012. "Liberal Protestants and the Occupy Movement's Critique of Inequality: A Culture Gap?" *Mobilizing Ideas,* November 15, 2012, Retrieved March 30, 2013 (http://mobilizingideas.wordpress.com/2012/11/15/liberal-protestants-and-the-occupy-movements-critique-of-inequality-a-cultural-gap/).

Lippert, Randy. 2005. *Sanctuary, Sovereignty, Sacrifice: Canadian Sanctuary Incidents, Power, and Law*. Vancouver: University of British Columbia Press.

Lippert, Randy and Sean Rehaag, eds. 2012. *Sanctuary Practices in International Perspectives: Migration, Citizenship, and Social Movements*. London: Routledge.

Lipsitz, G. 1998. *The Possessive Investment in Whiteness: How White People Profit From Identity Politics*. Philadelphia: Temple University Press.

Lofland, John and Rodney Stark. 1965. "Becoming a World-Saver: A Theory of Conversion to a Deviant Perspective." *American Sociological Review* 30:862–875.

Lorentzen, Robin. 1991. *Women in the Sanctuary Movement*. Philadelphia: Temple University Press.

Lorentzen, Lois Ann, Joaquin Jay Gonzalez, Kevin M. Chun, and Hien Duc Do, eds. 2009. *Religion at the Corner of Bliss and Nirvana: Politics, Identity, and Faith in New Migrant Communities*. Durham, NC: Duke University Press.

Luker, Kristin. 1985. *Abortion and the Politics of Motherhood*. Berkeley: University of California Press.

Mahmood, Saba. 2005. *Politics of Piety: The Islamic Revival and the Feminist Subject*. Princeton, NJ: Princeton University Press.

Marrow, Helen B. 2011. *New Destination Dreaming: Immigration, Race, and Legal Status in the Rural American South*. Stanford, CA: Stanford University Press.

Marsh, Charles. 2005. *The Beloved Community: How Faith Shapes Social Justice, From the Civil Rights Movement to Today*. New York: Basic Books.

Martinez, Lisa M. 2008. "'Flowers From the Same Soil': Latino Solidarity in the Wake of the 2006 Immigrant Mobilizations." *American Behavioral Scientist* 52:557–579.

———. 2011. "Mobilizing Marchers in the Mile-High City: The Role of Community-Based Organizations." Pp. 123–141 in *Rallying for Immigrant Rights*, edited by K. Voss and I. Bloemraad. Berkeley: University of California Press.

Marx, Karl. [1844] 1978. "Contribution to the Critique of Hegel's *Philosophy of Right*: Introduction." Pp. 53–65 in *The Marx-Engels Reader*, 2d ed., edited by R.C. Tucker. New York: W.W. Norton & Company.

Massey, Doug, ed. 2008. *New Faces in New Places: The Changing Geography of American Immigration*. New York: Russell Sage Foundation.

Matovina, Timothy. 2012. *Latino Catholicism: Transformation in America's Largest Church*. Princeton, NJ: Princeton University Press.

McAdam, Doug. 1982. *Political Process and the Development of Black Insurgency, 1930–1970*. Chicago: University of Chicago Press.

———. 1983. "Tactical Innovation and the Pace of Insurgency." *American Sociological Review* 48:735–754.

———. 1988. *Freedom Summer*. New York: Oxford University Press.

McAdam, Doug, John D. McCarthy, and Mayer N. Zald, eds. 1996. *Comparative Perspectives on Social Movements: Political Opportunities, Mobilizing Structures, and Cultural Framings*. Cambridge, UK: Cambridge University Press.

McAdam, Doug, Sidney G. Tarrow, and Charles Tilly. 2001. *Dynamics of Contention.* New York: Cambridge University Press.

McAlister, Elizabeth. 2001. *Rara! Vodou, Power, and Performance in Haiti and the Diaspora.* Berkeley: University of California Press.

McCarthy, Kate. 2007. *Interfaith Encounters in America.* New Brunswick, NJ: Rutgers University Press.

McCarthy, John D. and Mayer N. Zald. 1977. "Resource Mobilization and Social Movements: A Partial Theory." *American Journal of Sociology* 82:1212–1241.

McCammon, Holly J. 2003. "'Out of the Parlors and Into the Streets': The Changing Tactical Repertoire of the U.S. Women's Suffrage Movements." *Social Forces* 81:787–818.

McCammon, Holly J., Soma Chaudhuri, Lyndi Hewitt, Courtney Sanders Muse, Harmony D. Newman, Carrie Lee Smith, and Teresa M. Terrell. 2008. "Becoming Full Citizens: The U.S. Women's Jury Rights Campaigns, the Pace of Reform, and Strategic Adaptation." *American Journal of Sociology* 113:1104–1147.

McDaniel, Eric Leon, Irfan Nooruddin, and Allyson Faith Shortle. 2011. "Divine Boundaries: How Religion Shapes Citizens' Attitudes Toward Immigrants." *American Politics Research* 39:205–233.

Melucci, Alberto. 1980. "The New Social Movements: A Theoretical Approach." *Social Science Information* 19:199–226.

Mendieta, Eduardo and Jonathan VanAntwerpen, eds. 2011. *The Power of Religion in the Public Sphere.* New York: Columbia University Press.

Menjívar, Cecilia. 2007. "Serving Christ in the Borderlands: Faith Workers Respond to Border Violence." Pp. 104–121 in *Religion and Social Justice for Immigrants*, edited by P. Hondagneu-Sotelo. New Brunswick, NJ: Rutgers University Press.

Metcalf, Barbara Daly. 2004. *Islamic Revival in British India: Deoband, 1860–1900.* New York: Oxford University Press.

Meyer, David S. and Suzanne Staggenborg. 1996. "Movements, Countermovements, and the Structure of Political Opportunity." *American Journal of Sociology* 101:1628–1660.

Min, Pyong Gap and Jung Ha Kim, eds. 2002. *Religions in Asian America: Building Faith Communities.* Walnut Creek, CA: Altamira Press.

Milkman, Ruth. 2006. *L.A. Story: Immigrant Workers and the Future of the U.S. Labor Movement.* New York: Russell Sage Foundation.

———. 2011. "L.A.'s Past, America's Future? The 2006 Immigrant Rights Protests and Their Antecedents." Pp. 201–214 in *Rallying for Immigrant Rights*, edited by K. Voss and I. Bloemraad. Berkeley: University of California Press.

Minkoff, Debra. 1999. "Bending with the Wind: Strategic Change and Adaptation by Women's and Racial Minority Organizations." *American Journal of Sociology* 104:1666–1703.

Mirola, William. 2003. "Religious Protest and Economic Conflict: Possibilities and Constraints on Religious Resource Mobilization and Coalitions in Detroit's Newspaper Strike." *Sociology of Religion* 64:443–461.

Mooney, Margarita. 2007. "The Catholic Church's Institutional Responses to Immigration: From Supranational to Local Engagement." Pp. 157–171 in *Religion and Social Justice for Immigrants*, edited by P. Hondagneu-Sotelo. New Brunswick, NJ: Rutgers University Press.

———. 2009. *Faith Makes Us Live: Surviving and Thriving in the Haitian Diaspora.* Berkeley: University of California Press.

Morris, Aldon D. 1984. *The Origins of the Civil Rights Movement: Black Communities Organizing for Change.* New York: Free Press.

Munson, Ziad W. 2009. *The Making of Pro-Life Activists: How Social Movement Mobilization Works.* Chicago: University of Chicago Press.

Nepstad, Sharon Erickson. 2004a. *Convictions of the Soul: Religion, Culture, and Agency in the Central America Solidarity Movement.* New York: Oxford University Press.

———. 2004b. "Disciples and Dissenters: Tactical Choice and Consequences in the Plowshares Movement." *Research in Social Movements, Conflict, and Change* 25:139–159.

———. 2008. *Religion and War Resistance in the Plowshares Movement.* New York: Cambridge University Press.

Nevins, Joseph. 2010. *Operation Gatekeeper and Beyond: The War on "Illegals" and the Remaking of the U.S.–Mexico Boundary.* London: Routledge.

Offe, Claus. 1985. "New Social Movements: Challenging the Boundaries of Institutional Politics." *Social Research* 52:817–868.

Pallares, Amalia. 2010. "Representing La Familia: Family Separation and Immigrant Activism in Chicago." In *¡Marcha! Latino Chicago and the National Immigrant Movement*, edited by A. Pallares and N. Flores-González. Urbana: University of Illinois Press.

Pallares, Amalia and Nilda Flores-González. 2011. "Regarding Family: New Actors in the Chicago Protests." Pp. 161–179 in *Rallying for Immigrant Rights: The Fight for Inclusion in 21st Century America*, edited by K. Voss and I. Bloemraad. Berkeley: University of California Press.

Pallares, Amalia and Nilda Flores-González, eds. 2010. *¡Marcha! Latino Chicago and the Immigrant Rights Movement.* Urbana: University of Illinois Press.

Pantoja, Adrian D., Cecilia Menjivar, and Lisa Magana. 2008. "The Spring Marches of 2006: Latinos, Immigration, and Political Mobilization in the 21st Century." *American Behavioral Scientist* 52:499–506.

Parsley et al. v. Bentley, Civil Action File 2011, Retrieved November 30, 2012 (http://www.nytimes.com/2011/08/14/us/14immig.html?scp=1&sq=alabama%20immigration%20law%20clergy&st=cse).

Passel, Jeffrey. 2005. "Unauthorized Migrants: Numbers and Characteristics." Washington, DC: Pew Hispanic Center.

Passel, Jeffrey and D'Vera Cohn. 2008. "Trends in Unauthorized Immigration: Undocumented Inflow Now Trails Legal Inflow." Report 94. Washington, DC: Pew Hispanic Center.

———. 2009. "A Portrait of Unauthorized Immigrants in the United States." Report 107. Washington, DC: Pew Hispanic Center.

———. 2010. "U.S. Unauthorized Immigration Flows Are Down Sharply Since Mid-Decade." Washington, DC: Pew Hispanic Center.

Peacock, James L. 1978. *Purifying the Faith: The Muhammadijah Movement in Indonesian Islam.* Palo Alto, CA: Cummings Press.

Perla, Hector and Susan Bibler Coutin. 2009. "Legacies and Origins of the 1980s US-Central American Sanctuary Movement." *Refuge* 26:7–19.

———. 2012. "Sanctuary Movements and Practices in the United States: Old and New; Legacies and Origins of the 1980s US–Central American Sanctuary Movement." Pp. 73–91 in *Sanctuary Practices in International Perspectives: Migration, Citizenship and Social Movements*, edited by Randy Lippert and Sean Rehaag. London: Routledge.

Pew Forum on Religion & Public Life. 2012. The Global Religious Landscape. Washington, DC: Pew Forum on Religion & Public Life.

Pew Hispanic Center. 2007. Changing Faiths: Latinos and the Transformation of American Religion. Washington, DC: Pew Forum on Religion & Public Life.

Philibert, Paul J. and Dean R. Hoge. 1982. "Teachers, Pedagogy and the Process of Religious Education." *Review of Religious Research* 23:264–285.

Pichardo, Nelson A. 1997. "New Social Movements: A Critical Review." *Annual Review of Sociology* 23:411–430.

Pietersen, Willie. 2002. *Reinventing Strategy: Using Strategic Learning to Create and Sustain Breakthrough Performance.* New York: John Wiley & Sons.

Pitt, Richard N. 2010. "Fear of a Black Pulpit? Real Racial Transcendence versus Cultural Assimilation in Multiracial Churches." *Journal for the Scientific Study of Religion* 49:218–223.

Polletta, Francesca. 2002. *Freedom Is an Endless Meeting: Democracy in American Social Movements.* Chicago: University of Chicago Press.

———. 2004. "How Participatory Democracy Became White: Culture and Organizational Choice." *Mobilization* 10:271–288.

———. 2008. "Culture and Movements." *ANNALS of the American Academy of Political and Social Science* 619:78–96.

Polletta, Francesca, Pang Ching Bobby Chen, Beth Gharrity Gardner, and Alice Motes. 2011. "The Sociology of Storytelling." *Annual Review of Sociology* 37:107–128.

Polletta, Francesca and James M. Jasper. 2001. "Collective Identity and Social Movements." *Annual Review of Sociology* 27:283–305.

Prothero, Stephen, ed. 2006. *A Nation of Religions: The Politics of Pluralism in Multireligious America.* Chapel Hill: University of North Carolina Press.

Putnam, Robert D. and David E. Campbell. 2010. *American Grace: How Religion Divides and Unites Us.* New York: Simon & Schuster.

Ragin, Charles and Howard S. Becker, eds. 1992. *What Is a Case?: Exploring the Foundations of Social Inquiry.* New York: Cambridge University Press.

Rawls, John. 1997. "The Idea of Public Reason Revisited." *University of Chicago Law Review* 64:765–807.

Rehaag, Sean. 2009. "Bordering on Legality: Canadian Church Sanctuary and the Rule of Law." *Refuge* 26:43–56.

Rey, Terry and Alex Stepick. 2010. "Refugee Catholicism in Little Haiti: Miami's Notre Dame d'Haiti Catholic Church." Pp. 72–91 in *Churches and Charity in the Immigrant City*, edited by A. Stepick, T. Rey, and S.J. Mahler. New Brunswick, NJ: Rutgers University Press.

Ribuffo, Leo P. 1989. "God and Jimmy Carter." Pp. 141–159 in *Transforming Faith: The Sacred and Secular in Modern American History*, edited by M.L. Bradbury and J.B. Gilbert. New York: Greenwood Press.

Schmalzbauer, John. 2005. "Journalism and the Religious Imagination." Pp. 21–36 in *Quoting God: How Media Shape Ideas About Religion and Culture*, edited by C. Badaracco. Waco, TX: Baylor University Press.

Shaw, Randy. 2008. *Beyond the Fields: Cesar Chavez, the UFW, and the Struggle for Justice in the 21st Century*. Berkeley: University of California Press.

———. 2011. "Building the Labor-Clergy-Immigrant Alliance." Pp. 82–100 in *Rallying for Immigrant Rights*, edited by K. Voss and I. Bloemraad. Berkeley: University of California Press.

Sheik, Irum. 2008. "Racializing, Criminalizing, and Silencing 9/11 Deportees." Pp. 81–107 in *Keeping Out the Other: A Critical Introduction to Immigration Enforcement Today*, edited by D. Brotherton and P. Kretsedemas. New York: Columbia University Press.

Slessarev-Jamir, Helene. 2011. *Prophetic Activism: Progressive Religious Justice Movements in Contemporary America*. New York: New York University Press.

Smilde, David and Matthew May. 2010. "The Emerging Strong Program in the Sociology of Religion." Working Paper. New York: Social Science Research Council.

Smith, Buster G. and Byron Johnson. 2010. "The Liberalization of Young Evangelicals: A Research Note." *Journal for the Scientific Study of Religion* 49:351–360.

Smith, Christian. 1991. *The Emergence of Liberation Theology: Radical Religion and Social Movement Theory*. Chicago: University of Chicago Press.

———, ed. 1996a. *Disruptive Religion: The Force of Faith in Social-Movement Activism*. New York: Routledge.

———. 1996b. *Resisting Reagan: The US Central America Peace Movement*. Chicago: University of Chicago Press.

———, ed. 2003. *The Secular Revolution: Power, Interests, and Conflict in the Secularization of American Public Life*. Berkeley: University of California Press.

Smith, Christian, with Michael Emerson, Sally Gallagher, Paul Kennedy, and David Sikkink. 1998. *American Evangelicalism: Embattled and Thriving*. Chicago: University of Chicago Press.

Smith, Gregory A. 2006. *Attitudes Toward Immigration: In the Pulpit and the Pew*. Washington, DC: Pew Research Center.

Snow, David A. 2004. "Social Movements as Challenges to Authority: Resistance to an Emerging Conceptual Hegemony." Pp. 3–25 in *Authority in Contention: Research in Social Movements, Conflict, and Change*, edited by D.J. Myers and D.M. Cress. London: Elsevier.

Snow, David A., E.B. Rochford Jr., Steven K. Worden, and Robert D. Benford. 1986. "Frame Alignment Processes, Micromobilization, and Movement Participation." *American Sociological Review* 51:464–481.

Stark, Rodney and William Sims Bainbridge. 1980. "Networks of Faith: Interpersonal Bonds and Recruitment to Cults and Sects." *American Journal of Sociology* 85:1376–1395.

Stark, Rodney and Roger Finke. 2000. *Acts of Faith: Explaining the Human Side of Religion*. Berkeley: University of California Press.

Steensland, Brian, Jerry Z. Park, Mark D. Regnerus, Lynn D. Robinson, W. Bradford Wilcox, and Robert D. Woodberry. 2000. "The Measure of American Religion: Toward Improving the State of the Art." *Social Forces* 79:291–318.

Stepick, Alex, Terry Rey, and Sarah J. Mahler, eds. 2009. *Churches and Charity in the Immigrant City: Religion, Immigration, and Civic Engagement*. New Brunswick, NJ: Rutgers University Press.

Stout, Jeffrey. 2010. *Blessed Are the Organized: Grassroots Democracy in America*. Princeton, NJ: Princeton University Press.

Suárez-Orozco, Carola, Irina L.G. Todorova, and Josephine Louie. 2005. "Making Up for Lost Time: The Experience of Separation and Reunification Among Immigrant Families." Pp. 179–196 in *The New Immigration*, edited by M.M. Suárez-Orozco, C. Suárez-Orozco, and D.B. Qin. New York: Routledge.

Summers-Effler, Erika. 2010. *Laughing Saints and Righteous Heroes: Emotional Rhythms in Social Movement Groups*. Chicago: University of Chicago Press.

Swarts, Heidi J. 2008. *Organizing Urban America: Secular and Faith-based Progressive Movements*. Minneapolis: University of Minnesota Press.

Swidler, Ann. 1986. "Culture in Action: Symbols and Strategies." *American Sociological Review* 51:273–286.

———. 2001. *Talk of Love*. Chicago: University of Chicago Press.

Tarrow, Sidney. 1994. *Power in Movement*. Cambridge, UK: Cambridge University Press.

Taylor, Verta and Nella Van Dyke. 2004. "'Get Up, Stand Up': Tactical Repertoires of Social Movements." Pp. 262–293 in *The Blackwell Companion to Social Movements*, edited by D. Snow, S. Soule, and H. Kriesi. Malden, MA: Blackwell Publishing.

Thornton, Patricia H. and William Ocasio. 1999. "Institutional Logics and the Historical Contingency of Power in Organizations: Executive Succession in the Higher Education Publishing Industry, 1958–1990." *American Journal of Sociology* 105:801–843.

Tichenor, Daniel J. 2002. *Dividing Lines: The Politics of Immigration Control in America*. Princeton, NJ: Princeton University Press.

Touraine, Alain. 1981. *The Voice and the Eye: An Analysis of Social Movements*. Cambridge: Cambridge University Press.

Tramonte, Lynn. 2009. "Debunking the Myth of 'Sanctuary Cities': Community Policing Policies Protect American Communities." Washington, DC: Immigration Policy Center.

Tweed, Thomas A. 1997. *Our Lady of the Exile: Diaspora Religion at a Cuban Catholic Shrine in Miami.* New York: Oxford University Press.

———. 2006. *Crossing and Dwelling: A Theory of Religion.* Cambridge, MA: Harvard University Press.

Uecker, Jeremy E. and Glenn Lucke. 2011. "Protestant Clergy and the Culture Wars: An Empirical Test of Hunter's Thesis." *Journal for the Scientific Study of Religion* 50:692–706.

Vaisey, Stephen. 2009. "Motivation and Justification: Toward a Dual Process Theory of Culture in Action." *American Journal of Sociology* 114:1675–1715.

Van Dyke, Nella, Sarah A. Soule, and Verta A. Taylor. 2004. "The Targets of Social Movements: Beyond a Focus on the State." Pp. 27–51 in *Authority in Contention: Research in Social Movements, Conflict, and Change,* edited by D.J. Myers and D.M. Cress. London: Elsevier.

Vásquez, Manuel A. and Marie Friedmann Marquardt. 2003. *Globalizing the Sacred: Religion Across the Americas.* New Brunswick, NJ: Rutgers University Press.

Voss, Kim and Irene Bloemraad, eds. 2011. *Rallying for Immigrant Rights: The Fight for Inclusion in 21st Century America.* Berkeley: University of California Press.

Warner, Michael. 2002. *Publics and Counterpublics.* Brooklyn, NY: Zone Books.

Warner, R. Stephen. 2005. *A Church of Our Own: Disestablishment and Diversity in American Religion.* New Brunswick, NJ: Rutgers University Press.

———. 2006. "The De-Europeanization of American Christianity." Pp. 233–255 in *A Nation of Religions,* edited by S. Prothero. Chapel Hill: University of North Carolina Press.

Warner, R. Stephen and Judith G. Wittner, eds. 1998. *Gatherings in Diaspora: Religious Communities and the New Immigration.* Philadelphia: Temple University Press.

Warren, Mark R. 2001. *Dry Bones Rattling: Community Building to Revitalize American Democracy.* Princeton, NJ: Princeton University Press.

———. 2010. *Fire in the Heart: How White Activists Embrace Racial Justice.* New York: Oxford University Press.

Weber, Max. [1904] 2002. *The Protestant Ethic & the Spirit of Capitalism,* 3d ed. Trans. Stephen Kalberg. Los Angeles: Roxbury.

Weiner, Matt. 2010. *Working the Roots.* Unpublished Manuscript.

Weiss, Robert S. 1994. *Learning from Strangers: The Art and Method of Qualitative Interview Studies.* New York: Free Press.

Wellman Jr., James K. 2008. *Evangelical vs. Liberal: The Clash of Christian Cultures in the Pacific Northwest.* New York: Oxford University Press.

Wilcox, Clyde. 2006. *Onward Christian Soldiers?: The Religious Right in American Politics.* Boulder, CO: Westview Press.

Wilde, Melissa J. 2004. "How Culture Mattered at Vatican II: Collegiality Trumps Authority in the Council's Social Movement Organizations." *American Sociological Review* 69:576–602.

———. 2007. *Vatican II: A Sociological Analysis of Religious Change.* Princeton, NJ: Princeton University Press.

Williams Jr., J. Allen. 1964. "Reduction of Tension through Intergroup Conflict: A Social Psychological Interpretation." *Pacific Sociological Review* 7:81–88.

Williams, Raymond Brady. 1996. *Christian Pluralism in the United States: The Indian Immigrant Experience.* Cambridge, UK: Cambridge University Press.

Williams, Rhys H. 1995. "Constructing the Public Good: Social Movements and Cultural Resources." *Social Problems* 42:124–144.

———. 1996. "Religion as Political Resource: Culture or Ideology?" *Journal for the Scientific Study of Religion* 35:368–378.

———. 2002. "From the 'Beloved Community' to 'Family Values': Religious Language, Symbolic Repertoires, and Democratic Culture." Pp. 247–265 in *Social Movements: Identity, Culture, and the State*, edited by D. Meyer, N. Whittier, and B. Robnett. New York: Oxford University Press.

———. 2004. "The Cultural Contexts of Collective Action: Constraints, Opportunities, and the Symbolic Life of Social Movements." Pp. 91–115 in *The Blackwell Companion to Social Movements*, edited by D. A. Snow, S. A. Soule, and H. Kriesi. Malden, MA: Blackwell.

———. 2007. "Liberalism, Religion, and the Dilemma of Immigrant Rights in American Political Culture." Pp. 16–34 in *Religion and Social Justice for Immigrants*, edited by P. Hondagneu-Sotelo. New Brunswick, NJ: Rutgers University Press.

———. Forthcoming, 2013. "Civil Religion and the Cultural Politics of National Identity in Obama's America." *Journal for the Scientific Study of Religion*

Wilson, Catherine E. 2008. *The Politics of Latino Faith: Religion, Identity, and Urban Community.* New York: New York University Press.

Wiltfang, Gregory L. and Doug McAdam. 1991. "The Costs and Risks of Social Activism: A Study of Sanctuary Movement Activism." *Social Forces* 69:987–1010.

Wood, Richard L. 1999. "Religious Culture and Political Action." *Sociological Theory* 17:307–332.

———. 2002. *Faith in Action: Religion, Race, and Democratic Organizing in America.* Chicago: University of Chicago Press.

Wuthnow, Robert. 1988. *The Restructuring of American Religion: Society and Faith Since World War II.* Princeton, NJ: Princeton University Press.

———. 2005. *America and the Challenges of Religious Diversity.* Princeton, NJ: Princeton University Press.

———. 2006. *American Mythos.* Princeton, NJ: Princeton University Press.

———. 2009. *Boundless Faith: The Global Outreach of American Churches.* Berkeley: University of California Press.

———. 2010. "H. Paul Douglass Lecture: Heaven Is a Wonderful Place: The Role of Reasonableness in Religious Discourse." *Review of Religious Research* 52:5–20.

———. 2011. "Taking Talk Seriously: Religious Discourse as Social Practice." *Journal for the Scientific Study of Religion* 50:1–21.

Wuthnow, Robert and John H. Evans, eds. 2002. *The Quiet Hand of God: Faith-Based Activism and the Public Role of Mainline Protestantism.* Berkeley: University of California Press.

Yamane, David. 2000. "Narrative and Religious Experience." *Sociology of Religion* 61:171–189.

Yoshikawa, Hirokazu. 2011. *Immigrants Raising Citizens: Undocumented Parents and Their Young Children.* New York: Russell Sage Foundation.

Young, Michael P. 2006. *Bearing Witness Against Sin: The Evangelical Birth of the American Social Movement.* Chicago: University of Chicago Press.

Yukich, Grace. 2010. "Boundary Work in Inclusive Religious Groups: Constructing Identity at the New York Catholic Worker." *Sociology of Religion* 71:172–196.

———. 2011. "Beyond Religion as Resource: Expanding the Study of Religion and Activism." Presented at the Society for the Scientific Study of Religion Annual Meeting.

———. 2012. "'I Didn't Know If This Was Sanctuary': Strategic Adaptation in the U.S. New Sanctuary Movement." Pp. 106–18 in *Sanctuary Practices in International Perspectives: Migration, Citizenship and Social Movements*, edited by Randy Lippert and Sean Rehaag. London: Routledge.

———. 2013. "Constructing the Model Immigrant: Movement Strategy and Immigrant Deservingness in the New Sanctuary Movement." *Social Problems* 60(3).

Zaman, Muhammad Qasim. 2007. *The Ulama in Contemporary Islam: Custodians of Change.* Princeton, NJ: Princeton University Press.

Zubrzycki, Geneviève. 2006. *The Crosses of Auschwitz: Nationalism and Religion in Post-Communist Poland.* Chicago: University of Chicago Press.

INDEX